CULTURES OF **Transnational Adoption**

Xiangyin
Xiushui
HANGSHA
Xiangtan
Liuyang
Wanzai
Fengcheng
Yichun
Liling
Xinshao
Pingxiang
Hengshan
Anfu
Ji'an
Youxian
Chaling
Nanfeng
Anren
Leiyang
FUJIAN
Yongxing
Zixing
Ganzhou
Chenzhou
Guiyang
Jiahe
Ningyuan
Dayu
Longnan
Jianghua
Lianxian
Lianping
Qujiang
Xinfeng
Heyuan
Yingde
Fogang

CULTURES OF **Transnational Adoption**

Edited by Toby Alice Volkman

Duke University Press

Durham and London

2005

2nd printing, 2006
© 2005 Duke University Press

All rights reserved

Printed in the United States of America on acid-free paper ∞
Designed by Erin Kirk New
Typeset in Sabon with Scala Sans display by Keystone
Typesetting, Inc.

Library of Congress Cataloging-in-Publication Data appear
on the last printed page of this book.

Earlier versions of several essays in this volume originally
appeared in *Social Text*, volume 74. Copyright 2003, Duke
University Press.

Kay Johnson's essay originally appeared in her book
*Wanting a Daughter, Needing a Son: Abandonment,
Adoption, and Orphanage Care in China* (St. Paul: Yeong
and Yeong, 2004), and is reprinted here with permission.

FOR LUCIA XINGWEN

Contents

Acknowledgments

In 1994, soon after my husband and I returned from China with our newly adopted daughter, I found myself immersed in a community in which fellow New Yorkers, (mostly white) adoptive parents with Chinese daughters, celebrated Chinese holidays, took toddlers to Mandarin language or Chinese dance classes, and talked long and hard about "Chinese culture," "identity," or their sudden transformation into an "Asian American family." As an anthropologist, I knew I should be taking field notes. As a foundation program officer responsible for an initiative called "Crossing Borders," I saw my own experience as an instance of global border-crossing enacted in an intimate space. As a parent, I was simply busy.

I am grateful, then, to Rayna Rapp and Faye Ginsburg, friends who listened to my stories and first encouraged me to write — as an ethnographer and a mother — about this phenomenon. Six years later, a generous Ford Foundation grant to New York University made possible both my own research and the more collective project that led to this book. I thank Alison Bernstein and Janice Petrovich at the Ford Foundation for their support and appreciation of the links between this endeavor and "Crossing Borders." At New York University, Faye Ginsburg provided me with a dual home in the Anthropology Department and the Center for Media, Culture and History. Faye also organized "The Traffic of Kinship," a small but exciting conference at NYU in 2001 that brought together several of the contributors to this book and began our collective conversations. Eleana Kim served as my research assistant at NYU, and through her work on Korean adoptee movements helped me to see the recent waves of adoption from China and elsewhere in a more global and historical frame.

Thus when Cindi Katz invited me to guest edit a special issue of *Social Text,* where several of the essays in this volume first appeared, I welcomed the opportunity to broaden the geographic and temporal scope of this project. Subsequently, Ken Wissoker graciously guided this book through many stages at Duke University Press. I thank all the contributors, who in addition to their essays offered thoughtful responses to one another's work, along with a good mix of patience and enthusiasm. On a personal level, I thank Charles Zerner for his myriad contributions to this project. Lucia, my daughter, inspired it.

Toby Alice Volkman

Introduction

New Geographies of Kinship

TOBY ALICE VOLKMAN

Sierra Song E, Marty, and I sat with our noses pressed against the glass straining to see the land as it intermittently appeared and vanished through the clouds. Almost in a whisper she [Song E] confided, "I think that place right down there may be where my birth parents live, Mommy. I think maybe they might be looking up and wishing that their little girl could fly down to them for a visit. Someday, maybe I will look for them. I'm sending them a wish now. It is that I hope they have enough to eat and they are happy. I hope they are not missing me too much. I wish I could tell them that I will come back to China again and again."
— JANE BROWN, 2002

n the early 1990s the adoption of children across national borders began to accelerate at an extraordinary rate. Although transnational adoption originated more than fifty years ago in the aftermath of World War II and the Korean War, the current wave of adoption is unprecedented in magnitude and visibility. The number of children adopted from abroad to Western nations rose steadily in the final decade of the twentieth century, a period in which close to 140,000 transnational adoptions occurred in the United States alone. The roster of "sending countries" also changed dramatically during these years, reflecting a complex mix of political, economic, and social upheavals, sometimes linked to the shifting reproductive policies of the state. At the end of the 1990s China and Russia each sent about five thousand children a year to the United States. South Korea, Guatemala, Ukraine, Romania, Vietnam, and Kazakhstan followed, and, to a lesser degree, India and Cambodia. With the exception of South Korea, most of these countries became active players on the transnational adoption stage only in the 1990s.[1]

What are the implications of this massive and almost entirely unidirectional movement of young children from poor nations to the more affluent West? And what are the implications of more recent countermovements whereby adoptees revisit the countries of their birth? The "transnational" dimensions of these phenomena entail ongoing, crisscrossing flows in multiple directions, in space that is both real and virtual. There is, for example, the remarkable fact that the "international movement of two thousand South Korean children to foreign countries [for adoption] is matched by a reverse movement of two thousand or more Korean adoptees who as adults return to South Korea every year" (Kim, this volume). These returning adoptees, like the little girl described in the epigraph above who sends an airborne wish to her Chinese birth parents, are striking instances of a larger set of transnational processes, or what Aihwa Ong (2003, 87) has called the "disembedding from a set of localized relations in the homeland nation and re-embedding in overlapping networks."

A focus on the "transnational" allows the contributors to this volume to probe the effects of the nation and those processes that challenge it: South Korea's current embrace of "globalization," for example, and its parallel but sometimes stifling embrace of adoptees as "overseas Koreans." Travel in its many forms, the rise of the Internet and the global cyberspatial communities it produces, and efforts to create international legal frameworks all produce new forms of family and new articulations of identity that may not coincide easily with notions of the nation.

In this volume transnational adoption is explored as a form of circulation that creates new geographies of kinship. As authors, we draw on our diverse disciplinary roots (anthropology, communications, art history, politics). In our personal lives, we have come to this topic in different ways. Some (although not all) of us are adoptive mothers, but no one occupies the two other positions in what has come to be known as the "adoption triad" of birth parents, adoptive parents, and adopted children. We are acutely aware that the voices of birth parents and adoptees are largely absent from the academic literature on this topic, as they have been, until recently, from most representations of adoption.[2] Our project, nonetheless, treats adoption as a social and cultural phenomenon in which all parties must be understood in relation to one another. We write, then, of birth parents who relinquish, abandon, or simply circulate their children; of adoptive parents and adopted children; of adult adoptees; and of representations of adoption.

In North America, transracial domestic adoption and Native American adoption cross somewhat different borders. While in this collection we do not treat these forms of adoption, we acknowledge that they share with transnational adoption a number of structural issues. Indeed, all adoption that crosses borders — of culture, race, ethnicity, nation, or class — is shaped by profound inequities in power, by contradictions and ambivalence. Pauline Turner Strong (2002, 471), writing about extratribal (Native American) adoption, captures this eloquently: "Adoption across political and cultural borders may simultaneously be an act of violence and an act of love, an excruciating rupture and a generous incorporation, an appropriation of valued resources and a constitution of personal ties."

Issues of belonging and difference — central to the experience of adoption and even more salient in transnational adoption — are at the heart of part 1 of this volume, "Displacements, Roots, Identities." In the opening essay, Barbara Yngvesson explores these issues as she follows Chilean adoptees who with their parents return as a group to the country of their birth. A different sort of "return" is then examined by Eleana Kim, who looks at Korean adoptees traveling to Korea for "cultural training" under the auspices of the Korean government. My own essay at the end of part 1 examines a younger generation of adopted children from China and their North American parents, who grapple with the question of what "Chinese" or "Chinese American" identity might mean for their children.

In much of the adoption literature, nations that provide children for adoption are referred to as "sending countries," in contrast to "receiving countries" that provide families for children. The contributors to part 2, "Counterparts," question this simple dichotomy and trace a more complex circulation — of bodies, laws, scholarship, and fantasies — within and across national borders. Kay Johnson's essay reveals the struggles of Chinese parents in China who adopt Chinese children, thereby confounding stereotypes in the West about "cultural" resistance to adoption in China while also demonstrating the mutual entanglements of state and international policies and practices. Claudia Fonseca's essay conveys the textured, fluid nature of kinship in a Brazilian community; a fluidity that is undermined by pressures from the state, which in turn reacts to pressures to conform to global, "modern" adoption conventions. In the final essay in part 2 Laurel Kendall muses on her layered relationships as a scholar of gender in Korea, an anthropologist in the field, a fictive daughter in a Korean family, and as the adoptive mother of a Korean son.

In part 3 Lisa Cartwright illuminates how, in the 1990s, documentary news media and new technologies of visual imagery constituted the "global social orphan" and mobilized a "transnational politics of pity" through humanitarian efforts to rescue suffering children. Cartwright's discussion of media representations — the immediacy of the visual and the "death of distance" it produces — provides a frame for understanding the dramatic upsurge in transnational adoption in the 1990s, especially from China, the former Soviet Union, and Romania, all of which were newly opened to the global "borderless" economy.

Part 3 concludes with a reflection on narrative representation. Elizabeth Honig explores the disjunctions between master narratives (e.g., the Korean "master narrative of national maternity"), counternarratives (the lack of options beyond adoption), and the plural and often discrepant narratives of possibility that adoptees and adoptive parents may tell themselves and one another. Woven together of disparate strands — assumptions about history, culture, and politics, and fantasies about the personal — the stories of a new generation of adopted children, Honig suggests, are likely to one day have "formidable political power." Other essays in this volume invoke this possibility as well: ten-year-old adopted girls from China who participate in Playshops and panel discussions and write poems for the newsletter of *Families with Children from China* (Volkman); or young adult Korean adoptees whose collective "countermemories" are mobilized as a political voice (Kim).

Shifting Discourses

Questions of belonging, race, culture, and subjectivity loom large in contemporary discourses of transnational adoption. In an earlier era, adoption across borders was assumed to be straightforward. A child traveled to a new country and stayed there. A child born in Korea and adopted in Minnesota was expected to grow up and remain simply a (white) American. Parents and adoption organizations did not question that their acts were good deeds. The past was erased or contained in an abandoned "there"; the racialized trace of origins tended to be treated as manageable. Like race, adoption was not discussed and loss was rarely acknowledged. All this has changed significantly over the last few decades.

By the late twentieth century, the idea of the social construction of identity had assumed a prominent place in the culture of adoption in North America, Europe, and Australia. Adoptees were expected, or at least invited, to explore their multiple identities: to retain a name, to imagine their birth families, to learn about "birth cultures," perhaps to visit their birth country and seek out relatives. Many Korean adoptees had grown up and had shaken off their sense of isolation as they met other adoptees like themselves. They began to speak forcefully, sometimes with anger and pain, about how they were not simply the white Minnesotans (or Swedes, or Californians) whom their parents and the culture as a whole had expected them to be. Some articulated their sense of dislocation, uncertainties about where they fit as they struggled to reconcile their outer appearance and inner sense of self, the ambiguities of simultaneously belonging and not belonging. Many called for a radical new openness about both race and adoption. Some challenged the very practice and premises of transnational adoption, asking in whose "best interest" is it, after all?

In sending nations as well, questions were posed — whether by adoption professionals or within the legal system, the press, or the government. Efforts to reform an array of disparate and sometimes irresponsible practices in the early 1990s led to the Hague Convention on Protection of Children and Co-operation in Respect of Intercountry Adoption, a gathering of representatives of sixty-six sending and receiving countries. In 1993 the Hague Convention was signed. The Convention urged countries to do whatever necessary to enable a child to remain in his or her family of origin or, if impossible, with a family in that country. Transnational adoption was agreed to be the third best option. Considerable debate, in the words of Barbara Yngvesson (2002, 417), "focused on reconciling the apparent 'need' for the adoption of children transnationally with the reassertion of nationalisms, ethnicities, and identities grounded in a particular national soil." In drawing on an increasingly popular discourse of children's rights, the Convention insisted on a child's right to an "identity" and to the right to "grow up in a family environment, in an atmosphere of happiness, love and understanding" (1993 preamble, quoted in Yngvesson, 2002, 417). The tension between these assumed needs, rights, or aspirations — to a nationally or culturally rooted identity as well as a loving family — is a pervasive strand in the discourse of contemporary transnational (and, to some extent, transracial) adoption.

In 2004 members of a single Internet adoption listserv had adopted from thirty-six countries, from Albania to Vietnam, and lived in sixteen countries, mostly in the United States (forty states), Europe, and Australia, with a few members in several Asian countries.[3] The essays in this volume do not attempt to discuss transnational adoption in its many national variants worldwide, nor do they chart the striking ebb and flow of adoption from countries over time. In juxtaposing the essays in this volume, we seek to illuminate the distinctive features of what might be considered the "cultures" of transnational adoption in the late twentieth century and the early-twenty-first. These essays explore some of the ways that core ideas — identity, culture, community, family, roots — come into play and are actively questioned by participants in adoption. What is distinctively contemporary here is the process through which these ideas and practices are being shaped by conversations that are increasingly global, taking place across national spaces, and sometimes, as Kim (this volume) shows, in dialogue with or in opposition to the "state," as well as increasingly intergenerational, as cohorts of older adoptees position themselves as mentors to younger cohorts of adoptees or newer cohorts of adoptive parents. These conversations are shaped by an extraordinary degree of border crossing, as people, information, ideas, and imagery circulate with impressive velocity and intensity.

The fact that American adoptive parents are so concerned with questions of culture and identity, for example, cannot be understood without considering the interaction of these parents with earlier cohorts of Asian adoptees in the United States and Europe (Volkman, this volume). As a group, "Asian adoptees" have only recently begun to articulate both shared and distinct identities. Vietnamese adoptees, for example, have come of age and have drawn inspiration from their slightly older Korean counterparts. Swedish families who travel to Chile to encounter their children's "roots" participate in a trip that is made possible by changes in political relationships between Sweden and Chile. What makes this trip desirable and compelling, however, is the larger adoption discourse that encourages such journeys (Yngvesson, this volume). On the Internet, a proliferation of electronic mailing lists and Web sites connects adoptive parents, adopted people, and, potentially, birth parents from all over the world, while a profusion of images of "waiting children" on the Web incites desire and creates new kinds of adoption markets (Cartwright 2003). New global news media have played a major role in constituting what Cartwright (this volume) calls the "global social orphan" as a "transnational entity of riveting concern" by providing powerful visual imagery that collapses the distance — geographic, cultural, and personal — between "spectator and sufferer," between prospective adoptive parent and "waiting child."

Typically, in the adoption triad of child, adoptive parent, and birth parent it is the latter who is absent, the voice that is not heard. This is particularly the case in transnational adoption, where in addition to personal pain and loss, birth parents may face recriminations for unwed pregnancies that are considered deeply shameful or for acts of abandonment that are illegal or frowned on. In the United States in recent years there has been an outpouring of personal narratives of birth mothers (cf. Franklin 1998). In contrast, access to the voices and experiences of birth parents abroad is profoundly limited, and research in this area is understandably difficult as well. In the absence of more certain knowledge, adoptive parents devote considerable energy to imagining the circumstances and lives of birth parents. The essays in this book on Korean birth mothers (Kendall), on Chinese adoptive parents (Johnson), and on the circulation of children in Brazilian families (Fonseca), illuminate some of the conditions and constraints that shape lives and choices in sending countries.

Preoccupations with culture, identity, roots, and origins suffuse adoption discourse. Another conversation, less pervasive but nonetheless intense, involves a critical interrogation of a global political economy that makes it possible for poor countries that cannot provide for their "own" children to send these children to families in wealthy Western nations. Even when there appears to be no evidence of corruption or trafficking in children, does the very existence of the transnational adoption as a practice create a demand and hence a supply of children? Recent media attention in the United States has focused on activists' efforts in India to curtail transnational adoption and to promote domestic adoption by Indian parents. Yet such critiques of transnational adoption are complicated by disturbing conditions in the sending countries as well — for example, at least some prospective adoptive parents in India consider disabled, dark-skinned, or female children unadoptable (Yngvesson, forthcoming).

In these conversations about culture and identity, and about the politics of adoption across borders, adoptees themselves have only recently insisted on having a voice. The founder of an organization of Vietnamese adoptees writes: "It had been 25 years since we had been together . . . we wanted to find our voice as a community and tell our own histories (instead of agency/orphanage workers doing it for us)." He adds: "We wanted to provide the second generation [of Vietnamese adoptees] with what we didn't have growing up — someone to look up to, someone that looked like them, talked like them, and LIVED what they were/are living" (Brownlees 2003). On one electronic mailing list, adult adoptees repeatedly and with some frustration admonish adoptive parents to stop talking and writing so much about their own issues, or what they imagine their children feel, and just to listen. And, further, a "transracial abductees" Web site (www.transracialabductees.com) challenges the very existence of transnational adoption with intense anger.

As increasing numbers of adopted children grow up and become adults, will these critiques proliferate? Adoptive parents sometimes wonder if they are doing things differently, having learned lessons from mistakes made by the generations that preceded them. They see themselves as creating a more open space — for expressing anger, mourning loss, embracing birth parents, acknowledging difference, respecting culture, and the like. We may speculate that critiques of transnational adoption voiced by the younger generations of adoptees might assume a more political form, less driven by personal anger and isolation and more by concerns for social justice and equality.

Roots, Identities, Birth Culture

In her dual role as anthropologist and interpreter accompanying a group of Chilean adoptees and their Swedish parents who traveled "home" to Chile, Barbara Yngvesson tracks one exploration of "roots" in her essay. Journeys such as this, Yngvesson suggests, actually unsettle the narrative of exclusive belongings, the notion of a singular identity and a self that can be made whole. Contemporary adoption discourse echoes the ambivalences discussed by Yngvesson: the contradictory narratives of, on the one hand, the child "rooted" in her or his original culture and, on the other, the child as freely transferable to new kin and culture in the global marketplace.

The popular culture of adoption has begun to acknowledge the impossibility of what Yngvesson calls "exclusive belongings." An American mother wrote on the Internet of her hopes to give her daughter "what she would need to have a fulfilling, but divided life." The daughter, the six-year-old Sierra Song E, echoed her mother's thoughts: "Part of me lives here now and part of my heart is in China now, you know?" Her mother replied: "That is the way it should be — you are a daughter of each of the two lands you rightfully claim as yours" (Brown 2002). Like the passage quoted above in the epigraph — Sierra Song E's whispered thoughts upon leaving China at the end of her first "homeland visit" — this dialogue would have been unimaginable even a decade ago.

This theme is emerging in new children's literature as well, much of which has been written by adoptive parents. *Mommy Near, Mommy Far*, for example, tells a story of a little adopted Chinese girl with two mothers, one in the United States and one in China (Peacock 2000). A slightly older readership (six to nine years) is targeted in *At Home in This World: A China Adoption Story* (MacLeod 2003). The author describes the book as an exploration of the way "a transracial adoptee walks between worlds," a book that would help the child "begin to 'move beyond conventional understandings' of self identity." The book concludes: "I still wonder about my life in China. I love my parents very much and I wouldn't want any other family, but I think I will always miss knowing the parents that weren't mine to keep. My mom says that I am a brave kid and my life has been an amazing adventure — that I have experienced enormous changes, and I have survived them all. I like to think about it that way; it helps me bring both my sides together. I was born in China and now I'm from here, and my before and after is all part of who I am: one girl from two places who is growing up to be at home in this big, wide world" (unpaginated).

Questioning the cosmopolitanism implied in the idea of "at home in this big, wide world," Indigo Williams (2003), an adoptee who was born in Vietnam, raised in Australia, and came to the United States as a graduate student, writes: "But 'global' and 'world' descriptions fail to center [adoptees'] particular experiences and histories . . . I think as adoptees mature, regional and then local locations of self become more important than global ones. Be it North Asia (China) or Southeast Asia (Vietnam) or South Asia (India) — the distinct differences of those areas contribute to how adult adoptees re-construct their self-knowledge and history."

The state may stake its own claim to the adoptee, as Eleana Kim describes in a quite different version of the "roots" journey. As the leading sending country in the world for decades, South Korea's internal debates about adoption have long been inflected with considerations of national shame. In a dramatic public statement in 1998, President Kim Dae Jung apologized to a group of visiting Korean adoptees from eight nations. Reversing the direction of fifty years of Korean adoption, thousands of young adult Korean adoptees have traveled to South Korea in recent years, where some attend "cultural training" camps sponsored by a government now eager to recast Korean adoptees — once seen as outcasts — as "overseas Koreans." In this process, Kim shows, adoptees have resisted appropriation by the state and are struggling to create alternative identifications. Those struggles are part of a larger, self-consciously global movement in which Korean adoptees are encountering "Korea" in complex ways, wrestling with their own fantasies of origins and articulating new forms of "cultural citizenship" and understandings of what it might mean to be both Korean and not Korean.

The voices of these Korean adoptees, adopted at a time when for the most part their Koreanness was suppressed, have been extraordinarily influential in shaping the consciousness of adoptive families in the 1990s. Long silenced, Korean adoptees are now seen as articulate pioneers. Kim (2001) has written eloquently of their prolific production of "autoethnographic" films and videos, and of their work to create such collective practices as the worldwide Gathering of Korean adoptees, a movement that has inspired similar efforts elsewhere, especially by "first generation" or "Operation Babylift" Vietnamese adoptees. On the Internet a mother whose son was adopted from India thirty years ago wrote simply: "Everything I've learned has been from the Korean adoptees."

Changes in the culture of adoption have been especially dramatic since the 1990s. Aware of the experiences of earlier generations of adoptees, and caught up in the rhetoric of multiculturalism, adoptive parents of younger children self-consciously strive to embrace difference rather than assimilation, and attempt to help their children fashion multiple or fluid identifications. The intense involvement of these parents with what they have defined as "birth culture" brings to the fore tension between the affirmation of difference (cast sometimes as culture, sometimes as race) and its reinscription. Parents of children adopted from China have been especially active in promoting this involvement, but similar concerns are also evident in adoption groups from other parts of the world. These practices may provoke quite heated debates about what "culture" can possibly mean in this context, why it is deemed so important, how to attain "cultural competence," and the desirability (or difficulty) of "connecting" with the "community." In the case of children adopted from China, for example, is the desired "community" Chinese American, or Chinese, or more broadly Asian/Asian American? A fascination with the performance or embodiment of "Chinese culture," I argue in my essay, may represent displaced longing for the unknowable narrative of the child's past and the imagined figure of the birth mother.

In a message on the Internet, a single mother of four children in Australia described how she had changed her life in order to do what seemed best for her youngest daughter from China. "I will tell her I thought long and hard about adopting a child from another country. How I read all the literature I could find in my university library, how I talked to many adult internationally adopted people from India, Vietnam, Taiwan, and the Philippines for over 3 years before I began the process . . . When they told me do not ever let your child be the only child born in her country in her class, I began to think about schools . . . and made a commitment that my child will always go to school with a significant group of other children with her ethnic background. She is. When they told me the importance of bringing up my child to know her own culture I made plans to move house to a more diverse area and I have. When they told me my child will need adults born in her country to mentor her and teach her to deal with racism I listened and we have a growing number of Chinese friends . . . We are both learning Mandarin informally from one of our Chinese friends, who also teaches me to cook Chinese food properly . . . Our lives are very rich indeed" (Carrison 2003).

This account invokes many aspects of what is often presented as a model for parenting transnationally adopted children. Still, this model, however admired, may provoke frustration and guilt about how hard it is to do all of these things, to do them well, or even do them at all. What if one cannot readily locate the "culture" of one's child? Elizabeth Honig, who adopted from Kazakhstan, wrote to fellow electronic mailing list members that she does not have the option of finding connections to her children's culture, either in the United States or in their birthplace, where the Soviets forced ethnic Kazakhs from their land, destroyed their churches, and are now trying to recreate an ersatz Kazakh culture. In her effort to give her children a "cultural connection" Honig studied Russian, which her daughters had spoken along with Kazakh in their orphanage, only to discover that many Russians whom she met were profoundly prejudiced against orphans. In their Russian language class in California her daughters were treated as fundamentally inferior. "So what do I do?" she asked. "Do I keep trying to connect the kids with the Russian community, where they DO feel somewhat at home? My children are infinitely more accepted and appreciated in the broader cultures in Berkeley and Amsterdam than they are among Russians" (Honig 2003).

Even the presumed vitality or tangibility of something one might call "culture" is not enough to resolve these problems. An adult Korean adoptee responded to Honig: "As KADS [Korean adoptees, an acronym invented by Korean adoptees], we have the same issues, perhaps shown in a more subtle manner. Native Koreans often feel 'sorry' for us, pity us, but still don't want us marrying their son/daughter. I have ambivalent feelings towards them. Wanna be with them, feel left out and resentful of them. Blame them for having the attitude, yet want to be like them. That's why fellow KADS have my love, my respect, and my word that I will always defend and fight for them. They are more real to me than Koreans and every other group. They are my nation, and through them I have a country of my own" (Eun Mi 2003).

Adoptive families and adopted people are not isolated actors but rather are engaged in some form of larger community—the travel group mediated by the Swedish agency, the emerging global Korean adoptee movement and state-orchestrated stagings of identity, hundreds of large and small organizations such as Families with Children from China (or Vietnam, or Russia, or Guatemala), and the Internet, the most distinctive contemporary form of community making. The proliferation of Internet-based adoption discussion groups has contributed to the production of the type of idealized models discussed above. While some electronic mailing lists have strong representation from adoption social workers, these are no longer the only "experts" in the field, as new parents and experienced parents and adoptees of different generations and birth countries participate and speak with authoritative voices. The Internet has also produced the possibility of multiple affiliations. There is no limit to the number of electronic mailing lists to which a person may subscribe, no end to the exchange of information and the flow of cyber conversation — at once anonymous and intimate — on every conceivable aspect of adoption.

The Internet has facilitated the formation of new communities that also go beyond the virtual. The Vietnamese Adoptee Network (VAN), for example, was started in 2000 by first-generation Vietnamese adoptees after several agency-sponsored reunions. The VAN group is now working to develop "real world" activities such as conferences and connections with Vietnamese American communities, and its members are at the same time joining other adoption lists. "We are just starting to really tackle community building and forming an identity," explained VAN's president. "I wanted to learn from some of the more established TRA [transracial adoption] identities out there, and to really keep abreast of TRA issues that may not be currently discussed in our circles" (Brownlee 2003).

Media and new technologies may create or shape communities of discourse, but they have other, complicated, effects as well. Media attention may create adoption "hot spots," as when television viewers were catapulted into action in the rush to adopt in Romania; or, conversely, reports of scandals may help halt adoptions from a particular country. As Lisa Cartwright argues in this volume, the news media and "its compelling visual evidence" may serve as "vehicles for intimate encounters and for private, even familial, transformations" that have transnational political implications. Elsewhere, Cartwright has shown how advances in digital technology have made possible the creation of a staggeringly vast visual archive of available children from certain parts of the world, especially from Russia, the former Soviet republics, and Eastern Europe. Images of "waiting children" are used to incite desire, to classify and grade and diagnose, and to serve as "identity's most legible representation" (Cartwright 2003, 90). Such images may also provide potential adoptive parents with "choice," a topic in adoption discourse that is fraught to the degree that it implicates the possibility of the child as commodity.[4] One American social worker (Brown 2003) argues against any kind of choice on the part of prospective parents, asserting that to express even a gender preference is to succumb to racist (perhaps unconscious) assumptions (desirable Asian femininity, threatening black masculinity, and the like).

Until the mid-1970s when the "open adoption" movement was born in the United States, adoptive parents were pressured to create "as if begotten" biological families (Modell 1994). These practices were premised on the forgetting of a child's past, and especially on the erasure of birth parents. In dramatic contrast, contemporary adoption discourse encourages, even exhorts, adoptive families to imagine, to grieve for, and at times to search for those parents. These changes are sometimes read as a progressive opening up, an unsettling of the constraints of conventional kinship and the idealized white, nuclear family. The wish to normalize the nonnormative family is captured in the cartoon frontispiece to Adam Pertman's book *Adoption Nation*, where two women are chatting at a cocktail party, and one says to the other, who is visibly pregnant, "Oh, I'm sorry . . . You couldn't adopt?" (2000, xi).[5]

The sense that a different kind of family is in the making is especially pervasive in accounts of transnational adoption. Writing about her new granddaughter from China, journalist Ellen Goodman describes a little girl who came to America and "reminded us how small our world is and how vast: a village you can traverse in a day and a place of stunning disconnects and differences, haves and have nots" (2003, A13). Goodman asserts: "*We have embraced her with a loyalty that is all the more tenacious for having not been preordained by biology.* We have the sort of attachment that the word 'adoption' cannot begin to describe. . . . We have made her an American, and she has made us part of the global village" (A13, emphasis added).

Are we indeed witnessing a fundamental transformation? Or, alternatively, might the desire to connect with biological origins—in the form of what many now call "birth culture," birth kin, or country—represent a reemergence of the dominant American ideology of "blood," recast in a more contemporary idiom of DNA?[6] Cartwright (n.d., 48) argues that the late-twentieth-century turn toward the social construction of family was quickly followed by a return to genetics in adoption discourse, wherein the adoptive family is seen as a "set of genetic legacies" linked through choice, "a network of blood lines that closely cross but do not mix." Tensions between these visions complicate adoptive parents' pleasure in creating new forms of kinship. "Yes, but are they *really* sisters?" ranks high on a long list of frequently asked, infuriating questions from strangers, in this case directed at parents of two adopted children. Parents respond with a repertoire of well-crafted replies, each affirming the validity of socially constructed sisterhood, even as they or their fellow adoptive parents may anxiously pursue (or imagine pursuing) the remote possibility of finding "true" DNA sisters and other birth relatives.

Preoccupations in the West that impel parents and adoptees to seek connections with the country or the culture of origin have stimulated an array of reverse flows: culture camps, charitable initiatives, orphanage visits, birth family searches, organized "gatherings," and other forms of travel. These countermovements are promoted by social workers and agencies, the adoption community, Internet discussions, a growing number of travel agencies that specialize in adoption "heritage" tours, and even in some instances by the policies of sending states, most notably South Korea. Vietnam and other countries have begun to encourage travel as well. In Beijing, China's Center for Adoption Affairs recently created a unit within its office known as "Bridge of Love," which in actuality is a travel bureau for adoptive families who would like to visit their children's orphanages, or home towns, or travel elsewhere in China.

Counterparts

In spite of all of these reverse flows, most adoptive families in the West know very little of the experiences of birth parents who have relinquished their children, of the conditions that have pressed them to do so, or of the other options they might have chosen. Several of the essays in this volume attempt to illuminate the experiences of adoptive parents' counterparts — the shadow figures on the other side of the transnational flow — and to contextualize that experience in broader terms. By drawing on encounters in the course of research in Korea on other matters, and on her own "thickened" relationships with Korean friends that developed after she adopted her Korean son, Laurel Kendall reflects on the experiences of Korean birth mothers and children twenty or thirty years ago, affirming the value of "describing the humanity of otherwise unknown lives and the conditions of class, gender, and global and national politics that inform the living of those lives." These narrative fragments, Kendall contends, belong within "the counternarrative to the assumed fixity of family bounda-

ries" and blur the presumed divisions of time and space. Like the motherland tours and birth mother reunions discussed by Barbara Yngvesson,
these narratives also shake up and open up the premises of identity. The
stories foreground the contingency of outcomes—the taxi that turned
around and changed the life of a child who would have been adopted—
and of the choices made by birth parents. Claudia Fonseca's essay makes a
similar point, as she recounts the stories of Luciana and her siblings:
Luciana, brought home from the Brazilian orphanage to care for a new
baby; her two brothers, who simply left the orphanage and walked home;
and a third brother, an infant too young to walk or to choose, adopted to
an unknown place yet still expected by his family to return some day.

Imaginings about birth mothers occupy a large space in contemporary
adoption discourse, both domestic and transnational. Social workers and
peers encourage adoptive parents to talk about birth parents and create
rituals of remembrance beginning at the moment of adoption. More organized venues, such as the adoption Playshops created by social worker
Jane Brown (see Volkman, this volume) provide children as young as
five or six with spaces in which to fantasize—through drawings, notes,
wishes, and stuffed items such as Lily, an "adopted" flower with multi-
colored roots—about their first parents. Older children play with more
sophisticated ideas. At a New York City Playshop, for example, nine-year-
old adoptees gave a drawing of a stick figure named "Irving" words to
describe what he got from each of his two sides: the birth parents provided
such things as looks and genes (along with memories and dreams), the
adoptive parents provided love and jeans (and memories and dreams). In
Irving's heart, which encompasses both sides of his duality, the children
wrote "power."[7]

In asking who are the "counterparts" of American parents of children
born in China, Kay Johnson's essay explores less familiar terrain: Chinese
parents in China who adopt abandoned children. Johnson shows how it is
Chinese laws and regulations that make in-country adoption difficult in
China and not, as is popularly assumed, that adoption is against the supposed grain of "Chinese tradition" or Confucianism. Such laws and regulations, like other birth planning policies in China, are intended to imple-
ment the population policies of the state rather than to protect rights of
the child. The consequences can be tragic, in some cases resulting in a

double abandonment when parents find it impossible to keep the child whom they tried to adopt.

While the international community welcomed the openness and liberalization of China's Adoption Law of 1992, the same law, ironically, restricted the opportunities of Chinese couples to adopt children in their own country, as well as served to inflict still greater suffering on adoptive Chinese parents and their children. In exposing this bitter underside to the passage of a law that was celebrated with enthusiasm in the West, Johnson's research is likely to provoke soul searching within China adoption circles.[8] Academic research on these topics enters into ongoing debates about the ethics and politics of transnational adoption among "practitioners" — adoptive parents and adopted people — those who are, paradoxically, "advocates for international adoption while simultaneously working to make it unnecessary" (Register 1991, 212).

The sometimes vexed relationship between transnational and domestic adoption in the realm of law and policy is also treated in Claudia Fonseca's essay, which highlights discrepancies between global legal frameworks and local understandings and practices. As Brazilian legislation was revised to conform to "modern" global frameworks for adoption (articulated in the Hague convention), it insisted on plenary adoption — that is, a complete rupture or "clean break" with the past. The possibility of such a permanent and total rupture, Fonseca argues, is profoundly discrepant with local Brazilian understandings, values, and practices involving the circulation of children — practices she portrays in rich ethnographic detail.

Although there is a voluminous, well-established body of adoption literature in psychology and social work (to a large extent focused on adjustment and "outcomes") in other disciplines adoption is an emergent field of study. As sociologist Katarina Wegar (1997, vii) notes at the beginning of her study of the debate over sealed records: "As I was quite astonished to discover, the subject of adoption has been largely neglected by sociologists." Until the recent publication of several important studies (Berebitksy 2000; Melosh 2002; Novy 2001), the same might have been said of history and literature.

In anthropology, even given its traditional core focus on kinship and the question of "what makes a relative" (cf. Rapp, Heath, and Su-Taussig 2001), the study of adoption, except in faraway places like Oceania and East Asia, has been for the most part oddly absent.[9] In the 1990s, feminist anthropology began to address topics such as new reproductive technologies (Strathern 1992) or gay and lesbian kinship (Lewin 1993; Weston 1991), creating openings for a critical analysis of adoption. In this volume we build on these studies as well as on scholarship that addresses the politics of reproduction at the intersection of the local and the global, situating adoption within a framework of "transnational inequalities on which reproductive practices, policies, and practices increasingly depend" (Ginsburg and Rapp 1995, 3). Transnational adoption, we contend, is fertile ground on which to explore the double aspect of reproduction articulated by Ginsburg and Rapp: "Reproduction is inextricably bound up with the production of culture" even as it "provides a terrain for imagining new cultural futures and transformations" (ibid., 1,2). In writing about adoption as cultural production and transformation, we also seek to raise questions about race, culture, and nation; about kinship, biology, and belonging; and about the politics of sending and receiving nations, poor and rich, powerless and powerful.

For those of us who are adoptive parents (including several authors in this collection), writing about adoption also raises methodological questions. We live daily with the ambivalences and ambiguities of adoption, and we have struggled with how to position our research and writing: how to cast an eye that is both critical and sympathetic, attuned to our own profoundly personal connections to these questions and to an analysis of the cultural and political contexts within which adoption must be situated. As partial "insiders" in the role of adoptive mothers our position may offer special access or insights, but it is also our vulnerability. Is our scholarship somehow less serious, less critical, less clear? As parents, how can we write about the adoption triad; where are the voices of adoptees and birth parents? On the other hand, those of us who are not members of the triad may struggle with "outsider" status, even in the academic community. "Mine is a delicate position," Fonseca writes, "because not only are many of my colleagues adoptive parents, but much of our audience is also in this category. I don't have the same ongoing personal engagement. I think, how do I dare enter into this debate?" (personal communication 2004).

The contradictions articulated by Pauline Turner Strong — love and violence, rupture and incorporation — are always present in adoption, sometimes prominently and sometimes quite hidden, whether in our lived experience or in our scholarship. We anticipate that children and friends as well as colleagues will read what we write. We present these essays, then, as the opening of a field of inquiry and the beginning of a dialogue not only with scholars but also with many others who are imagining and actively shaping creative forms and new geographies of kinship.

Notes

For their helpful comments on this introduction I thank Cindi Katz, Erika Duncan, and Charles Zerner.

1. Altstein and Simon (1991) identify several major "waves" of transnational adoption. In the first, following World War II, close to six thousand children orphaned in Europe (mostly Germany and Greece) and nearly twenty-five hundred in Asia (mostly Japan) were adopted by Americans. The second wave began with the adoption of Korean War orphans in the early 1950s; adoptions from South Korea continued for other reasons in the following decades. In the 1970s a third wave originated from Central and South America, followed by a fourth wave from Central and Eastern Europe, beginning with the fall of the Ceausescu regime in Romania in 1989.

2. For recent scholarly work by adoptees, see Wegar 1997; Williams 2004; and Hubinette 2004. See Kim 2001 for a discussion of films by Korean adoptees. Popular writing by U.S. birth mothers is an expanding genre, including the 2002 film by Sheila Ganz, *Unlocking the Heart of Adoption* (San Francisco: Pandora's Box Productions).

3. International-Adopt-Talk, or I-A-T, was formed early in 2001 as a forum for both adult adoptees and adoptive parents. Unlike most electronic mailing lists for adoption that are constituted by shared geography (e.g., families with children from China), I-A-T was created with the intention of bringing together people from different adoption communities.

4. Yngvesson (2002) offers an insightful discussion of the "gift child."

5. Pertman (2000, 5) writes about the "adoption revolution" through which adoptees and birth parents can now find each other, and "single women, multiracial families, and gay men and women . . . are bringing a rainbow of children from abroad into their predominantly white communities. This rather ecstatic portrayal of "happy hybridity" (cf. Lo 2000) is challenged by many adoptees and others who

contend that "race is the salient issue," and that to "celebrate the rainbow world" is to deny the reality of lived experience in a racist society (Brown 2003).

6. See, for example, Korean adoptee Jane Trenka's 2003 memoir, *The Language of Blood*, about finding her birth family.

7. This description is based on Jane Brown's summary, for parents, of a Playshop held in Brooklyn in November 2003. No parents or adults (other than Jane Brown and several young adult adoptee "helpers") participate in or observe the Playshop, which is defined as a space in which chidren can share thoughts or wishes freely with each other.

8. Johnson's (1998) earlier research on infant abandonment in China was widely read by adoptive parents and helped shape the adoption/abandonment narrative for countless girls.

9. Judith Modell's work on domestic adoption in the United States is the important exception, especially her books from 1994 and 2002.

References

Altstein, Howard, and Rita Simon, eds. 1991. *Intercountry Adoption: A Multinational Perspective.* New York: Free Press.

Berebitsky, Julie. 2000. *Like Our Very Own: Adoption and the Changing Culture of Motherhood, 1851–1950.* Lawrence: University Press of Kansas.

Bonner, Raymond. 2003. "A Challenge in India Snarls Foreign Adoptions." *New York Times,* June 23.

Brown, Jane. 2002, 2003. International-Adopt-Talk@yahoogroups.com.

Brownlee, Chris. 2003. International-Adopt-Talk@yahoogroups.com.

Cartwright, Lisa. 2003. "Photographs of 'Waiting Children': The Transnational Adoption Market." *Social Text* 74: 83–109.

———. n.d. "On the Bodies of Children: Media and Communication Technology in the Construction of the Child Subject." Unpublished manuscript.

Eun Mi. 2003. International-Adopt-Talk@yahoogroups.com.

Franklin, Lynn C. 1998. *May the Circle Be Unbroken: An Intimate Journey into the Heart of Adoption.* New York: Three River Press.

Ginsburg, Faye D., and Rayna Rapp, eds. 1995. *Conceiving the New World Order: The Global Politics of Reproduction.* Berkeley: University of California Press.

Goodman, Ellen. 2003. "Cloe's First Fourth." *Boston Globe,* July 3, A13.

Honig, Elizabeth. 2003. International-Adopt-Talk@yahoogroups.com.

Hubinette, Tobias. 2004. "Adopted Koreans and the Development of Identity in the 'third space.'" *Adoption and Fostering* 28 (1): 16–24.

Johnson, Kay, with Huang Banghan and Wang Liyao. 1998. "Infant Abandonment and Adoption in China." *Population and Development Review* 24: 469–510.

Kim, Eleana. 2001. "Korean Adoptee Autoethnography: Refashioning Self, Family and Finding Community." *Visual Anthropology Review* 16: 43–70.

Lewin, Ellen. 1993. *Lesbian Mothers: Accounts of Gender in American Culture.* Ithaca: Cornell University Press.

Lo, Jacqueline. 2000. "Beyond Happy Hybridity: Performing Asian-Australian Identities." In *Alter/Asian*, ed. Ien Ang, Sharon Chalmers, Lisa Law, and Mandy Thomas. London: Pluto Press.

MacLeod, Jean. 2003. *At Home in This World: A China Adoption Story.* Warren, NJ: EMK Press.

Melosh, Barbara. 2002. *Strangers and Kin: The American Way of Adoption.* Cambridge, MA: Harvard University Press.

Modell, Judith S. 1994. *Kinship with Strangers: Adoption and Interpretations of Kinship in American Culture.* Berkeley: University of California Press.

———. 2002. *A Sealed and Secret Kinship: The Culture of Policies and Practices in American Adoption.* New York: Berghahn Books.

Novy, Marianne, ed. 2001. *Imagining Adoption: Essays on Literature and Culture.* Ann Arbor: University of Michigan Press.

Ong, Aihwa. 2003. "Cyberpublics and Diaspora Politics among Transnational Chinese." *Interventions* 5: 82–100.

Peacock, Carol Antoinette. 2000. *Mommy Near, Mommy Far: An Adoption Story.* Morton Grove, IL: Albert Whitman and Co.

Pertman, Adam. 2000. *Adoption Nation: How the Adoption Revolution Is Transforming America.* New York: Basic Books.

Rapp, Rayna, Deborah Heath, and Karen Su-Taussig. 2001. "Geneaological Dis-Ease: Where Hereditary Abnormality, Biomedical Explanation, and Family Responsibility Meet." In *Relative Values: Reconfiguring Kinship Studies*, ed. Sarah Franklin and Susan McKinnon. Durham: Duke University Press.

Register, Cheri. 1991. *"Are Those Kids Yours?" American Families with Children Adopted from Other Countries.* New York: Free Press.

Strathern, Marilyn. 1992. *Reproducing the Future: Anthropology, Kinship, and the New Reproductive Technologies.* New York: Routledge.

Strong, Pauline Turner. 2002. "To Forget Their Tongue, Their Name, and Their Whole Relation: Captivity, Extra-Tribal Adoption, and the Indian Child Welfare Act." In *Relative Values: Reconfiguring Kinship Studies*, ed. Sarah Franklin and Susan McKinnon. Durham: Duke University Press.

Trenka, Jane Jeong. 2003. *The Language of Blood.* Saint Paul, MN: Minnesota Historical Society Press.

Wegar, Katarina. 1997. *Adoption, Identity, and Kinship: The Debate over Sealed Birth Records*. New Haven: Yale University Press.

Weston, Kath. 1991. *Families We Choose: Lesbians, Gays, and Kinship*. New York: Columbia University Press.

Williams, Indigo. 2003. Not Quite/Just the Same/Different: The Construction of Identity in Vietnamese War Orphans Adopted by White Parents. M.A. thesis, University of Technology, Sydney.

Yngvesson, Barbara. 2002. "Placing the 'Gift Child' in Adoption." *Law and Society Review* 36 (2): 401–30.

———. Forthcoming. "National Bodies and the Body of the Child." In *Cross-Cultural Approaches to Adoption*, ed. Fiona Bowie. New York: Routledge.

PART I   **Displacements, Roots, Identities**

Going "Home"

Adoption, Loss of Bearings, and the Mythology of Roots

BARBARA YNGVESSON

An angel with no face embraced me
And whispered through my whole body:
"Don't be ashamed of being human, be proud!
Inside you vault opens behind vault endlessly.
You will never be complete, that's how it's meant to be."
— TOMAS TRANSTRÖMER, "Romanesque Arches"

n the world of intercountry adoption, two stories predominate: a story of abandonment and a story about roots. In the
abandonment story, a baby is found in a marketplace, on a
roadside, outside a police station, or in the "tour" of an orphanage;[1]
alternately, a child is left by its mother at a hospital or is relinquished or
surrendered to child welfare officials, a social worker, or the staff of a
children's home. After passing through the hands of social workers, law-
yers, and/or orphanage staff, and perhaps in and out of hospitals, foster
homes, and courts, this child may ultimately be declared free for adoption,
a process that requires a second, legal separation that constitutes the child
as a legal orphan. Similarly, a mother who relinquishes her child to state
agents must consent to the irrevocable termination of her rights to the
child. In international adoptions, the child will also be separated from its
state of origin (a procedure that in some nations involves sealing the
record of this severance and altering the child's birth certificate) so that it
can be connected to a new family, a new name, a new nation. The child is
given a new identity. It now *belongs* in a new place.

This story of separation is a story about loss and the transformation of
loss into a "clean break" (Duncan 1993, 51) that forms the ground for

starting anew. The clean break separates the child from everything that constitutes her grounds for belonging as a child to *this* family and *this* nation, while establishing her transferability to *that* family and *that* nation. With a past that has been cut away — an old identity that no longer exists — the child can be reembedded in a new place, almost as though she never moved at all.

Even as this legal story of separation is the official ground for constituting adoptive identities, another story competes with it in both law and adoption practice. This other story was a persistent counterpoint to the movement for "strong" adoptions that prevailed at the Hague Conference in the early 1990s (Duncan 1993) and was incorporated into the Hague Convention as children's right to the preservation of their "ethnic, religious and cultural background" (Hague Convention 1993). The preservation story implies that there is no such thing as a clean break and underpins the search movement in domestic adoptions, the debate over sealed records, and the movement in the United States to keep adoptions open (Yngvesson 1997; Carp 1998; Verhovek 2000). In this story, identity is associated with a root or ground of belonging that is inside the child (as "blood," "primal connectedness," and "identity hunger") (Lifton 1994, 67–71) and is unchanging. But it is also outside the child in the sense that it is assumed to tie him or her to others whom he or she is like (as defined by skin color, hair texture, facial features, and so forth). Alienation from this source of likeness produces "genealogical bewilderment" (Sants 1964, cited in Lifton 1994, 68) and a psychological need for the adopted child to return to where he or she "really" belongs.

The story of a freestanding child and the story of a rooted child appear to be mutually exclusive and are associated with different adoption practices. The former is associated with race and other forms of matching that are intended to produce "as if" adoptive families that mimic natural ones (Modell 1994). Even in international transracial adoptions, where race matching is impossible, adoption practices in the 1960s and 1970s emphasized complete absorption of the adopted child into the new family and nation (Andersson 1991). By contrast, the story about roots is associated with the recognition of adoption as a distinct family form (Kirk 1981) and involves acknowledging (even underscoring) the differences between an adoptee and his or her adoptive parents, constituting the adoptive family as a site of tension because of its inclusion of a child who "naturally" belongs to another person or place.

Both practices are versions of a familiar and powerful (Western) myth about identity as a matter of exclusive belonging and of belonging as a matter of "an active proprietorship" (Strathern 1988, 135).[2] In the clean break version of this myth, the adopted child is set free from the past (constituted as "abandoned" or "motherless") so that he or she can be assimilated completely into the adoptive family. In the preservation story, on the other hand, the child is imagined as a part of his or her birth mother or birth nation, imagined as being constantly pulled back to that ground.

In what follows I propose an alternative to the narrative of exclusive belongings as a way of thinking about the connections between adoptive parent and child, adoptive family and birth family, and sending and receiving nations. This alternative begins with the lived experience of adoptees, adoptive parents, and birth parents — that no one of them is freestanding vis-à-vis the others but that there is a pull toward the other parent, the other nation. The pull back is an effect of the closures and cutoffs of adoption law and has materialized in the practices of open adoption, roots trips, searches, and so forth. These trips and the reunions to which they sometimes lead reveal how compelling the myth of the return can be. But they also unsettle the idea that such journeys of self-realization are likely to produce completion for the adoptee, or that they constitute a "journey towards wholeness" (Lifton 1994). Rather, as Elspeth Probyn (1996, 114) suggests, "bringing forth beginnings can result in a loss of bearings."

This loss of bearings involves the discovery of a self both familiar and strange, of a "me" and "not me," a pull to the adoptive parent at the very moment one is in the arms of a birth mother, a pull toward the birth mother at the very moment that she is embracing one's child. The identity narrative and the concept of a child or a parent as a "part of me" are inadequate for capturing the contradictions of desire that constitute this state "in-between being and longing" (Probyn 1996, 35). Neither do they capture the *movement* — the "desire for becoming-other" (5) — that is part of the search for a root of belonging and that is provoked by the experience of seeing someone who "looks like me," by touching the native soil of an adopted son, or by the realization that there is a connection, not an unbridgeable gulf, between oneself and the birth mother of one's child. Each of these moments provokes "yet another journey" (Saffian 1998, 301–2), an opening rather than an experience of closure.

Roots trips reveal the precariousness of "I am," the simultaneous fascination and terror evoked by what might have been, and a longing for the safety of home. They materialize an unfathomable moment of choice, when one life that might have been was curtailed and another life that exists now came into being: "Why just me? It feels very strange. One wonders, 'What would have become of me if I had remained there? Who was I during the time I was there?'" (Sarah Nordin, interview, 22 August 1999).[3] Such moments interrupt the myth that the legal transformation to an "other" was free—that the child simply came home to a site of love where he or she always belonged—revealing instead the cost of belonging (and of love), its inseparability from the birth mother, the orphanage, the courthouse, the agency, and the histories linking nations that give children to those that receive them.[4] But they also interrupt the myth of the return as a form of completion or fulfillment in which one can find oneself in another (be consumed by an other) at a place or point of fusion, of "immanence regained" (Nancy 1991,59). Rather, interruption "occurs at the edge, or rather it constitutes the edge where beings touch each other, expose themselves to each other and separate from one another" (59). As Jean-Luc Nancy suggests, this edge that both connects and separates is where beings "come into being" (61).

The roots trip described below explores these issues, focusing on the experiences of adoptive parents as they seek to fill a gap in the belonging of their adopted children; the complex emotions of adoptees as they are pulled between a familiar self and an unknown other; and the position of adoptive parents as witnesses to the "labor of mourning" (J. Benjamin 1995, 113) in which their children (and the parents themselves) are involved. My analysis here is based on participant observation and on interviews conducted in 1998 and 1999 with adults adopted as children in Chile and with the Swedish parents who adopted them in the 1970s and early 1980s. I also interviewed staff members of Stockholm's Adoption Centre and Chilean adoption officials. This work is part of a larger study of Swedish international adoption in which I have been engaged since 1995.

Return to Chile

> The Greek work for "return" is *nostos*. *Algos* means "suffering." So nostalgia
> is the suffering caused by an unappeased yearning to return.
> — MILAN KUNDERA, *Ignorance*

In April 1998 I accompanied a group of twelve Swedish families (nineteen parents and sixteen children ranging from ten to twenty-one years of age) to Santiago, Chile, on a roots trip organized by Stockholm's Adoption Centre (AC). No one in the families spoke Spanish, and because I am fluent in both Spanish and Swedish it was agreed that I would serve as one of the three interpreters for the group. I had lived in Santiago as a teenager but had not been back since that time, and in many ways the trip felt like a return to roots for me as well as for the adopted children.

The adoptions had taken place during the middle years of the Pinochet dictatorship, and for the parents this was their first visit to Chile. Some of them had adopted other children from countries such as Thailand or El Salvador, where they had journeyed to fetch their child. As I discuss below, such trips are charged, often difficult moments for adopting parents and many consider them a key piece in the work of transforming themselves into their adopted child's "real" parents. Tense political relations between Sweden and Chile during the 1970s and early 1980s — Sweden was a place of refuge for a significant number of Chileans who fled their country during Pinochet's dictatorship — meant that children adopted from Chile at that time were not picked up by their adoptive parents but rather arrived with escorts.

To complicate matters further, Swedish adoptions from Chile ended in 1991 under strained circumstances. A new adoption law introduced in Chile in 1988 as a result of concerns about child trafficking changed the relationship between AC's representative in Santiago and the tribunals in southern Chile that were responsible for approving international adoptions. Chile was one of Sweden's principal sending nations between 1974 and the early 1980s, with the number of adoptions exceeding two hundred annually in the late 1970s and remaining in excess of one hundred annually until 1985. In the late 1980s, Swedish adoptions from Chile dropped off steeply, and after 1991 they stopped completely.

Marta García, head of the adoption division of SENAME (Servicio Nacional del Menor), Chile's child welfare office, explained to me in an interview on 15 April 1998 the circumstance behind the ending of Chilean adoptions to Sweden:

> Before 1988, the Swedish Adoption Centre had its representative here and [the system] worked very well through an arrangement involving direct coordination with the tribunals [family courts], especially those in the south. . . . The babies were transported from the south to Santiago, and in Santiago they were placed in the care of the Adoption Centre, an institution which always guaranteed excellent care for the children: seriousness, transparency. No fault with the Swedish Adoption Centre, none! They had good foster mothers, good social workers who were in contact with the families, everything. But everything was very easy, also. The babies came to Santiago—almost all were from Temuco—and were entered in the civil register in Santiago with the names of the adoptive parents, with Swedish surnames. So everything was very easy for them.
>
> When SENAME was established in 1988, I had to deal with AC's representative in Santiago and we had many clashes trying to make her understand that things had changed and that now the business of international adoption was to be regularized.

The tensions surrounding Swedish adoptions from Chile are suggested in García's observation that the processing of Chilean babies for adoption in Sweden was "very easy" for the Adoption Centre. Her comment hints at the complications that, in her opinion, should surround the conversion of a child, who is assumed to be by nature Chilean, into a Swedish child, while tacitly acknowledging the power of state officials to effect such arbitrary conversions—the babies were simply "entered in the civil register in Santiago with the names of the adoptive parents, with Swedish surnames." The "Chilean child" thus in effect disappeared before it even left the country.

García's unease gestures toward the implicit assumption that underpins such transactions in children: they can only take place if the Chilean and the Swedish child are treated "as if" they are directly exchangeable for one another—that is, "as if" they are the same. Clearly, the child who might have grown up in Chile and whose mother was compelled or perhaps "chose" to relinquish, abandon, or place her child for adoption is not "the same" child who grows up in Sweden and whose mother was unable or chose not to give birth to a child, or who adopted a Chilean baby for political, humanitarian, or other reasons. The exchange is only possible, however, if this knowledge is bracketed. The adoptable child is treated "as if" it were not a material object that bears traces of its passage in the world but rather a "sublime" object that can "endure all torments with its beauty immaculate" (Žižek 1989, 18). The sublime object is treated " 'as if it were made of a special substance over which time has no power' " (Sohn-Rethel 1983, cited in Žižek 1989, 18). It was this assumption and the seeming transparency of transactions that obscured it that were disturbing to Marta García, no less than the concern that some foreign adoptions were set in motion by money, or that there was a clandestine network of caring women through which the movement of babies from Chile to Sweden was occurring.[5]

By contrast, for Swedish parents who adopted from Chile at this time the ease of the transaction was part of its appeal: there was little delay, the children were very young, and the parents assumed that there was little of their child's developmental history that they were missing. The only thing needed to complete the child was his or her "culture," something that could be passed on through stories, albums, and eventually visits to a distant land with its exotic tastes, smells, and customs. For Swedish parents, the ease of the transaction eased the process of the baby becoming their own child.

García's discomfort and the satisfaction of the parents are both an effect of the power of the market in constituting any chid—any person—as an entity that "qualifies . . . for life" in a market economy.[6] The discomfort it occasioned for García suggests how important it is to our consistency as subjects that we be blind to this truth (like the parents). Child adoption brings us face-to-face with this needed blindness and the myth it produces: that the circulation of children in a global economy is free, leaving no traces on the body of the child. The clashes with the local representative of AC over the ease with which Chilean children were becoming Swedish disrupted this myth and in doing so brought to an end Sweden's complex relationship with Chile as a sending country for adoptive children. For Chilean adoptees and their families, this meant that there was indeed a clean break with the past, one that was no less significant than the official cutoff instantiated by adoption law. The informal relationships of communication and cooperation that tie agencies in receiving countries to orphanages, foster parents, social workers, and child welfare officials in sending countries were disbanded. These relationships, which are crucial to the movement of children from nations that send to nations that receive, are no less important (as I argue in more detail below) to the memories, desires, and (re)constructions that constitute an adopted child's identity. They provide the grounds through which adoptees (and their adoptive parents) can "seize" (W. Benjamin 1969, 255) and "own" (Petcheskey 1995) a past in which the prevailing characteristic is only fleetingly and problematically captured in the metaphor of a search for roots from which children have been "cut off."

The search for roots assumes a past that is there, if we can just find the right file, the right papers, or the right person. This kind of search is part of a familiar story of belonging and of lost belongings in which an alienated self must be reconnected to a ground (an author, a nation, a parent) that constitutes its identity. By contrast, seizing the past involves not so much finding a ground as piecing one together, a process that is more material than intellectual, an active (re)inhabiting of events in order to lay claim to them (and in this sense to "own" them). Reinhabiting encompasses a broad range of processes that adopted children and their families are presently involved in, but it always involves bringing the "past" into dialogue with the present rather than collapsing present into past (or privileging one over the other).[7]

In my analysis here I am particularly interested in the revisitation of sites of involuntary displacement, separation, and (sometimes temporary) emplacement through which a child who is "abandoned" and placed for adoption undergoes the complex transformations in identity necessary to make an *adoptable* child, a "precious resource" for the nations that receive it and for those that give it away (Yngvesson 2000). Laying claim to the past in this way may shake up identity in the very moment of grounding it by revealing the interruptions, contradictions, and breaks through which the process we know as "identity" takes shape.[8] The informal relationships that bind (Northern) agency to (Southern) orphanage are crucial to this process of simultaneously making and shaking up identity.

In the case of Swedish adoptions from Chile, seizing the past required what Birgitta Löwstedt, the AC representative in charge of the agency's Resor och Rötter (Trips and Roots) division for South America, describes as "true detective work" (interview, 18 May 1998). During the first months of 1996, Löwstedt received over fifty calls from families who had adopted from Chile inquiring about adoptee backgrounds or requesting assistance in making contact with Chilean adoption officials. As a result, she renewed AC's contact with SENAME and, in late 1996, made a trip to Santiago. She took with her a suitcase filled with letters and photographs from 250 adoptive families with Chilean-born children and the name and address of one of the foster mothers who had cared for the Swedish adoptees. She was cautiously hopeful that she could contact social workers and foster mothers and possibly the doctor who had delivered many of the children.

The SENAME office was unexpectedly helpful in this process, in part because of its own interest in rethinking the relationship between Chile and its children adopted abroad. Indeed, this rethinking of the relationship of adopted children to their birth nations has become increasingly important to officials in all of the major sending nations. While SENAME had originally had no contact with the foster mothers, Löwstedt located one whose (incorrect) address she had with the help of a determined taxi driver. Through this foster mother, Löwstedt was able to locate other relations such as sisters, daughters, aunts, and in-laws, bringing them news of children they had been told to "forget" once those children had left the country. Because the Swedish foster mother system was unofficial—although not clandestine—in the 1970s and 1980s, and because Sweden's activities as an adopting nation at that time were regarded with suspicion by the Pinochet government, the women had kept a low profile and had simply disappeared as a "system" when adoptions to Sweden came to an end. They had never expected to hear of the children again.

The success of Birgitta Löwstedt's trip led to plans for a group tour to Chile in April 1998. The aim of the tour was in part simply to see the country because none of the parents had been there before and the children had left when they were infants. More significantly, however, Löwstedt saw the trip as an opportunity for parents and children to visit the hospitals, orphanages, courts, foster mothers, social workers, doctor, judges, and government offices that had been involved in the adoption of the children to Sweden. For some families, there was the possibility of locating a birth parent; for all, there would be access to court records that contained details of the birth and relinquishment, key materials for piecing together a story of the early weeks or months of their child's life.

Going Back

> What do you mean, go "back"? I want to travel there as if it were any other
> country. I want to see the *country*.
> — NINA, eighteen-year-old Chilean-born adoptee

While adoptees sometimes respond negatively to the idea that they might
want to return to their birth country, insisting that they are "completely
Swedish" (Clara, interview, 20 May 1998; see also von Melen 1998, 116)
and that for them a visit is not a "return," adoptive parents on the Chile
trip expressed a powerful desire to go to the birth country of their children. This was especially notable in the stories of parents who received
their first adopted child in his or her home country but were unable to do
so for the second child. Two such parents, who traveled to Chile with their
sixteen-year-old daughter, explained why they felt this way:

> MOTHER: For my part, I missed not having been in Chile. I wanted some time in
> my life to come to Chile, especially because we had been in El Salvador when
> we adopted Daniel [their eldest child] and saw how it was there. That piece
> was missing, I thought, when we got Maria, because we hadn't been in Chile.
> But then, we have always said that the compensation was that she was so
> young.
>
> FATHER: I felt that because we traveled to El Salvador we could be a means for
> passing on some of that to him [Daniel] [*förmedla något till honom*]. So we
> wanted to do the same for Maria, later.
>
> MOTHER: We missed being able to pass on to her our sense of the sounds and
> smells, what one has experienced oneself. That's not something you see on
> TV, you can't experience it on the TV. And it's the same thing, being able to see
> the Andes from the hotel window, the buses they drive. (interview, 15 May
> 1998).

The use by these parents of the Swedish word *förmedla*, (for which
there is no good English translation in this context) is telling: *Förmedla*
means to mediate, to go between. It also means to make peace, restore
harmony, bring into agreement. For them, going to Chile or to El Salvador
was a way of bridging the experienced gap, of restoring harmony in the
experienced dissonance of having a child who belongs on (whose roots are
in) the other side of the world. The parents become a bridge between there
and here — they become, in other words, a kind of "back" for their child
by virtue of having been there to fetch the child. The album with photo-

graphs of the orphanage, the caretakers or foster mother, and other scenes from the birth country — or in more recent adoptions, a video of the arrival at the orphanage and the stay (typically lasting weeks or months) in the child's birth country — are a visual prop for this "back." Because none of the parents on the Chile trip had been able to make the voyage to Chile when they adopted their children, the roots trip became, in the words of another adoptive mother, "my *own* life's trip [*min livs resa*]. It was very powerful." It provided for her (and she assumed for her daughter), "something concrete on which to grasp [*någonting att ta på*]. If someone asks about Chile, then you can tell about it, that you have been there, you have a photographic memory of it, you have powerful experiences associated with it" (interview, 19 May 1998).

Here, the adoptive parent becomes — like Walter Benjamin's (1969, 83, 87) storyteller — someone who "exchanges" experience, who "takes what he tells from experience . . . and makes it the experience of those who are listening to his tale." In the stories told to their children by adoptive parents, "it is not the object of the story to convey a happening *per se*, which is the purpose of information; rather, it embeds it in the life of the storyteller in order to pass it on as experience to those listening. It thus bears the marks of the storyteller much as the earthen vessel bears the marks of the potter's hand" (159). The adoptive parents' "powerful experiences" associated with the trip to receive (or revisit the birth country of) their child become embedded in both parent and child through the telling of the story. By recounting experiences that might provide their adoptive children with something concrete on which to grasp about their native land, parents thus become engaged not only in the work of completing a child who (it is assumed) might otherwise remain fragmented but in completing themselves as parents as well.

"Completion" here (unlike the conventional understanding of completion as fulfillment or making "whole") is a spatial and temporal process of "infolding" (Rose 1996, 43).[9] Through travel to a child's birth country and retelling the story of bringing the child home, powerful experiences associated with that distant landscape (the long journey to reach it, its associated sights, tastes, and smells) become a "part of me" for the parent in a process that places the adoptive child "within" the parent as well. For another family on the Chile trip, this infolding of an "exterior" place was accomplished not only by stepping together with their son onto Chilean ground but by collecting in a small plastic bag some soil from outside the hospital where he was born. The moment of gathering the soil was highly charged for the little boy's parents, who returned in tears to the bus on which they were traveling. The child himself, at ten years of age the youngest on the trip, appeared to have little interest in this event. For his parents, on the other hand, their son's past was made present in the plastic bag of soil that they took back with them to Sweden because it contained fragments of a place and was powerfully associated with the memory of their son's birth — and it would become part of the story of their return.[10]

In words that are familiar from countless stories told by adoptees, a mother on the Chile trip spoke of her daughter's need for completion in terms that applied no less (and perhaps even more) to adoptive parents. For both, adoption is a process that can never be complete. It is a response to, but also continually reproduces for parent and child, a "hole in their lives that must be filled if they are to be whole people" (interview, 19 May 1998). The trip to Chile and the memories it made possible in stories, photograph albums, and handfuls of soil were a way of attempting to fill this void. At the same time, these embodied memories were a constant reminder of what the adoptee had left behind, of what he or she lacked. In the words of another adoptee who had chosen not to revisit her birthplace, this lack — which she described as "some kind of empty space" — does not go away. It remains as "some kind of pull towards an origin [*en slags strävan mot urprunget*]" (cited in von Melen 1998, 166).

As this comment suggests, roots trips, journeys by parents to the birth country of the child they plan to adopt, and the stories that are told about these movements to bring a child home or take him or her back are not only a way of bridging a narrative gap in the relation of adoptive parent to child or completing a "break" in the child's narrative (Lifton 1994, 36–37): these practices also create gaps and narrative breaks. Journeys "back" materialize a moment of abandonment by a return to the physical spaces (orphanages, foster homes, and courtrooms) in which this break was made concrete. They constitute a kind of "time travel" (Saffian 1998, 296) that displaces "home" (even as homes are made through such journeys) and split the present with powerful memories from the past (Aronson 1997). Finally, they reveal the impossibility of ever being fully integrated, of having anything that, in the words of Astrid Trotzig (1996, 214), "constitutes both an outer and inner place where I belong."

Roots trips propel adoptees and their parents into what one Swedish social worker, in a talk about her work with adoptive parents, describes as "the eye of the storm" (Stjerna 1996). They bring the adoptive family and the adoptee face to face with the terror and the promise of confronting an "other" who is experienced as a "part of me" by the adoptee but who cannot be fully contained and remains irredeemably other for the adoptive family. In adoption practice, the birth mother embodies this other, but the birth country is also a powerful site where the potential and the impossibility of full belonging may be experienced (Trotzig 1996; Liem 2000; Yngvesson and Mahoney 2000). A confrontation with this impossibility shakes up the idea of a coherent "I" and the illusion of autonomous families, nations, and selves on which this "I" is contingent, gesturing instead toward the dependence of receiving nations and adoptive parents on the dispossessed for their *self*-possession and at the irreducible distance and asymmetry involved in this relation of difference and of nonpossession. The stories below illuminate these contingencies of belonging, focusing on the ambivalence and discomfort experienced by adult adoptees, while opening a space in which a more complex understanding of the relationship of self and other can materialize.

"This Is Your Country"

> I don't think I had so many expectations. I didn't know what to expect of the country, except maybe that in some way I would get to know myself, but then of course one knew that one was into [*in på*] two different places, that one belongs in two different places. I already knew that before I went.
> — MARIA, sixteen-year-old Chilean-born adoptee

Like adoptive parents, for whom the journey to Chile was a way of placing their (unknown) child within themselves, for adoptees coming to know Chile was a way of connecting to an unknown part of themselves, a part that they weren't even sure was themselves. For example, Maria talked about how she had wondered, before going on the trip, "Do I really come from Chile?" By contrast to a friend from Colombia, whom she described as "having more of a Mapuche-like appearance," she herself was not obviously "from Latin America."[11] With her light skin, "I could have been something else." Maria described a ceremony held at the offices of SENAME on one of the last days of the trip, when the director said to all of them, " 'This is your country.' It was, I think it was for everyone, it was a conviction that, 'OK, I am from Chile, too!' It was like a confirmation from a Chilean and from the country itself that I am from Chile. It was so big in some way. That was why we dared to respond and began to cry" (interview, 15 May 1998).

Clara (an eighteen year old) described an evening gathering with the foster mothers as the moment when "I began to realize that I was really there." She had fantasized about Chile before the trip, but "it felt strange to be there. It felt as though I myself was left in Sweden although my body was in Chile, and so was somewhere in between, *where one didn't know where one was.* It was really strange. But when we met the foster mothers, I found myself" (interview, 20 May 1998; emphasis added).

Like Maria, whose light skin made her wonder if she "really" came from Chile (as though, her father commented wryly, "we had fooled you"), Clara worried at times about who she was, but in her case it was her dark skin that occasioned doubts. She recalled a time in the second grade when some people came up to her and began speaking Spanish, and she "couldn't grasp what they were saying. And then I began to think, 'they see me as an immigrant, when actually I am Swedish.' " Anti-immigrant incidents in Stockholm made her feel "scared, since it isn't obvious on the outside that one is adopted." She continues: "There is that feeling of unease [*en sådan här oroskänsla*], that others see one as though one is dark, those around you, those you know, and you know yourself that you are completely Swedish. And you know, sometimes I forget that I am dark skinned. When I sit with friends and chat. And then when one looks in the mirror: 'Aha! That's how it is!' " (interview, 20 May 1998).

This sudden sense of "aha!" was intensified on the roots trip to Chile and was a key element in the repeated (re)discovery by adoptees that one is not "completely Swedish." This discovery was mediated, in part, by its collective dimension and by the support experienced from other adoptees and from parents.[12] As Clara explained, regarding the close bonds developed among adoptees on the trip, "one didn't need to explain how one felt, because everyone felt the same." This "same" feeling was on the one hand exhilarating. It involved a kind of grounding of an intuited self as Chilean that had always seemed just out of reach in Sweden, until one "looked in the mirror." But it was complicated by the inseparability of being Chilean (of being "dark-skinned," of being "Mapuche-like") from the experience of abandonment that was rediscovered in the physical spaces of hospitals, orphanages, and courtrooms, in the spoken words of social workers and government officials, and in the writing on "papers" that finalized the separation of each adoptee from her mother and from the country to which she was now returning in order to find or know her self. The carefully cultivated experience of pride in being Chilean, transmitted by the Swedish parents of the adoptees and connected to their own experience of the trip as "my life's trip," was contingent on the adoptees' displacement to Sweden, on their being able to imagine Chile in the way their parents did, as part of a tour of Chile or a temporary visit from afar. Adoptees could in part share this imagined Chile with their parents, but their parents could only act as witnesses to a part of Chile that their children had once experienced firsthand and up close. This complex, emotionally explosive Chile was in the rooms and beds of an orphanage, in the feel and smell of a rosary that belonged to an adoptee's birth mother, and in the written words and physical presence of a doctor or a matron who had recorded the details of a particular child's birth. As one twenty-year-old woman described her feelings after reading through a file of documents at the Temuco court, and after visiting the orphanage where she had spent three weeks as an infant and driving by the house where her mother once lived, "It was the most tumultuous day of my life. I found out about everything! [*Det var det mest omtumlande dag av mitt liv. Jag fick veta allt*]" (interview, 9 April 1998).

Two Mothers

> FATHER: How do they choose which children will be adopted? What criteria does the court have for accepting or rejecting a child?
>
> SOCIAL WORKER: There are no criteria for accepting or rejecting a child, but the mother is advised of her rights. Before the child is born, we explain what it means to place the child "in a state of abandonment" [*en situación de abandono*]. It will be like the child is dead to her. She will never hear more about the child.
>
> — Field notes from visit to Temuco court, 18 April 1998

Central to the meaning of the Chile trip for each adoptee, in one form or another, was some attempt to grapple with the experience of abandonment and with what Jessica Benjamin (1995, 113) describes as "the labor of mourning." For some, this desire was more clearly formulated than for others. Clara went to Chile together with her adoptive mother in the explicit hope of meeting her birth mother. She had learned her mother's name from documents in Sweden and she carried with her a letter in which she wrote, "Although I don't know you, I feel as though in spite of everything, you are a part of me." Clara explained how much she longed to know what her mother looked like and who she was. With the cooperation of SENAME and the assistance of a distant relative who had cared for her mother when she became pregnant and was forced to leave home, the woman was located after a week's search, and Clara's letter was delivered to her. A meeting was arranged for the day prior to Clara's departure for Sweden. Clara explained her feelings about this meeting during an interview in Stockholm a month later:

> CLARA: I felt so strange, and wondered how I would react, if I would stay in one piece [*sitta helt*], that is, if I would not start to cry or if I would immediately begin to cry when she came. . . . But when she saw me, she began to cry and then . . . but it was as though, because I have always had a hole inside, or however one might say it, and then when I saw her, immediately I cried and then it [the hole] was filled again. I still don't understand that feeling, that it went so fast. I was almost a little scared.
>
> AUTHOR: That the thoughts were gone, you mean?
>
> CLARA: Yes, or rather, the thoughts, the fantasy of how she would look. Now I had a picture of how she looked and how she was, how the house was. So everything fell into place in an hour. It was such a short time.
>
> ADOPTIVE MOTHER: It was a very strong experience. I had also imagined what she would be like, that she was probably very poor and had lived a hard life and would be marked by that. But that wasn't the way it was. Well, she was poor, but not very poor. One understood how much she had suffered.
>
> CLARA: One thing I had thought a lot about was sitting in the same room with two mothers. I thought it would feel very strange.
>
> AUTHOR: And when it actually happened?
>
> CLARA: It felt good, partly because I could speak Swedish with my mother from Sweden, and then I had you, who could translate. I felt supported to have Mamma along, someone from Sweden. It was something one could return to, that one wasn't alone in Chile. (interview, 20 May 1998)

The meeting with Clara's "mother from Chile" was held in the modest house of the woman who had cared for her eighteen years previously and was attended by Clara's cousins, a half-sister, a nephew, and other extended kin, as well as by her adoptive mother and a social worker from SENAME. I was also present at the meeting, to interpret for Clara and for her birth mother. As they cried themselves out together and I leaned toward them to catch their whispered words, there was a kind of breathless silence. Clara's mother caressed her daughter's face and begged her forgiveness. I felt like the thinnest of membranes connecting the two women (linguistically, physically) — and separating them from (joining them to) Clara's Swedish mother who stood nearby. I struggled to maintain my composure. Even the youngest children seemed to be suspended in the tension that caught us all up in this collective moment of recognition, in which Clara said she felt as though she were "more or less the same and yet not the same [as her birth mother], since she is mother to me and I am daughter to her."

Afterward we all sat down to a long meal together where gifts were exchanged and addresses written down. On leaving, Clara took with her a rosary that was a gift from her birth mother. She described this later as a wonderful present: "I could see that it had been used, and it had a special smell. It smelled like her." It was "something one knows about that one can make something of [later], on one's own."

This notion that "one can make something of" an object surely includes moments of completion or of "filling a hole," as in Clara's meeting with her mother. Similar moments were experienced by other adoptees in the midst of the turbulence of the return, as they walked on the streets in the neighborhoods where their mothers once lived, visited the maternity wards of the hospitals where they were born, or held the files containing details about the time and place of their birth, the name and age of their mother, and the date on which she formally consented to their abandonment. But return trips and other efforts at recovering or confronting the past are always ambiguous, and moments of clarity are typically just that — mere moments in a process of self-constitution that is ongoing, painful, and turbulent, challenging any sense of a stable ground of belonging.

One woman, elated finally to be touching the papers in her court file and overwhelmed with the sense that finally she had "found out about everything" — the hour of her birth, her mother's name, the address where her mother had lived when she was born — became distraught when she was advised not to make contact with the woman. She insisted on driving by her house, lingering on the street where she imagined she had once lived, and photographing the area. When I spoke to her a month later, she was still shaken by the experience. She had also become worried about the issue of how babies are chosen for adoptive parents. Her own parents expressed shock at the discovery that children today are carefully monitored by the agency for defects, and that their other child, an adopted son who suffers from Asperger syndrome, would surely have remained in his Thai orphanage had his affliction been known. Another adoptee, who hoped to contact her mother and brother in Chile, was told by a court social worker that this move would be unwise because the woman was "extremely aggressive" and had threatened to harm herself and the baby had she not been permitted to surrender her for adoption nineteen years earlier.

These events, no less than the meeting of Clara with her birth mother, disturb the notion of return as completion or closure, revealing the distance and asymmetry separating women who give their children away and those who receive them as acts of love. They expose the work involved in producing a child who can be chosen (by the agency, by the parent) so that it can be loved as though it were "one's own" and underscore the key role of a legal clean break in securing the ground on which exclusive belonging is forged: the freedom of the child, the adoptive parent, and the birth parent vis-à-vis one another. Return trips unsettle these freedoms, revealing the powerful dependencies that underpin them. On the Chile trip, these dependencies were pieced together from fragments of a past that each person seized in an effort to make sense of an event that could never make sense and that would forever remain, "somewhere beyond the reach of the intellect," even as it was "unmistakably present" in papers, places, and the ambiguities and silences of a court document (Walter Benjamin 1969, 158).

In each of these situations, the mediating presence of others (adoptive parents, other adoptees, AC staff, the kin of Clara's mother, the children in an orphanage, myself as interpreter) was crucial to the process of seizing the past. We became both witness and bridge, a potential space in which the complex and contradictory meanings of being "the same as me" (or "different from me") could materialize in places that were saturated with meaning for the adoptees and their families (the hospital, the maternity ward, the orphanage, the court, the house of a foster mother, and so forth). These places, perhaps more than any words that were spoken, infused present encounters with meanings that were linked to memories and fantasies of what had once taken place there. At the same time, these fantasies, and the work of constructing an account of the adoptee's abandonment, depended on her capacity to "return to [them]" in Sweden, a return that was possible because "one wasn't alone in Chile."

The Eye of the Storm

> An area like a hole or column in the center of a tropical cyclone marked by only light winds or complete calm with no precipitation and sometimes by a sunlit clear sky (the eye of a hurricane).
> — *Webster's Third New International Dictionary*

Ingrid Stjerna, a Swedish social worker who works with prospective adoptive parents, describes how important it is to awaken in the adoptees "positive, warm, empathic feelings for this person who could not take care of her child. It is important for the child that they have these positive feelings." Stjerna notes that this is harder to accomplish when "you became a parent standing at Arlanda [the Stockholm airport] with money in your hands—none of this traveling to difficult countries." Meeting the mother, by contrast, "awakens anxiety. Background and country and decorations and songs, all that is fine—but the mother: no. That puts them into the eye of the storm. That forces them to come to terms with the pain and misery" (Stjerna 1996).

Coming to terms with the fact that "there is no such thing as a motherless child—even if she is dead, she is important" has been crucial to the transformations that have taken place in adoption over the past two decades and in international adoption during the past ten years. That such children are not motherless implies that their adoptive parents must accept the fact that they are not actually their children, Stjerna argues. What I understand her to mean by this is not that these children belong to somebody else but that they are not freestanding—that they came from someone, and from somewhere, and bear the traces of that elsewhere just as they bear the traces of the pull or the desire that links them to their adoptive parents and adoptive country. Accepting that the adoptees belong to no one means accepting that they are neither rooted nor freestanding but rather marked by an existential condition of being thrown into the world as much as by the need for connection, for hands to catch them so that they can take their "place" in the world (Merleau-Ponty 1968, paraphrased in Doyle 1994, 210). The return trip to Chile illuminated the contradictory truths that the adopted child—like other children—has been thrown into the world, but that she or he is not motherless. The condition of being thrown marks the child as "not me," as fundamentally "other than me," while the condition of being "not motherless" marks the child's proximity, his or her openness to an encounter with a stranger who can say, "This is my child, too."[13]

Ingrid Stjerna's insistence that the adoptee is not a motherless child in spite of the breaks mandated by adoption law captures (in different words) Marilyn Strathern's (1997, 301) idea of the double-evocative power of the gift—the gift child of adoption has been freed for exchange and links the giver and receiver as partners in the exchange. These partners are embedded in a complex web of connections, a web that broke down when adoption from Chile to Sweden ceased in 1991. This web binds orphanage to agency and adopting mother to abandoning mother, tying those developing nations with an "excess" of children to the overdeveloped nations that need these children. The physical movement of a child in adoption—the routes he or she takes from "there" to "here"—is a part of this interdependence and the exchanges through which it is played out. To be "in the eye of the storm" is to enter, imaginatively and in practice, the space of these exchanges.

Entering this space involves more than having warm, positive feelings about the birth mother or pride in the birth nation of a child. These benevolent feelings evoke the sense that the eye of the storm is a site of calm, but they ignore the relationship of this center of calm to the chaos that produces it. To enter the eye of the storm is to take risks: that a background story will be too hard to bear, that the pull "back" will be too powerful, that boundaries will be lost—the edges that make our families complete. The challenge for international (and other forms of) adoption today is in the ways it has opened a space that is structured by adoption law but not fully contained by it. This space has revealed a kind of chaos that shakes up (and opens up) families, individuals, and nations in the world that created international adoption and that international adoption helped to create. While adoption is the focus of this opening up, the questions it raises remind us that we are all in one way or another close to the eye of the storm, which is where life is lived.

Notes

The research on which this article is based was supported by the National Science Foundation (grant no. SBR-9511937) and by faculty development grants from Hampshire College. It was made possible by the cooperation and generosity of adoptive parents, adoptees, staff members at Stockholm's Adoption Centre, and Chilean child welfare officials. I thank Michelle Bigenho, Maureen Mahoney, Beth Notar, Jeff Roth, Janelle Taylor, Sigfrid Yngvesson, and in particular Nina Payne for their helpful comments on earlier drafts.

1. The "tour," or "wheel," was a device initiated in early nineteenth century France that enabled women who had given birth and were unable or did not want to keep their child to deposit the child anonymously at a foundling home. The device has also been documented in other parts of Europe (such as Italy, Spain, and Portugal), where it is known as the "roda" or "rota." It is still in use today in some countries, and in the latter years of the twentieth century was proposed in parts of the United States as a means of preventing infanticide. For a discussion of the tour, see Isabel dos Guimaraes Sa (1991).

2. As Strathern notes (1988, 158), there is no comfortable space for the presence of an "other" in this concept of identity, except as supplanted authorship or proprietorship. See also Farrell-Smith's (1983, 205, 208) discussion of the exclusion of others as fundamental to the idea of "proprietary or possessive control over another thing or person." For a discussion of the ways in which adoption policy and practice work to constitute adopted children as the adoptive parents' "own," see Ragoné 1996, 359; Hoelgaard 1998, 229–31; Yngvesson 1997, 67–76; and Yngvesson and Mahoney 2000.

3. The interviews from 1998 and 1999 cited in this essay were recorded either in Spanish or in Swedish and were translated by the author.

4. The phrase "came home," or "will come home" is widespread in Internet discussion groups for the parents of internationally adopted children and in magazines and brochures published by and for adoptive parents.

5. The argument about the exchange value of a child is persuasively developed by Zelizer (1985) and by Kopytoff (1986), both of whom build on Simmel's (1978 [1908], 390–91) seminal insights about the complex relationship between desire for an object and the object being "set into motion" by money. As Zelizer (1985, 14) argues, the priceless child presents a legal quandary that is no less a cultural and social quandary: "How could value be assigned if price were absent?" Kopytoff (1986, 75) points to this same paradox, noting that to be " 'priceless' in the full possible sense of the term" can as easily refer to the uniquely worthless as to the uniquely valuable. To acquire value, Kopytoff argues, the "patently singu-

lar" must become part of a "single universe of comparable values" — that is, it must be placed into circulation, made "common" (68–72).

6. The quote is from Butler (1993, 2). The argument here draws on my reading of a range of works relevant to this issue, including Strathern 1988 (135–59); Kopytoff 1986; and Žižek 1989. The crucial point is that entry into the symbolic order of culture and law is an arbitrary legal process on which our "naturalization" as whole persons (as civil subjects) is contingent.

7. Here I build on Lyotard's (1984, 22) insight about the "ephemeral temporality" that accompanies narrative knowledge. Lyotard argues: "The narratives' reference may seem to belong to the past, but in reality it is always contemporaneous with the act of recitation."

8. For a discussion of identity processes in adoption narratives, see Yngvesson and Mahoney 2000.

9. Drawing on the work of Deleuze, Rose (1996, 143) describes the "fold" as indicating "a relation without an essential interior, one in which what is 'inside' is merely an infolding of an exterior."

10. See Walter Benjamin's (1969, 158) discussion of how "the past is 'somewhere beyond the reach of the intellect, and unmistakably present in some material object (or in the sensation which such an object arouses in us)' " (quoting Proust, *A la recherche du temps perdu*). Similarly, Rose (1996, 143) suggests that "memory of one's biography is not a simple psychological capacity, but is organized through rituals of storytelling, supported by artefacts such as photograph albums and so forth."

11. Note here the stereotyped linking of Latin America more generally with the "indigenous" and the use of "Mapuche" as a trope for a person of color.

12. By contrast, see Swedish adoptee Astrid Trotzig's (1996) account of her trip alone to Pusan, South Korea, where her experience of not belonging there was no less intense than in Sweden.

13. These words were spoken by an Ethiopian woman as she smoothed the bed covers over a friend of her birth daughter during a visit of the two Swedish women to Ethiopia. Both had been adopted by families in Sweden.

References

Andersson, Gunilla. 1991. *Intercountry Adoption in Sweden: The Experience of 25 Years and 32,000 Placements*. Sundbyberg, Sweden: Adoption Centre.
Aronson, Jaclyn C. 1997. "Not My Homeland." Senior thesis, Hampshire College, Amherst, MA.
Benjamin, Jessica. 1995. *Like Subjects, Love Objects: Essays on Recognition and Sexual Difference*. New Haven: Yale University Press.

Benjamin, Walter. 1969. "The Storyteller." In *Illuminations: Essays and Reflections*, ed. Hannah Arendt, trans. Harry Zohn. New York: Schocken.

Butler, Judith. 1993. *Bodies That Matter: On the Discursive Limits of Sex*. New York: Routledge.

Carp, E. Wayne. 1998. *Family Matters: Secrecy and Disclosure in the History of Adoption*. Cambridge, MA: Harvard University Press.

dos Guimaraes Sa, Isabel. 1991. "The 'Casa da Roda do Porto': Reception and Restitution of Foundlings during the Eighteenth Century." In *Enfance Abandonée et Société en Europe XIVe–XXe Siécle*. École Francaise de Rome: Palais Farnèse.

Doyle, Laura. 1994. *Bordering on the Body: The Racial Matrix of Modern Fiction and Culture*. New York: Oxford University Press.

Duncan, William. 1993. "Regulating Intercountry Adoption: An International Perspective." In *Frontiers of Family Law*, ed. Andrew Bainham and David S. Pearl. London: John Wiley and Sons.

Farrell-Smith, Janet. 1983. "Parenting and Property." In *Mothering: Essays in Feminist Theory*, ed. Joyce Treblicot. Totowa, NJ: Rowman and Allanheld.

Hague Convention. 1993. Hague conference on private international law, final act of the seventeenth session, 29 May 1993, 32 I.L.M. 1134.

Hoelgaard, Suzanne. 1998. "Cultural Determinants of Adoption Policy: A Colombian Case Study." *International Journal of Law, Policy, and the Family* 12: 202–41.

Kirk, David. 1981. *Shared Fate: A Theory of Adoption and Mental Health*. New York: Free Press.

Kopytoff, Igor. 1986. "The Cultural Biography of Things: Commoditization as Process." In *The Social Life of Things*, ed. Arjun Appadurai. Cambridge, MA: Harvard University Press.

Liem, Deann Borshay. 2000. *First Person Plural*. San Francisco: NAATA. Video.

Lifton, Betty Jean. 1994. *Journey of the Adopted Self: A Quest for Wholeness*. New York: Basic Books.

Lyotard, François. 1984. *The Postmodern Condition: A Report on Knowledge*, trans. Geoff Bennington and Brian Massumi. Minneapolis: University of Minnesota Press.

Merleau-Ponty, Maurice. 1968. *The Visible and the Invisible*. Evanston, IL: Northwestern University Press.

Modell, Judith. 1994. *Kinship with Strangers: Adoption and Interpretations of Kinship in American Culture*. Berkeley: University of California Press.

Nancy, Jean-Luc. 1991. *The Inoperative Community*. Minneapolis: University of Minnesota Press.

Petchesky, Rosalind P. 1995. "The Body as Property: A Feminist Re-Vision. In *Conceiving the New World Order: The Global Politics of Reproduction*, ed. Faye D. Ginsburg and Rayna Rapp. Berkeley: University of California Press.

Probyn, Elspeth. 1996. *Outside Belongings*. New York: Routledge.

Ragoné, Helena. 1996. "Chasing the Blood Tie: Surrogate Mothers, Adoptive Mothers, and Fathers." *American Ethnologist* 23: 352–65.

Rose, Nicolas. 1996. "Identity, Genealogy, History." In *Questions of Cultural Identity*, ed. Stuart Hall and Paul du Gay. London: Sage.

Saffian, Sarah. 1998. *Ithaka: A Daughter's Memoir of Being Found*. New York: Basic Books.

Sants, H. J. 1964. "Genealogical Bewilderment in Children with Substitute Parents." *British Journal of Medical Psychology* 37: 133–41.

Simmel, Georg. 1978. [1908]. *The Philosophy of Money*. London and New York: Routledge.

Sohn-Rethel, Alfred. 1983. *Intellectual and Manual Labor*. Atlantic Highlands, NJ: Humanities Press.

Stjerna, Ingrid. 1996. Address to visiting Adoption Centre representatives, Stockholm, 21 August.

———. 1997. "Partners and Consumers: Making Relations Visible." In *The Logic of the Gift: Toward an Ethic of Generosity*. New York: Routledge.

Strathern, Marilyn. 1988. *The Gender of the Gift*. Berkeley: University of California Press.

Trotzig, Astrid. 1996. *Blod är tjockare än vatten* (Blood is thicker than water). Stockholm: Bonniers.

Verhovek, Sam H. 2000. "Debate on Adoptees' Rights Stirs Oregon." *New York Times*, 5 April.

von Melen, Anna. 1998. *Samtal med vuxna adopterade* (Conversations with adult adoptees). Stockholm: Raben Prisma/NIA.

Yngvesson, Barbara. 1997. "Negotiating Motherhood: Identity and Difference in 'Open' Adoptions." *Law and Society Review* 31: 31–80.

———. 2000. "Un Niño de Cualquier Color: Race and Nation in Intercountry Adoption." In *Globalizing Institutions: Case Studies in Regulation and Innovation*, ed. Jane Jenson and Boaventura de Sousa Santos. Aldershot, Eng.: Ashgate.

———. 2004. "National Bodies and the Body of the Child: 'Completing' Families through International Adoption." In *Cross-Cultural Approaches to Adoption*, ed. Fiona Bowie. London: Sage.

Yngvesson, Barbara, and Maureen Mahoney. 2000. " 'As One Should, Ought, and Wants to Be': Belonging and Authenticity in Identity Narratives." *Theory, Culture, and Society* 17: 77–110.

Zelizer, Viviana A. 1985. *Pricing the Priceless Child: The Changing Social Value of Children*. Princeton: Princeton University Press.

Žižek, Slavoj. 1989. *The Sublime Object of Ideology*. London: Verso.

Wedding Citizenship and Culture

Korean Adoptees and the Global Family of Korea

ELEANA KIM

On a hot August afternoon in a bucolic setting on the outskirts of Kwangju, South Korea, a palanquin was hoisted up and brought to the site of a canopy tent, under which was a table laden with food, alcohol, and two live chickens. An elderly Korean man intoned directions into a microphone and an interpreter called out the translation in English. Around fifty Koreans, the women dressed in Korean *hanbok*, surrounded the tent, and all eyes were on the heavily made-up bride as she was helped out of the palanquin, her face turned down into her hands, elbows raised to either side of her head. She and the bridegroom knelt on opposite sides of the table, rising awkwardly to kowtow several times, pouring and ceremoniously sipping alcohol from carved-out gourds — and thus endured the elaborate ritual of a traditional Korean wedding ceremony.

In this pastoral location, the authenticity of the ritual performance was made conspicuous by tennis shoes and sports sandals peeking out from beneath the hanbok (which were poorly fitted — some too large and some too small for their wearers) and by men in tank tops and shorts looking on from a distance. As the spectators stood on tiptoe and craned their necks to observe the careful gestures of the bride and groom, their gazes were frequently interrupted by the aggressive movements of television camera crews. Some onlookers were elbowed out of the way by camera operators getting into position, another was hit in the head more than once by a camera being wielded on the operator's shoulder.

This was not, by any means, a typical Korean wedding — in fact, it was not even a legitimate union between a man and a woman.[1] The presence of the cameras and their intrusiveness on the experience of those watching suggested that the intended audience was elsewhere, on the other side of the lens. The audience here was being captured as part of the same spectacle, ultimately to be consumed by the Korean public.

In fact, the "wedding" was staged for a group of overseas Korean adoptees, who had been invited and were hosted by the South Korean government under the auspices of the Overseas Koreans Foundation (OKF), a division of South Korea's Ministry of Foreign Affairs and Trade. The roles of bride and groom were played by Korean adoptees, and the onlookers were, for the most part, other adoptees, or, like myself, camp counselors.[2] It was the seventh day of a ten-day program attended by thirty adoptees, who ranged in age from sixteen to thirty-four and hailed from North America, Europe, and Australia. On this day, perhaps aggravated by the heat, frustrations had mounted, and the presence of the media only made things worse. Later, some complained to me that they felt like "animals in a zoo"; that they had been made a spectacle of as they were transported from location to location on what one adoptee called "the orphan bus," which was emblazoned with a banner stating "2001 Summer Cultural Awareness Training Program for Overseas Adopted Koreans" (*kugoe ibyang tongp'o moguk munhwa yônsu*) in Korean and English.

The Motherland

I begin this essay with the story from the 2001 OKF summer program to suggest how government attempts to grant 'Koreanness" to overseas Korean adoptees can come into conflict with the desires and experiences of adopted Koreans themselves.[3] The OKF program was in many ways an attempt to wed Korean adoptees to "Korea,"[4] an invitation to the "motherland" so that they might, as offered by the president of OKF, "begin to feel the breath of Korea's rich culture." The OKF program was cohosted by Global Overseas Adoptees' Link (GOA'L), a then three-year-old organization established by adoptees, and Bridge of Adoptees from Chonnam Kwangju (BACK), an independent Korean organization headed by a local businessperson and run by volunteers.

This motherland tour occupied the participants with activities that included trips to ancient palaces and courses on Korean "traditional" food and customs, thus introducing them to a folklorized vision of Korean culture. Attendees were largely discouraged from experiencing contemporary urban South Korean life, with the exception of one afternoon of sightseeing in Seoul, several hours at Korea's largest amusement park, and a presentation of the Republic of Korea's military prowess at the demilitarized zone. One day of the program was devoted to the third annual GOA'L conference, where issues were addressed such as the search for and reunion with birth families and the human rights of adoptees. The conference, however, was the only adoption-related activity on the itinerary.

Motherland tours are a means of offering a safe way for adopted Koreans to return to their country of birth, and can also provide an opportunity for adopted Koreans to meet others like themselves from all over the world. The 2001 tour was unexceptional in that the tensions that arose around the desire to search for birth families, the lack of spare time, and the restrictions on participants from experiencing the "real" Korea are reportedly common with other tour programs.[5] What was exceptional about the OKF tour, however, was the intensity with which these conflicts played out, especially with respect to the participants' perceptions of the Korean state and its orchestrating role in their experience. These conflicts help to illuminate the complex dynamics of adoptee identity in a transnational context, particularly with respect to Korea.

Since the Seoul Olympic Games in 1988, adoptees have been returning to Korea in increasing numbers. Globalizing forces and transnational phenomena — in the form of South Korean products, media and immigration to other parts of the world — have rendered South Korea imaginable as a place of actual return for adoptees and have also been key in shaping the boundaries of the Korean government's recognition of adoptees as Koreans. Transnationally adopted Koreans have recently been legally incorporated into the "global family" of Korea as part of the cultural and economic "globalization" policy (*segyehwa*) nominally inaugurated under President Kim Young Sam and expanded under President Kim Dae Jung (see S. Kim 2000). The OKF, established in 1997, is the prime government agency for incorporating overseas Koreans (*chaeoe tongp'o*). In its 2001 summer program training guide, the OKF statement of mission is "to serve as the spokesperson on behalf of overseas Koreans worldwide. We recognize their immense contributions, which [have] provided a tremendous boost, not only to the Korean economy during the 1997 economic crisis, but also the morale of Koreans everywhere."

The ritual ceremony described above, I argue, reveals how Korean adoptees' "identity," existing as it does between available diasporic categories, both in the West and in South Korea, is brought into visibility at moments when state practices come into contradiction with the lived, felt experiences of adoptees in their "birth country," as they unearth their pasts, recover embodied memory, and confront the "elsewhereness" of their "authentic" identities. Encounters with the South Korean state — through Motherland tours, official ceremonies, or official state discourses — may thus reveal awkward weddings of "culture" and "citizenship" wherein stagings of identity provoke unintended and unanticipated effects among adoptees, thereby opening up the possibility for resistant practices and alternative senses of belonging. Based on my observations as a participant in the summer 2001 OKF program and in September 1999 at the first Gathering of the First Generation of Korean Adoptees, my research suggests that a collective adoptee consciousness is surfacing in a transnational field, provoked in part by "disidentification" with hegemonic versions of being "Korean."

The OKF program is a government-sponsored "motherland" tour, and the Gathering is an adoptee-organized biannual conference that has planted the seeds for what is emerging as a self-consciously global movement. Despite this important difference, both sites provide views of the complex ways in which Korean adoptees encounter "Korea." Moreover, both show that the diversity of Korean adoptees' experiences frustrates attempts at broad generalization. Not only do differences among them cut across personal histories and nationalities, they also transgress boundaries of class, race, and gender and sexuality, as well as religion, generation, and region.[6]

As adults, adopted Koreans negotiate a complex relationship to Korea in a globalized economy that has made it possible for them to recognize their own ethnic identity in new ways, both individually and collectively. This identity is also being reformulated by the South Korean government, in light of a broader political and social transformation that places Korean adoptees in the ambiguous position of being at once reminders of a difficult past and beacons of an ideal global future (cf. Hubinette 2002). In this essay I explore this dialectical relationship by posing questions about cultural citizenship and national belonging for a transnational group that is being newly (re)valued as a "diaspora" by the South Korean state.[7]

Disidentification

José Muñoz (1999) employs the concept of "disidentification" to reference a strategy of cultural survival in which subaltern performances of difference become "rituals of transformation" that render visible the boundaries of symbolic meaning and the constructedness of naturalized social categories. From a less psychoanalytically inflected perspective, Lisa Lowe (1996, 103–4) writes that "disidentification expresses a space in which alienations, in the cultural, political and economic senses, can be rearticulated in oppositional forms. . . . [and] it allows for the exploration of alternative political and cultural subjectivities that emerge within the continuing effects of displacement." I draw on both Muñoz and Lowe (extending their discussions of minoritarian cultural politics in the United States into a transnational context) to argue that it is precisely in the moments of "disidentification" with the official narrative of the South Korean state that the adult adoptee as a problematic social category becomes visible.[8]

Against the attempted enrollment of adoptees into the mythic national narrative or into an ahistorical folklorist spectacle, Korean adoptee "auto-ethnographies" and what I call "sites of collective articulation" (E. Kim 2001) constitute individual and group visibility through expressive forms and social practice. I interpret these practices as inscriptions of an unofficial history of adoption from South Korea, one in which histories of dislocation and displacement reveal the possibilities for counterhegemonic reimaginings of social relations. It is through translocal practices that Korean adoptees are constructing and questioning their "roots," against the autochthonic master narrative proffered by the Korean state.

Ritual performances produced under the South Korean state, like the wedding ceremony, encourage Korean adoptees to participate in enactments of Koreanness, yet they also produce a conflicted sense of cultural belonging, often provoking feelings of inauthenticity and alienation—and, sometimes, active resistance. Moreover, the welcoming embrace offered to Korean adoptees by the South Korean government is also a stifling one, one that requires "forgetting" in order to present adoptees as harbingers of the global future of Korea.

For many adoptees who go to South Korea the past weighs heavily, whether as something to actively explore through birth family searches or as something to defer. Many confront their individual histories and understandings of cultural identity and belonging in ways that they may never have done before. This sense of belonging is, in some ways, connected to "Korea" as nation-state and ethnic-cultural paradigm, but it is also produced out of a disjuncture from "Korea." The social memory of transnational Korean adoptees is necessarily fractured, diverse, and deterritorialized. And, because Korean "adopteeness" is increasingly articulated by a collective, global, and deterritorialized community, collective histories that are constructed through shared storytelling constitute a kind of "disidentificatory" practice out of which Korean adoptee cultural citizenship emerges.

For most of the participants, the OKF program was an opportunity to travel to South Korea, to meet other adoptees, and to share their stories. For some it was a chance to seek information about their birth families or to try to meet their foster parents. The program, however, was ultimately geared toward "cultural training." Under pressure from ministry officials the director of the program laid out very strict rules for attendance and curfews, thereby making many participants, who were adults in their twenties and thirties, feel infantilized. Not a few participants, therefore, felt that their desires were frustrated or ignored by the camp organizers, who planned an exhausting and tightly packed itinerary that kept participants occupied in "cultural training" activities for twelve to fifteen hours a day. Because of the tight schedule, groups of adoptees often stayed awake until four or five o'clock in the morning to socialize in a relaxed atmosphere and to share their personal stories.

According to the OKF Web site, its aim is "to promote Korea's rich cultural heritage, and to give the resident Koreans abroad a chance to explore their motherland and gain better understanding of Korea through language study, cultural training and touring. Through such training, [OKF] aspire[s] to help Korean adoptees understand and appreciate their Korean identity." The program thus constructs the adoptees as tourists, with an emphasis on their lack of cultural competence, over the acknowledgment of their intimate and embodied ties to Korea and to their biological families.[9] Moreover, the OKF statement points to an underlying assumption that Korean adoptees have a "Korean identity" that they need to "understand and appreciate," and thus to a central tension between opposing notions of identity as either biologically given or culturally achieved.

In addition, the OKF program is an opportunity for the Korean media to dramatize adoptee stories, to spectacularize their lack of cultural knowledge, and to highlight the Korean government's efforts to welcome adoptees back to their "motherland." The media thus becomes a problematic presence, underscoring for many adoptees the instrumentalizing logic behind the program itself. Indeed, the "adoption problem" in Korea is one that the major broadcasting stations have exploited in recent years. The increasing numbers of adopted Koreans returning to South Korea every year are particularly vulnerable to the voracious media appetite for melodramatic content, especially that surrounding family separation, cultural loss, and transnational contingency.[10]

For some adoptees, traveling in a group that clearly marks them as "tourists" made asserting their rights to Koreanness very important. For example, during the trip to the amusement park, one adoptee from France was talking animatedly with other French-speaking adoptees as they were being harnessed into an adventure ride. The ride attendant, clearly curious about their cultural backgrounds, asked if they were Japanese or American. I was about to answer that they were from France, when the French adoptee, fluent in French and English and competent in basic Korean, pointing to himself emphatically, asserted, in Korean and English: "I'm Korean! *Hanguk saram!*"

In encounters between adoptees and "Korea" a play of authenticity and difference merges and collides with discourses of nationalism and globalization, thereby creating a range of contradictions, in the midst of which, I argue, an increasing number of adoptees are finding a place to inhabit and make claims to being "Korean." Conferences and roots tours serve as sites for performances of "culture," as well as for the articulation of multiple losses — of birth family, cultural "authenticity," psychic wholeness, personal history and memory, and legitimate citizenship. These counterdiscourses oppose the attempts of state institutions and adoption agencies to imbue adoptees with "cultural roots" or diasporic "identities." "Korea" as the site of primary dislocation thus also becomes a site of conflicting identifications. Through these encounters we can begin to see the ways that the Koreanness of Korean adoptees is being conjured, appropriated, and incorporated, and how their complicated histories both comply with and resist those appropriations. Adoptees' disidentification from offical constructions of Koreanness fuels a counterhegemonic production of Korean adopteeness, and the proliferation of "sites of collective articulation" — activity in cities around the world and on the Internet — constitutes alternative locations for the production of Koreanness, Korean adopteeness, and for the emergence of a collective history.[11]

The Global Movement of Korean Adoptees (I)

The history of adoption from South Korea spans five decades, which makes South Korea the country with the longest continuous foreign adoption program in the world. Harry Holt, an evangelical Christian and logging magnate from Oregon, became a legendary figure in Korean adoptee history when he and his wife, Bertha, adopted eight GI babies in 1955. Largely because of their efforts, both the Korean and the U.S. governments hastily passed legislation to facilitate the rescue of these children (Sarri, Baik, and Bombyk 1998). The Holts soon established the Holt Adoption Agency (now Holt International Children's Services), which continues to be the leading agency for transnational adoption today. Following the first wave of mixed-race children came full-blood Korean "orphans," relinquished in large part due to extreme poverty, a lack of social service options, and a staunchly patrilineal "Confucian" society that placed primal importance on consanguineous relations, especially on the status that comes with bearing sons. According to Altstein and Simon (1991, 4), South Korea allowed the "almost unrestricted adoption" of orphaned and abandoned children from the 1950s through the 1970s.

Whereas the women who relinquished their children in the 1960s and 1970s tended to be poor factory workers, by the 1980s, as South Korea's economic boom took off, unmarried college-age women were giving up their babies. Today, a trend in teen pregnancies has supported the supply of adoptable children. No doubt, factors such as South Korea's rapid industrialization, uneven economic development, patriarchal attitudes about women's sexuality, residual gender ideologies that are in contradiction with liberal sexual practices, and the recent IMF crisis serve to perpetuate the social conditions that contribute to the abandonment or relinquishment of children in South Korea.

Since 1954, more than 200,000 children have been adopted from South Korea to foreign countries. Approximately 150,000 of those adopted were sent to American families, with the rest adopted into families in Europe and, in recent years, Australia. In the United States, South Korean adoption accounted for over half of the total international adoptions during the 1980s and early 1990s. In 1989, with most countries sending less than one-tenth of 1 percent of live births abroad, South Korea was sending 1 percent of live births (Kane 1993, 336); at its peak, this totaled over 8,000 children in one year alone.

North Korea had already criticized the South Korean government for its liberal adoption policies in the late 1970s, and the government subsequently took steps to reduce the numbers of foreign adoptions by instituting the Five Year Plan for Adoption and Foster Care (1976–1981), which included measures to promote domestic adoption (Sarri, Baik, and Bombyk 1998). When South Korea achieved international recognition and honor as the host of the 1988 Summer Olympics in Seoul, it also received negative scrutiny from the American press for exporting its "greatest natural resource," its children. Reportedly bringing in $15 to $20 million per year, adoption in South Korea had become a business and a cost-effective way of dealing with social welfare problems (Rothschild 1988; Herrmann and Kasper 1992; Sarri, Baik, and Bombyk 1998).

Due to growing ignominy in the eyes of the international community, the government soon announced a plan to gradually phase out adoption by implementing a quota system to reduce the number of children sent abroad by 3 to 5 percent a year. In addition, state policies in the early 1990s encouraged domestic adoptions through tax incentives and family benefits and gave preference to foreign couples willing to adopt mixed-race or "special needs" children. An eleven-year decline in transnational South Korean adoption was reversed with the IMF crisis, which caused a concomitant crisis of overflowing orphanages. In 1996, approximately five thousand children were placed in state care, and that figure was projected to double in 1998, leading the Ministry of Health and Welfare to announce that it "has no choice but to make changes to recent policy which sought to restrict the number of children adopted overseas" (C.-k. Kim 1999).

Adoption from South Korea has proven to be extremely sensitive to economic fluctuations and concerns over the nation's international reputation. As recently as July 2002, following the successful cohosting of the

2002 World Cup games, the government announced a series of measures to further bolster the nation's image, which included a plan to end overseas adoption (Shim 2002). It is too soon to determine whether this new plan will, in fact, lead to the end of international adoptions from South Korea or whether it, too, will be set back by economic pressures, as has been the case with other such plans over the past four decades.

What is certain is that South Korea, with the lowest social welfare spending of any OECD country (S. Kim 2000, 26), holds aspirations for advanced-nation status that render problematic its continued reliance on foreign adoption. Economic and material realities suggest that these periodic abatement plans will continue to be shortsighted and ineffectual unless adequate resources are developed for the welfare of women and children. Other problematic hurdles to the curtailment of adoption are related to the deeply embedded patriarchal ideologies of Korea — the social stigma associated with single parenthood, the low status of women, and the "Confucian" rejection of nonagnate adoption — and they render single motherhood in Korea to be a hazardous or wholly unfeasible choice for most women.

Domestic adoptions have been on a slow yet steady increase since 1995, with 1,726 adoptions by South Koreans in 1999, yet those South Korean adoptive parents can only partially alleviate the problem of the 7,000 children in need of welfare intervention each year (Jang 2000). Public education campaigns encouraging greater receptiveness to domestic adoption have been instituted by adoption agencies in South Korea, and increasing openness among parents of adopted children has helped to reduce some of the stigma of adoption in South Korea. Foreign adoptions from South Korea have dropped to around 2,000 per year, yet the nation continues to rank third in the world — after Russia and China — in the number of children adopted by Americans annually.[12] This international movement of 2,000 South Korean children to foreign countries is matched by a reverse movement of 2,000 or more Korean adoptees who as adults return to South Korea every year.

The Global Movement of Korean Adoptees (II)

With generations of adopted Korean children having come of age since the 1950s, a number of elaborations of a distinctive "Korean adoptee" identity have begun to emerge over the past few years. Many adoptees are now excavating their own pasts and critiquing assimilationist models to ask questions about kinship, social relations, biological ties, and "family" ideology. Against the dominant discourses provided by Korean, American, and Korean American communities, they are actively exercising a Korean adoptee "voice" in the process of naming and constituting what one Korean American adoptee has dubbed a "fourth culture" (Stock 1999).[13] Their experiences as "pioneers" of transnational adoption have made them valuable resources for rethinking adoption policy and practice. Some individuals and groups are participating in the current and future practice of Korean and transnational adoption as advisors and consultants to agencies and parents or as mentors for younger adoptees. And some adoptees are now adopting children from South Korea themselves, building multigenerational Korean adoptive families.

The "fourth culture" of Korean adoptees is one based on a common core experience of being adopted and Korean. Yet the balance of these two categories of identity varies among individuals, and for adoptees at both the Gathering and on the OKF tour, other vectors of identity, such as regional commonalities, seemed more relevant than being either Korean or adopted. Nevertheless, the potent pull of "roots" has drawn a significant number of Korean adoptees to sites such as these.

The ability for overseas adopted Koreans to imagine themselves as "Koreans" and as part of a transnational community of adoptees has only recently been made possible through global flows of communication and media and also through the direct intervention of the state, which has begun to publicly acknowledge adoptees as part of the modern "global family" of Korea. Transnational flows of information and people have created more opportunities for adoptees and biological families to find and meet each other, with electronic registries and the Internet providing faster and more efficient means of tracking and disseminating information.

In addition, over the past decade the Internet has facilitated the growth of organized groups of adult Korean adoptees around the world. Since the early 1990s, at least a dozen adult adoptee organizations and support groups have sprung up worldwide — in Europe, Australia, the United States, and South Korea. Along with numerous electronic mailing lists, Web sites, newsletters, magazines, and literary anthologies, these "sites of collective articulation" provide spaces for the voicing and exploration of shared historical origins and common experiences with assimilation, racism, identity, and dual kinship. Adoptees of Korean descent are producing and managing a growing sense of collectivity from the available cultural and ethnic categories. They are performing their own form of cultural work on the borderlands "beyond culture" (Gupta and Ferguson 1992) and asserting their position in a global "ethnoscape" (Appadurai 1996) constructed out of discourses of Korean diaspora and transnationality.

Developing out of a common history and a growing globalized consciousness, this "imagined community" (Anderson 1991) negotiates and brings to light a complicated and troubled relationship to "Korea" as nation-state, culture, and place. Common feelings of disorientation and alienation from Korean culture are expressed by adoptees who go back to Korea, and desires for "authentic" personhood (Yngvesson and Mahoney 2000) frequently surface in adoptee activities of self-narration. These narratives suggest that the ideal of building bridges, of being "flexible citizens" (Ong 1999) or postcolonial hybrid subjects, may be more compelling in theory than in lived practice (cf. Maira 1999). Transnational Korean adoptees have historical, biological, and ethnic connections to their country of birth, yet for many of them those connections are abstracted from their everyday lives, having been raised in majority-white cultures in American and European Caucasian homes. A concern with identity and loss emerges in much adoptee artwork, in which expressive practice enacts a recuperative (re)production or (re)creation of a memory of Korea that has been severed or forgotten (E. Kim 2001).

The Korean adoptee "movement" has been both a community-building project and a political one, exhibiting concerns with both cultural struggle and social policy. Sites of collective articulation and searches for self and identity through different aspects of adoptee experience contribute to the production of what Teshome Gabriel (cited in Xing 1998, 93) refers to as "a multi-generational and trans-individual autobiography, i.e., a symbolic autobiography where the collective subject is the focus. A critical scrutiny of this extended sense of autobiography (perhaps hetero-biography) is more than an expression of shared experience, it is a mark of solidarity with people's lives and struggles." The Gathering and the OKF program help to illuminate some of the translocal conjunctures that form the broader context for the emergence of Korean adoptee "hetero-biography," constituted by their discursive and symbolic practices.

The Gathering

In September 1999, over four hundred Korean-born adoptees from thirty-six U.S. states and several Western European countries congregated for three days in Washington, D.C.[14] Heralded as the "first significant and deliberate opportunity for the first generation of Korean adult adoptees to come together," the Gathering of the First Generation of Korean Adoptees, or simply the Gathering, as it was called by participants, did not purport to advance a specific political or ideological agenda, but rather was desecribed in the program notes as "a time for us to celebrate that which we all share." Restricted to adoptees over the age of twenty-one (and their spouses or partners), with some spaces reserved for "adoption researchers" and adoption agency "observers," the Gathering was one of three major international public events of 1999 that together represent a growing Korean adoptee presence,[15] and a self-conscious production of what Nancy Fraser (1992) calls a "counterpublic."[16]

The Gathering was touted as the first conference organized by, and exclusively for, adult Korean adoptees. For many there, it symbolized an important moment of self-determination in which they asserted their autonomy from families, agencies, and governments — institutions that since their relinquishment, had decided their fates and mediated their realities. The framing of adoption as an accomplishment was continually emphasized in the opening remarks of the conference, often with a sense of wonder, pride, or gratitude. No doubt, these dominant representations exclude the negative experiences that many adoptees have endured due to displacement, anti-Asian racism, and the social stigma that accompanies transracial adoption.

The informal title of the conference, "the Gathering," carries with it connotations of communalism, nonpartisanship, and quasi religiosity, underscored by the Korean translation that accompanied it, *da hamgae* (*ta hamgge*). Translated as "all together," this phrase is suggestive of a collective voice or chorus singing in unison. As articulated by Susan Soon-Keum Cox — then vice president of public policy and external affairs for Holt International, conceiver and primary organizer of the conference, and herself a Korean Caucasian who was adopted in 1956 — the intention of the conference was to "focus on us" — that is, the adoptees, for whom the "connection to the birth country is forever."

This connection to the birth country for individual adoptees, however, has been fraught and difficult, and has only recently been acknowledged by the South Korean state. For some adoptees, their actual experiences in South Korea have been marked by perceived rejection, outright discrimination, and painful alienation. After returning to their birth country, for many adoptees "Korea" becomes demystified as a place of nostalgia or "home" as they come to accept that they are, as one American adoptee put it, "genetically Korean, but culturally American." At the Gathering, "Korea" — as nation-state, as "culture," and as memory — was diversely articulated by government officials, adoption agency professionals, and adoptees. An essentialized Koreanness was being drawn on by all of those constituencies but in very different ways, bringing out conflicting interpretations of whether or not Korean adoptees are "Korean," and, if they are, how they are so.

The Global Family of Korea

In tandem with this recent proliferation of adult adoptee activity, the Korean government in the late 1990s under President Kim Dae Jung demonstrated a remarkably open attitude toward adoptees — through policy reforms, public recognition of Korean adoptees in South Korea, and official statements such as at the Gathering. A symbolic break occurred in 1998, shortly after President Kim's inauguration, when he invited twenty-nine Korean adoptees to the Blue House and offered them an unprecedented public apology. Along with visa rights extended to adoptees, the opening of the Adoption Center in Seoul in 1999 indicated the government's interest in openly addressing the public stigma of adoption in South Korea.[17] This recognition of overseas adopted Koreans was credited in part to the advocacy and encouragement of President Kim Dae Jung's wife, First Lady Lee Hee-ho. At the Gathering, First Lady Lee, presented via video in Korean with English subtitles, provided a matronly face for the symbolic "motherland," embracing adoptees as a source of pride for adoptive parents, Korean culture, and the South Korean state.

Lee Hee-ho's video address emphasized the ethnic roots of Korean adoptees, exhorting them to "forget your difficult past and renew your relations with your native country in order to work together toward common goals based on the blood ties that cannot be severed." Lee emphasized the role of adoptees in the future of South Korea, which, as she stated, is "developing day by day to become a first-rated nation in the twenty-first century. It will be a warm and reliable support for all of you." In drawing on globalization ideology, coupled awkwardly with metaphors of nurturance, her message was embedded in an economic discourse in which the South Korean nation continues to aspire to First World status. In this narrative, South Korea, which may have been unable to take care of its own in the past, is now capable of incorporating and "supporting" her abandoned children.

South Korean Ambassador Lee Hong Koo echoed the First Lady's sentiments, adding that the role of Korean adoptees would be to build a bridge "between the country of birth and the present country of citizenship." These statements reveal a significant proactive shift on the part of the position of the South Korean state in defining the ambiguous position of Korean adoptees, who are, through their constitutive origins and potential allegiances, at once eminently and incompletely transnational. To instill ethnic pride and identification among adopted Koreans, the government, through OKF, offers the adoptees a chance to experience "Korea" as the motherland — a distinctly modern, transnational projection of the nation. The Korean motherland capitalizes on a trope of gendered nationalism that naturalizes the presumed biological and emotional ties that adoptees must feel for the nation, as it also implicitly constructs "Korea" as temporally prior and spatially originary.

In an interview with a television reporter, one adoptee on the OKF program was asked whether she thought Korea was her motherland. She answered, "I think of Korea as my motherland because this is where I was born, and America as my fatherland, because it's where I was raised." This division of the adoptee's identity across transnational space and time is symbolically accomplished through the transposition of kinship relations onto geopolitical and historical ones. And this specific form of objectification resonates with statements by Korean state officials, wherein blood and original belonging are first rhetorically separated from citizenship and present-day belonging and then formulated to suggest their symbolic conjoining through the mechanisms made possible by "globalization."

At the Gathering an explicit opposition was posed between the birth country to which, as Susan Cox stated, "the connection . . . is forever," and the adoptive country in the West, which is the contingent, "present" one of citizenship rather than of blood. The birth country is constructed as an "authentic" source of Koreanness, an inalienable tie that binds Korean adoptees to the motherland and, more overtly now, the state. And the rhetoric of "success" that echoed throughout the opening plenary statements was undoubtedly influenced by the elevated class status of these adoptees as indexed by their college educations and professional occupations.[18] As Ambassador Lee noted in his speech, "You demonstrate the capacity to transform oneself from humble beginnings to success." In many ways, then, adoptees would seem to reflect the same progress and development model offered by the narrative of South Korea's miraculous and meteoric rise out of a colonial past through the devastation of war to its ascendance as a newly industrialized "Asian Tiger," boasting in 1996 the world's eleventh largest economy.

These expressions are tokens of a larger national project that seeks to interpellate and co-opt adoptees as overseas Koreans to be integrated into a modern, hierarchically structured Korean "family," even as the state and adoption agencies frequently discourage or frustrate adoptee searches for their biological families. This national project indicates a desire to construct certain overseas Koreans as productive links between South Korea and the global economy, writing them into a narrative of neoliberal capitalism that excludes "other" Koreans — women, mixed-race Koreans, and nonaffluent diasporic Koreans in the global South (see Park 1996). These adopted children, now adults, are framed as cultural and economic bridges to the West, as representatives of Korean culture, and as potential mediators of global capital. The position of the Korean adoptee vis-à-vis the state is one that is deeply embedded in the context of South Korea's globalization policies and state-sponsored nationalism.[19]

What emerged during the Gathering, however, was a disidentification between the rhetoric of the South Korean state and the lived experience of adoptees who feel disconnected, culturally foreign, and ontologically displaced in South Korea. What constitutes their ties to South Korea is precisely those memories of the "difficult past" that Lee Hee-ho exhorted the adoptees to "forget"; unearthing those memories is part of the process of return, search, and reunion for many of the adoptees. As Lisa Lowe (1996, 26–27) points out, "*political emancipation* through citizenship is never an operation confined to the negation of individual *private* particulars; it requires the negation of a history of social relations." The "forgetting" of personal and national trauma is encouraged not only in American multi-culturalist ideologies, but also in the recent attempts by the South Korean government to produce a homogeneously "Korean," yet heterogeneously dispersed, "family" based on shared ancestors or "blood."

Against the narrative of "success" and "achievement" that character-ized the Gathering's opening plenary session, the adoptee-centered work-shops complicated the meanings of that "success," with attendees sharing intimate and painful memories of Korea, their childhoods in America, and the negative experiences of living in a white culture with a "white" name and family but an Asian physiognomy.[20] The experiences of adoptees in South Korea, as expressed in a workshop I attended,[21] reflected a sense of disappointment in the failure of the fantasy of "home" to live up to reality. For some it was a very painful time as they faced their pasts, confronted their feelings about being adopted, and worked out complicated issues about race, ethnicity, and culture. Many expressed amazement at finally being in a place where they looked like everyone else, but also spoke of the difficulty of not "relating" to Koreans or Korean culture. Others had more positive experiences, with one attendee insisting that one or two trips would not be enough; he had been back to Korea six times, because "you have to go several times to understand your relationship to [Korea]."

Overwhelmingly, across all of the workshop groups, adoptees ex-pressed feelings of discrimination from Americans and feelings of rejec-tion from both South Koreans and Korean Americans. The perception of being "looked down on" was linked by adoptees to interactions with South Koreans who treated them as objects of pity. Other adoptees men-tioned meeting South Koreans who were surprised at how well they had grown up, for they had only heard sensationalist stories about sexual abuse and slavery of adopted children by foreigners.

A survey of participants at the Gathering found that 40 percent of respondents said that they identified as Caucasian in their adolescence and perceived Asians as "the other" (Evan B. Donaldson Adoption Institute 1999). For adoptees like them who grew up isolated from others and who identified primarily as Americans, therefore, racial discrimination posed a particularly difficult form of double-consciousness. Even the most empa-thetic parents were perceived as unable to fully relate to the experience of racism, thereby intensifying feelings of alienation and racial differ-ence. Some described it as a pendulum swinging back and forth between

"Korean" and "American" sides. Many agreed with one attendee's sense that "Koreans reject the American side, Americans reject the Korean side," adding, "Koreans reject the adoption side. For them, I [have] no family, no history."

Adoptees who were encouraged by their adoptive parents during their adolescent years to make connections to their Korean "heritage" often rejected those attempts, with some feeling that the culture pushed on them was "overdetermined," as if they were "the only ones with an ethnic identity." As one adoptee said, "kids just want to fit in and be normal," and many agreed that they felt most comfortable in "mainstream" white culture. Another adoptee described her identity as being "about culture, and your culture is not your face — but you're pinpointed for that all your life." But the recognition of a broad historical and cultural shift was clear — as one adoptee stated, an "international identity is emerging," and another informed his cohort, "Don't you know? Asian people are 'in' now."

Much of the cultural work emerging at sites such as the Gathering is centered on the articulation of double-consciousness, as well as a double-orientalizing move, one based on reified understandings of "culture" and of "nation." Adoptees who may feel alienated from Korea, as well as from "traditional" Korean communities or those of Korean diaspora, often regard Korea as other even as they attempt to understand what it means "to be Korean." So, while many adoptees use the metaphor of a pendulum to describe the experience of swinging between Korean and American "sides," there is also a tendency to speak of being "Korean" in ethnicized and essentializing ways. At the same time, however, the Korean state is invested in a self-orientalizing project that is tied to tourist discourses and its own vision of itself as an "Asian Tiger" (see Ong 1999).

This double-orientalizing move complicates any easy interpretations of Korean adoptee articulations of identity as subaltern interventions, and instead calls for an investigation of the dialectical relation between these practices and the dominant notions of being Korean in the diaspora and in South Korea. Louie (2000, 655) writes about Chinese American youth on "roots" tours to China, arguing that the tours raise "tensions . . . between historically rooted assumptions about Chineseness as a racial category and changing ways of being culturally, racially and politically Chinese (in China and the diaspora)." Adoptees, occupying an ambiguous and troubled place in the Korean imaginary, raise similar tensions. As reminders and remainders of South Korea's Third World past, the "illicit" sexual practices of Korean women, and American cultural and economic imperialism, they are the specters of a repressed history, one on which the official narrative of South Korean modernity utterly depends.

Yet adult adoptees now occupy a peculiarly privileged position in the context of the global economy. Having been reared in predominantly middle- to upper-middle-class white families, adoptees may lack cultural "authenticity" but this is seen as a necessary loss in return for the benefits of material wealth, "success," and the opportunities afforded by the West. In this way, international adoptees may be considered literal embodiments of the contradictory processes of "globalization." The play of identity and difference that characterizes Korean transnational transracial adoption is one in which Koreanness is a national, political, and cultural discourse that seeks to interpellate adult Korean adoptees into a productive role in the global economy, and one that Korean adoptees face when they encounter other overseas Koreans, and especially when they return to South Korea.

At the district office of Kangdong-gu in Seoul, South Korea, a conference room was set up for a special citizenship ceremony. A camera operator from the Educational Broadcasting System, who had been following the group everywhere they went, was joined in the room by other camera crews from other major stations. I was asked to explain to the adoptees that the reason they were invited to the ceremony was to receive an identification card and a certificate of "honorary citizenship" (myôngyegumin) to Kangdong-gu, an outlying district on the eastern edge of metropolitan Seoul. The adoptees were welcomed by the mayor of Kangdong-gu, who was a longtime, dedicated supporter of adoptees who return to Korea. Indeed, the mayor, in his ardently delivered speech, went so far as to suggest that each adoptee consider Kangdong-gu to be his or her "hometown" (kohyang): "If you get lost, you can tell people that you are from Kangdong-gu."[22] They should, he further stated, feel free to contact the district office if they had any problems while in Korea. Another counselor, who lives in the district, whispered to me, "They can't even help the people who live here — how are they supposed to help them [the adoptees]?" Each adoptee was ceremoniously given a certificate and an ID card with their picture and their Korean name — neither of which was an official document, but rather symbolic artifacts intended as a gesture of welcome to the adoptees.

A volunteer representative for the adoptees, a college student from Massachusetts, then rose and gave words of appreciation to the mayor on behalf of the group. She was overwhelmed with the district's show of generosity and broke down in tears. The group was then invited out to a celebratory dinner and karaoke party, after which I asked two American adoptees what they thought of the ceremony. One of them, echoing the sentiments of the woman from Massachusetts, said in earnest, "It was so nice of them. I can't believe it. They really didn't have to do this." The adoptee from France and another from Italy offered starkly different impressions, however—they had been offended by the ceremony and compared the ID cards to toys, agreeing with each other that "they are treating us like children."

Perhaps due to the stifling summer humidity or to their poor construction, the Kangdong-gu ID cards, laminated pieces of cardboard with passport-size photos pasted onto them, started to break apart within a few days. The tour itself began to show signs of fracture by the end of the trip, provoking the adoptees, despite differences in age, nationality, personal histories, and individual concerns, to join together to express collective outrage at the program organizers and the Korean government. After a lengthy meeting from which counselors were prohibited, as a united group they confronted the camp organizer with a list of demands. They felt that their camp experience had been co-opted and abused by the South Korean government, primarily through the media. They demanded to have a meeting with the president of OKF to present their concerns about the program. Many felt that they had been misinformed about the program, which had initially advertised on its Web site that assistance would be provided for birth family searches. They were thoroughly cynical, believing that "it's all about money." More than one adoptee said, "This is about the media and the World Cup. They're using us to show how great adoption is."

After the meeting, the group projected a strong sense of solidarity, and seemed to have overcome latent rifts due to cultural and linguistic barriers between the English-speaking and French-speaking adoptees. Yet upon further discussion with some participants, a degree of ambivalence also became apparent: some expressed gratitude to the Korean government for hosting the trip and to the director and counselors for their efforts and their friendship, whereas others were incensed enough to threaten to leave the group entirely. One adoptee from Chicago told me that the program was the first time he'd felt like he "fit" among a group of people, and for many of the adoptees on the trip, for whom this was the first time they had met other adoptees like themselves, it seemed to be a very memorable, if not a transformative, experience.

An Internet group was set up shortly after the trip ended, and some of the program participants organized a transatlantic reunion, as well as coordinated trips back to Korea. A lively exchange, maintained for well over a year, was full of information and advice about, among other things, living in Korea, language programs, job announcements, adoptee conference updates, talking to one's adoptive parents about the desire to search, and dealing with racism and discrimination in Korea and at home. The adoptee from Chicago also started an adoptee organization in that city where he networks with other Korean adoptee organizations.

The Diasporic Futures of Korean Adoptees

Korean transnational adoptees present a challenge to anthropological categories of diaspora and hybridity that are used to describe transnational subjects marked by dislocation and/or deterritorialization. Although similar to "exiles" or "refugees," adoptees are distinct because of their emigration as children. The aspect of agency that grants a measure of rational choice to exile, even under extreme duress, is arguably of a lesser degree and kind for the adoptee. The adoptees' connection to "homeland" is often embodied yet disconnected from practical consciousness, and they often lack any images or documents of their preadoption pasts. For this reason, in many Korean adoptee cultural forms, including the program for the Gathering, preadoption photos and documents are fetishized and present a talismanic aura. Often they are displayed as a juxtaposition of "before" and "after" photographs, outlining a trajectory from one location to another, from one name and possible identity to another.

Like Paul Gilroy's (1993) black Atlantic or the Sikh diaspora described by Brian Axel (2002), the diasporic imaginary or cultural identity of Korean adoptees is based less on memories of a mythic homeland and more on a shared experience of violence and loss. The pastoral mission of the

OKF program is invested in fostering an identification in adoptees with "Korea" and Korean culture in order to give them not only a sense of "roots" from which draw for personal strength but also to potentially benefit the economic and political position of South Korea in the world. Yet state-orchestrated returns to the "motherland" prove that returns to Korea may serve to further problematize the location and construction of "home."

Akhil Gupta and James Ferguson (1992, 11) discuss the power of imaginary "homelands" for diasporic or exiled peoples: "The relation to homeland may be very differently constructed in different settings. Moreover, even in more completely deterritorialized times and settings — settings where 'home' is not only distant, but where the very notion of 'home' as a durably fixed place is in doubt — aspects of our lives remain highly 'localized' in a social sense." Likewise, I argue here that the first Gathering and the OKF program were local sites in which notions of "home" were negotiated through explorations of individual subjectivity and group identity and mediated through available discourses on cultural citizenship and belonging. For adult adoptees located at the borderlands beyond "culture" Korea presents a problematic site of identity, memory, and desire, and for adoptees who have returned to their country of birth, the common experience of demystification, largely due to negative experiences with Korean ethnocentrism, leaves many with a stronger feeling of loss and of being without "home."

In discussing issues of national identity with an adoptee from Germany and with one from France, I asked, rather naively, if they couldn't imagine themselves as being both Korean and German, or Korean and French, in the way that I try to imagine myself as both Korean and American. In response the French adoptee asserted, "You need to be situated in a nation. It's too idealistic to think that you can live in between. You need to be sure in a concrete reality." As indicated by the cases of the OKF camp and the Gathering, hybridity, or dual belonging, is often felt to be an uncomfortable in-between state that is an undesirable, or even untenable, location. Unable to be fully "French" in France or even "American" in the United States, such adoptees are likewise unable to be fully "Korean" in South Korea or in the Korean diaspora. For another young French adoptee who declared "I don't like France and I don't like Korea," the question still remains, "Where can I go?"

A possible answer to this question might be that "home" is where you make it. Based on the research presented here I argue that, as Lowe (1996, 104) attests, "displacement, decolonization and disidentification are crucial grounds for the emergence of . . . critique" and for the emergence of alternative histories. And as Barbara Yngvesson (2000, 305) suggests, the potential for a "cosmopolitan, counterhegemonic consciousness among adoptees" is latent in the proliferation of discursive activity and shared social practice. Sharing stories and imagining community is, like the production of "public intimacy" in the disability community that Faye Ginsburg and Rayna Rapp (2001) describe, a form of "mediated kinship" that, in this case, offers a critique and remodeling of both kinship and national belonging in South Korea and elsewhere.

Following Stuart Hall (1996, 349), the emergence of ethnicity in the postcolonial era can be seen as a response to globalizing processes, wherein "ethnicity" is a local production of identity that is eminently political and positioned: "It has a relationship to the past, but it is a relationship that is partly through memory, partly through narrative, one that has to be recovered. It is an act of cultural recovery." This dual movement of recovering and creating memory is key to the construction of kinship and identity in the adoptee movement. Adoptees are producing their own "nation" out of available diasporic discourses and in relation to the South Korean state (Johnsen 2002). In the process of building a self-consciously global "community," competing notions of "home," ethnicity and belonging emerge and are negotiated in a variety of ways, through a variety of media.

Public recognition of adoptees in South Korea has also come about through the work of adoptee activists who have mobilized for greater awareness and sensitivity to adoptee issues. GOA'L is now recognized as a nongovernmental organization in Korea, and the chair of its Board of Directors is a member of the South Korean National Assembly. In South Korea adoption is a recurring political issue of major significance, and the continuing concern with the nation's global economic and political position may result in more attention to the role that adoptees can play in bolstering the nation's international reputation. In addition, an interest in overseas Koreans in general has been growing in South Korea, with special "diaspora" showcases in art exhibits and film festivals that seem regularly to include Korean adoptee work. There are a number of Korean adoptee artists living and working in South Korea, where they perform their own interventions and produce activist media related to their experiences in South Korea and as adoptees. Some Korean American adoptee groups also articulate a self-conscious bridge-building role between South Korea and the United States, thus echoing the rhetoric of the South Korean state.

This increasing visibility of Korean adoptees in South Korea and in the world carries with it the ambivalences and contradictions inherent in political representation and the concomitant dangers of co-optation and appropriation, especially because transnational Korean adoptees are currently being acknowledged by the South Korean government in unprecedented ways and with unclear motives. As adoptees are further accepted into the "global family" of Korea, their complex histories may become reduced to spectacles of national and cultural alterity, thus denying a history of violence and displacement in favor of homecoming and national reunion.

Adoption from South Korea is central to understanding South Korean modernity. It continues to be a part of its "postcolonial" history that is at once repressed, yet crucial to understanding how the official narrative of South Korea's "economic miracle" and "struggle for democracy" erases the violence of the military regime and of the draconian development and misogynistic population policies that produced South Korea's "successful" capitalist transformation. As Chungmoo Choi (1997, 349) writes; "Assuming South Korea to be postcolonial eludes the political, social and economic realities of its people, which lie behind that celebrated sign 'post' of periodization, without considering the substantive specificity of Korean histories." Adoptee narratives compose part of the "substantive specificity of Korean histories," in particular a history that has bodied forth in the past several years with the unexpected and unprecedented return of well over two thousand adoptees to South Korea every year, a previously unimaginable scenario for adoption agencies and the government.

Adoptees and social activists in South Korea have criticized the state's continued reliance on international adoption as a social welfare policy solution (Sarri, Baik, and Bombyk 1998) and its complicity in the perpetuation of gendered inequalities. Birth mothers — often working-class women, teen mothers, abandoned single mothers, sex workers, and victims of rape — represent the most subordinated groups in an entrenched patriarchy and misogynistic state welfare system, and are brought into the public gaze with the arrival of adoptees and their desire to locate their social and biological connections.

Adoption resulted from the initial crisis of orphans and mixed-race GI children during the Korean conflict and continued as a product of rapid economic and structural transformations, as a consequence of cold war population and development policies intended to build national "stability." It flourished as a profitable enterprise in the 1970s and 1980s, during a period of political repression and massive social unrest. As adoptees organize a political voice as adults, their collective countermemories — composed out of individual memories (and lack of memories) of Korea, oftentimes tragic and painful preadoption histories, and return trips to South Korea — are important articulations of personal and national history that demand further investigation.

Moreover, transnational Korean adoptees challenge dominant ideologies that conflate race, nation, culture, and language in the definition of what it means to be "Korean," and this distinctive subject position potentially disrupts facile culturalist and nativist assumptions about belonging and identity. There are a number of competing claims to the adoptee's "Koreanness" — from the state, adoption agencies, adoptee groups, and adoptee artists — wherein nostalgia, "authenticity," and "tradition" are mobilized in the production of Korean "culture" and "identity." These claims have important ramifications for other internationally adopted individuals and adoptive communities who are themselves negotiating the vexing question of cultural heritage.

As the cultural work of Korean adoptees demonstrates, Korean adoption has as much to do with reimagining kinship as it does with recasting diaspora. Transnational families are becoming commonplace in many areas of the world, and the deep ethical ambiguities of adoption are increasingly being publicly explored in transnational adoption communities, including that of Korean adoptees as adults (see Volkman in this volume for a discussion of the Chinese adoption community). Korean adoptees, with their adoptive families and their biological families, are building "superextended" families (Roe 1994) and also a sense of kinship among themselves. This community, based initially on common experience, is extending into one based on solidarity and shared experience. Recognized as Korean, they are making claims as Koreans but with a difference.

Notes

I gratefully acknowledge the James West Memorial Fund for Human Rights for supporting the research in South Korea on which part of this essay is based. A portion of this work was presented at Hampshire College in 2001 at the International Adoption Conference organized by Barbara Yngvesson and Kay Johnson. I appreciate their generous invitation to present my work there. Many thanks also to Toby Volkman for her important critical feedback, and for her invaluable work in making this volume possible. I'm also grateful to Elise Andaya, Jackie Aronson, Leo Hsu, and Jong Bum Kwon for their insightful suggestions and discussions on earlier drafts of this essay. And I owe special acknowledgment to Faye Ginsburg for her ongoing support and mentorship.

1. Folk weddings such as this one have long been out of fashion in South Korea, where since the 1960s syncretic "modern" wedding forms involve Western-style unions of individuals rather than the symbolic joining of households and patrilineages. Although there was a resurgence of traditional-style weddings in South Korea in the 1980s, a number of the South Korean counselors at this wedding ceremony were enthralled by the performance because they had never before witnessed one (see Kendall 1996).

2. The counselors were all native Koreans who spoke English, some of whom were volunteers for GOA'L. We were all paid nominally. As the only Korean American counselor, I was frequently asked to perform as a Korean-English interpreter and was relied on by the director of the program to make announcements to the adoptees in English. There was also a Korean-French interpreter. The group leaders were called "counselors" and the participants were often called "campers," underscoring the tour's similarity to a summer camp. The language used to refer to the staff and the participants, combined with the free-spiritedness of the participants, contributed to this effect.

3. I place "Koreanness" in quotes as an indication of the inherently unstable field of reference it attempts to denote. For reasons of style, however, I use the term Koreanness without quotes in the remainder of this essay.

4. "Korea" in this article designates an idealized concept of South Korea as a cultural entity, geographic region, and national political unity. I use "Korea" in quotes to indicate a reified notion that conflates place, culture, and identity, and I use South Korea (without quotes) wherever possible to specify the Republic of Korea as nation-state and bounded geopolitical territory.

5. Some specific issues related to the intrusiveness of the media and adoption agency visits were directly addressed through changes to the program the following year. Adoption agency visits are now one of the first activities on the itinerary, and interviews with the media are arranged for interested adoptees, either before

or after the tour schedule. Native Korean volunteers, mostly college students, have been integrated into the program and are paired up with adoptees for a three-day retreat for "intercultural exchange" that include sports, games, songs, and discussions of cultural difference.

6. There are clear differences in experience and racial formation between European adoptees and their North American counterparts that cannot be adequately addressed in an essay of this length.

7. Ong (2003, 87) notes the importance of maintaining an analytic distinction between "transnationality" and "diaspora." She writes: "Diaspora sentiments may linger but it may be more analytically exact to use the term 'transnationalism' to describe the processes of disembedding from a set of localized relations in the homeland nation and re-embedding in overlapping networks that cut across borders."

8. Certainly, overseas adoptees experience "disidentification" from the hegemonic cultural and racialized scripts in the countries where they were raised, and this alienation most likely contributes to the desire to connect to "Korea," to locate an "authentic" identity. This essay, however, focuses on the local encounters between adoptees and "Korea" and can only suggest the relationship between their feelings of alterity in majority-white societies of the West. For a comprehensive study of cultural identity issues among Korean adoptees in Minnesota, see Meier 1998.

9. The issue of the birth family search is a complex one that can not be fully explored here. Whether or not the government should provide services for birth searches is an open question. Although the 2003 tour incorporated adoption agency visits and also resulted in several reunions or meetings between birth relatives and adoptees, the program itself did not provide professional counseling or support services.

10. Reporters are a significant source of information and assistance for adoptees who search for their birth families. They can help adoptees who are unable to navigate the bureaucratic channels due to language barriers. Newspapers run advertisements with identifying information and television news programs show brief clips of adoptees doing searches. The arrangement seems to be mutually beneficial, for if the reporter can find the adoptee's biological family then they've clinched a story (see Adolfson 1999).

11. At the second Gathering it was reported that "some participants started thinking that they were part of their adoptive country and then they discovered the Korean culture. Today, they realise that they do not associate with being either Korean or their adoptive country [sic]; they begin to associate with people in Korean adoptee associations" (Sloth 2001, 30).

12. In 2002, however, this trend was broken by a significant increase in the num-

ber of Guatemalan children adopted into the United States, while South Korean adoptions, under the quota system, remained steady. For the first time, Guatemalan adoptions exceeded those from South Korea.

13. This "fourth culture" model does not take into account the Korean adoptees raised in Europe who comprise an active part of the global Korean adoptee community.

14. The large majority of the four hundred participants were from the United States, with around a dozen adoptees from European countries. For this reason, the perspectives of adoptees in the United States, tended to dominant the discussions. The Oslo Gathering in 2002 was primarily attended by European adoptees, mostly from Scandinavia.

15. The other events were the Global Overseas Adoptees' Link (GOA'L) Conference in Seoul and the Korean American, Adoptee, and Adoptive Family Network (KAAN) Conference in Los Angeles. Both are now annual events that bring together members of the Korean adopted community.

16. Fraser (1992, 110) writes: "Subaltern counterpublics have a dual character. On the one hand, they function as spaces of withdrawal and regroupment; on the other hand, they also function as bases and training grounds for agitational activities directed toward wider publics. It is precisely in the dialectic between these two functions that their emancipatory potential resides."

17. In December 2002, Roh Moo Hyun was elected to succeed Kim Dae Jung as South Korea's president. The presidential elections were overshadowed by the increasing tensions between the United States and North Korea following North Korea's announcement of its clandestine nuclear weapons program, and were accompanied by massive anti-American protests in South Korea over the acquittal of American military personnel who killed two Korean schoolgirls in a traffic accident. Many believe that Roh's successful campaign capitalized on the prevailing anti-American sentiments and widespread opposition to the Bush administration's handling of the North Korea situation. His election signals popular resistance to the paternalism that has characterized the relationship between the two nations since the Korean War. Adoption from South Korea to the United States has always depended on a close political alliance between the two countries, and recent tensions and shifts in this relationship will undoubtedly have significant effects on adoption policy and practice.

18. According to a survey of the Gathering participants, 70 percent had graduated from college, 24 percent had graduate degrees, and 15 percent were enrolled in university or postgraduate work.

19. See Park 1996 for a discussion of South Korea's state-sponsored globalization policy (segyehwa), which explicitly promotes ethnic identification with the nation. As Park argues, a deterritorialized community based on "long-distance

nationalism" (Anderson 1992), cannot escape the constraints and stratifications imposed by the regimes of law and economics.

20. It is important to note that although most of the adoptees at the conference were raised by white middle-class families, there was a great deal of diversity with respect to color, racial identification, class, and sexuality.

21. The adoptees were divided into six groups according to the years in which they were adopted, with a seventh group created for adoptees' spouses and partners. I sat in on one session of a group of over fifty adoptees who had left South Korea between 1967 and 1970.

22. Of course, the adoptees, all having been born in Korea, have their own *kohyang*.

References

Abelmann, Nancy. 2003. *The Melodrama of Mobility: Women, Talk, and Class in Contemporary South Korea*. Honolulu: University of Hawaii Press.

Adolfson, Nathan. 1999. *Passing Through*. San Francisco: NAATA. Video.

Altstein, Howard, and Rita Simon, eds. 1991. *Intercountry Adoption: A Multinational Perspective*. New York: Free Press.

Anderson, Benedict. 1991. *Imagined Communities: Reflections on the Origin and Spread of Nationalism*. New York: Verso.

Appadurai, Arjun. 1996. *Modernity at Large: Cultural Dimensions of Globalization*. Minneapolis: University of Minnesota Press.

Axel, Brian. 2002. "The Diasporic Imaginary." *Public Culture* 14: 411–28.

Choi, Chungmoo. 1997. "The Discourse of Decolonization and Popular Memory: South Korea." In *Formations of Colonial Modernity in East Asia*, ed. Tani Barlow. Durham: Duke University Press.

Clifford, James. 1997. *Routes: Travel and Translation in the Late Twentieth Century*. Cambridge, MA: Harvard University Press.

Evan B. Donaldson Adoption Institute. 1999. *Survey of Adult Korean Adoptees: Report on the Findings*. New York: Evan B. Donaldson Adoption Institute.

Fraser, Nancy. 1992. "Rethinking the Public Sphere: A Contribution to the Critique of Actually Existing Democracy." In *Habermas and the Public Sphere*, ed. Craig Calhoun. Cambridge, MA: MIT Press.

Gathering of the First Generation of Korean Adoptees. 1999. Conference program notes, Washington D.C., 10–12 September.

Gilroy, Paul. 1993. *The Black Atlantic*. Cambridge, MA: Harvard University Press.

Ginsburg, Faye, and Rayna Rapp. 2001. "Enabling Disability: Rewriting Kinship, Reimagining Community." *Public Culture* 13: 533–56.

Gupta, Akhil, and James Ferguson. 1992. " 'Beyond Culture': Space, Identity and the Politics of Difference." *Cultural Anthropology* 7: 6–23.

Hall, Stuart. 1996. "Ethnicity: Identity and Difference." In *Becoming National: A Reader*, ed. G. Eley and R. Suny. New York: Oxford University Press.

Herrmann, Kenneth J. Jr., and Barbara Kasper. 1992. "International Adoption: The Exploitation of Women and Children." *Affilia* 7: 45–58.

Hubinette, Tobias. 2002. "The Adoption Issue in Korea: Diaspora Politics in the Age of Globalization." Paper presented at the seventh annual Korean Studies Graduate Student Conference, Harvard University, 12–13 April.

Jang, Ok Joo. 2000. "Government Policy to Promote Adoption." Paper presented at the International Seminar to Promote Domestic Adoption, Holt Children's Services, Seoul, 29 September.

Johnsen, Sunny (Jo). 2002. "The Creation and Rise of KAD as a Separate Identity and Nation." www.geocities.com/kadnation/kadnation.html.

Kane, Saralee. 1993. "The Movement of Children for International Adoption: An Epidemiologic Perspective." *Social Science Journal* 30: 323–39.

Kendall, Laurel. 1996. *Getting Married in Korea: Of Gender, Morality, and Modernity*. Berkeley: University of California Press.

Kim, Chang-ki. 1999. "Foreign Adoption on the Increase." *Chosun Ilbo*, 11 January.

Kim, Choong S. 1988. *Faithful Endurance: An Ethnography of Korean Family Dispersal*. Tucson: University of Arizona Press.

Kim, Eleana. 2001. "Korean Adoptee Autoethnography: Refashioning Self, Family, and Finding Community." *Visual Anthropology Review* 16: 43–70.

Kim, Samuel S. 2000. *East Asia and Globalization*. Lanham, MD: Rowman and Littlefield.

Kim, Yeon-kwang. 2000. "Adoption Restrictions to Be Removed." *Chosun Ilbo*, 7 March.

Louie, Andrea. 2000. "Re-territorializing Transnationalism: Chinese Americans and the Chinese Motherland." *American Ethnologist* 27: 645–69.

Lowe, Lisa. 1996. *Immigrant Acts: Asian American Cultural Politics*. Durham: Duke University Press.

Maira, Sunaina. 1999. "Identity Dub: The Paradoxes of an Indian American Youth Subculture (New York Mix)." *Cultural Anthropology* 14: 29–60.

Meier, Dani. 1998. "Loss and Reclaimed Lives: Cultural Identity and Place in Korean American Intercountry Adoptees." Ph.D. diss., University of Minnesota.

Modell, Judith. 1994. *Kinship with Strangers*. Berkeley: University of California Press.

Moon, Seungsook. 2003. "Redrafting Democratization through Women's Representation and Participation in the Republic of Korea." In *Korea's Democratiza-tion*, ed. S. Kim. Cambridge: Cambridge University Press.

Muñoz, José E. 1999. *Disidentifications: Queers of Color and the Performance of Politics*. Minneapolis: University of Minnesota Press.

Ong, Aihwa. 1999. *Flexible Citizenship: The Cultural Logics of Transnationality*. Durham: Duke University Press.

——. 2003. "Cyberpublics and Diaspora Politics among Transnational Chinese." *Interventions* 5: 82–100.

Park, Hyun Ok. 1996. "Segyehwa: Globalization and Nationalism in Korea." *Journal of the International Institute* 4: www.umich.edu/īlnet/journal/vol4 no1/segyeh.html.

Rhee, Jong Hun. 2002. "Legal Issues of Overseas Adoption (*Haeoe ibyang goan-ryôl bôbryul munjeh*)." Paper presented at the Fourth Annual Conference of the Global Overseas Adoptees' Link, Seoul, 24 August.

Roe, So Yun. 1994. "My Husband's Families: Kinship in an International Korean Adoptive Superextended Family." Master's thesis, University of Southern California.

Rothschild, Matthew. 1988. "Babies for Sale: Koreans make them, Americans buy them." *The Progressive*. 52(1): 18–23.

Sarri, R. C., Y. Baik, and M. Bombyk. 1998. "Goal Displacement and Dependency in South Korean–United States Intercountry Adoption." *Children and Youth Services Review* 20: 87–114.

Shim Jae-yun. 2002. "Measures to Improve National Image Unveiled." *Korea Times*, 10 July.

Siu, Lok. 2001. "Diasporic Cultural Citizenship: Chineseness and Belonging in Central America and Panama." *Social Text* 69: 7–28.

Sloth, Kirsten. 2001. "Official Report of the Second International Gathering of Adult Korean Adoptees." Oslo, Norway: G2 Planning Committee. www .adopteegathering.org/2ndgathering/g2_report.pdf.

Soh, Ji-young. 2000. "Domestic Adoptions Growing." *Korea Times*, 6 August.

Stock, Kimberly K. H. 1999. "Rise of a Fourth Culture: Korean Adoptees." *Trans-cultured* 1: 11.

Strong, Pauline T. 2001. "To Forget Their Tongue, Their Name, and Their Whole Relation: Captivity, Extra-Tribal Adoption, and the Indian Child Welfare Act." In *Relative values: Reconfiguring Kinship Studies*, ed. Sarah Franklin and Susan McKinnon. Durham: Duke University Press.

Xing, Jun. 1998. *Asian America through the Lens: History, Representations, Iden-tity*. Walnut Creek, CA: AltaMira.

Yngvesson, Barbara. 2000. " 'Un nino de cualquier color': Race and Nation in

Intercountry Adoption." In *Globalizing Institutions: Case Studies in Regulation and Innovation*, ed. Jane Jenson and Boaventura de Sousa Santos. Aldershot, Eng.: Ashgate.

Yngvesson, Barbara, and Maureen Mahoney. 2000. "'As One Should, Ought and Wants to Be': Belonging and Authenticity in Identity Narratives." *Theory, Culture, and Society* 17: 77–110.

Embodying Chinese Culture

Transnational Adoption in North America

TOBY ALICE VOLKMAN

sabelle, who is six, makes a list of all the children she knows and begins to identify those among them who are, as she is, adopted. Naming three other Asian children in her New York City first-grade class, she pauses, then shakes her head: "No, but they look adopted." Isabelle's mother asks, "What does an adopted person look like?" Isabelle replies, "Chinese."[1]

In the 1990s, families in the United States began to adopt children from other regions of the world in unprecedented numbers. Although adoption across national borders had its beginnings in the 1950s in the aftermath of World War II and the Korean conflict, it remained for decades a relatively unnoticed phenomenon. "The quiet migration" is how a demographer writing in 1984 described the movement of children for adoption across national borders (Weil 1984). That description now needs to be revised. Over the past ten years, transnational adoption has become both visible and vocal. How has this shift occurred? And how might the contemporary practice of transnational adoption provoke new ways of imagining race, kinship, and culture in North America?

Visible and Vocal: Adoption from China

In 1994, when I traveled to China with my husband to adopt our daughter, I had no inkling that we were on the cusp of what would become an enormous wave of Chinese adoptions. Neither did I sense the tremendous changes in adoption practices that were then under way; the heightened attention to all aspects of adoption that would become so defining of this moment; or the ways in which my lived experience would so intimately touch on contested anthropological terrain. Soon after returning to New York, however, I realized that our very personal act of creating a family through adoption was simultaneously, if unwittingly, part of a larger, collective project. In that project "culture" figured both prominently and, for me, a bit uneasily. This essay is the fruit of my efforts to understand parents' fascination with the imagined "birth culture" of their adopted children. I argue here that this fascination may, in part, represent displaced longings for origins and absent birth mothers, and I attempt to situate such longings within historical and cultural shifts in adoption discourse and practices over the last ten years.

Adoptions from China to the United States soared from 115 in 1991 to 5,081 in 2000.[2] By the end of the 1990s, China had become the leading "sending" country of children to the United States and elsewhere in the world, and more than 30,000 adopted Chinese children, mostly girls, were growing up with their (mostly) white parents in North America. In February 2002, bookstore windows in Manhattan displayed Valentine's Day specials, among them *I Love You like Crazy Cakes* (Lewis 2000), a children's book about a single mother adopting a baby girl from China. The mainstreaming of Chinese adoption has occurred in part through the incessant media attention that has been lavished on adopted Chinese girls over the past decade.[3] This interest shows no signs of abating, as shown by the steady stream of articles published in disparate venues. On a page boldly titled "How America Lives," the *Ladies' Home Journal* featured "Citizen Amy," an adopted five-year-old Chinese girl in Kentucky, American flag in hand (Leader 2001).

Numbers and media attention do not in themselves suggest a profound transformation in, or the normalization of, adoption. They surely do not reveal the ardent embrace of a new transracial kinship; the *Ladies' Home Journal* knows that this is not really how most of America lives. Nonetheless, the phenomenal growth of adoption that crosses lines of nation and of race, and the proliferation of media representations of adoption, hint that interesting changes are in motion, changes that must be situated within larger processes of rewriting kinship, identity, and culture in North America. I focus here on adoption from China because it and the communities that have developed around it have become remarkably visible and vocal. Families with children from many other parts of the world, however, are dealing with similar issues, particularly when race visibly marks differences between parents and children.[4]

In contrast to the isolation and confusion articulated in recent years by many young adult Korean adoptees, adopted children from China and their (mostly) white parents are visible not just to the public but (intensely so) to each other, through the formation of play groups, dance troupes, culture celebrations and camps, reunions, Web sites, electronic mailing lists, and publications intended for the adoptive community. Visibility is entwined with vocality. In writing about the world of disability, Rayna Rapp and Faye Ginsburg (2001, 534) describe how publicly circulating narratives chronicling intimate experiences with disability have helped to shape "a more expansive sense of kinship across embodied difference." A similar proliferation of stories characterizes the world of transnational adoption.

Until the wave of Chinese adoptions there had never been another cohort of transnational, transracial adoptees that arrived in the United States in such large numbers, in so few years, of roughly the same age and largely the same gender. Many more Korean children had been adopted into U.S. families — a total of approximately one hundred thousand — but they were widely dispersed over a period of fifty years and across urban, rural, and small-town America. Operation Babylift, in which two thousand babies were flown out of Saigon to the United States in a few days in April 1975, was a dramatic moment, but these children also were dispersed throughout the country and were not followed (until recently) by other Vietnamese adoptees. For most adoptees from Asia, stories such as those told in recent years in films made by Korean adoptees were far more typical: the only Asian child growing up in a largely white small town somewhere in middle America (Adolfson 1999; Liem 2000). Adoption was not freely discussed, and racial assimilation was the goal. There must have been many parents like Nathan Adolfson's mother in Minnesota, who simply wanted her child to be, as she declares in her son's film, "a little Scandinavian" (Adolfson 1999).

Adoptive parents themselves have a distinctive demographic profile. Those who adopt from China are "older" (until 1999, China required parents to be at least thirty-five) and often share a sense of generational history and sensibility.[5] "We came of age in the sixties, we told our stories in the women's movement," one New York mother said. Especially in urban areas, where the largest numbers of children adopted from China live, such parents typically postponed childbearing, are relatively affluent and well educated, and see themselves as active citizens of the world. Many are not married. Although China's politics have recently changed to prohibit adoption by gay and lesbian parents and to limit single-parent adoptions, during most of the 1990s China's openness was striking and coincided with the increasing acceptance of single parenting and other nontraditional ways of making families in North America.[6] Unconventional parents easily forged connections out of the networks in which they already participated, such as support groups for single women contemplating motherhood. Such parents are often conscious of their delicate and difficult roles. A mother in a discussion group mused, somewhat anxiously: "We are older, we are Jewish, we are two mommies, we are white. Just how much difference can we give them?"

The experience of traveling to China to adopt has also catalyzed the growth of organizations beyond the family. Whereas Korean babies typically arrived on planes, delivered by escorts to expectant parents in North American airports, families who adopt from China must travel there to meet their child, in groups as large as a dozen families arranged by adoption agencies. A family spends two weeks in China with this group, sharing momentous experiences: the emotionally charged moments of the delivery of their children, visits to the orphanage, and myriad anxieties, difficulties, joys, and surprises. These trips create powerful bonding experiences, which those involved subsequently seek to reproduce and reinforce through reunions and little rituals like annual photo shoots of children lined up on someone's couch. Ties forged in travel groups may focus on intimate connections: parents of babies who shared an orphanage crib may decide to nurture their daughters' friendship as they grow, even to return to China together when the girls are older. Sometimes the sense of kinship extends in the other direction to a sort of bonding with "China," a China that is imagined yet somehow palpable, embodied in the child, archived in photographs and other tangible souvenirs.

Perhaps most critical in shaping the visibility and vocality of adoption in China is the historical moment. The discursive celebration of multiculturalism of the 1990s is worlds apart from the earlier emphasis on assimilation. If we live now in an era of "Rainbow Kids," as one adoption magazine is called, this was not the case when transnational adoption began in the 1950s. Then, the all-American white bread family was very much the desired norm, and green-eyed, freckled, Irish Catholic babies were supposed to be matched with green-eyed, freckled, Irish Catholic moms and dads. The "as if begotten" biological family was the goal (Modell 1994), a "clean break" with the past achieved by rewriting birth certificates with the names of adoptive parents and erasing the identity of birth parents by sealing records (Carp 1998). In the 1950s, when Oregonians Harry and Bertha Holt launched adoption from South Korea as a Christian "rescue" mission for mixed-race orphans fathered by American soldiers, it seems that little thought was given to how such children would fit into a society where sameness was the unquestioned norm. The prevailing "clean break" model of domestic adoption was transposed, in intercountry adoption, into a "clean break" from biological progenitors and from the national or cultural origins of the child (Shanley 2001; Yngvesson 2000).

The civil rights movement sparked some adoptions in the late 1960s of black or biracial children by white parents. But in the early 1970s, in part because of the strong stance of the National Association of Black Social Workers against transracial adoption, race again became an explicit barrier in domestic adoption. Around this time Americans began increasingly to embrace adoption from other nations. This turn coincided with dramatic changes that were unfolding within the domestic adoption community. The silence and secrecy that had surrounded adoption were beginning to dissolve, as adoptees began to assert their rights to be told truthfully about their past, their "roots," and the parents who relinquished them. As adoption became "open" — both in the sense of specific and legal forms of "open adoption" in which information is disclosed, records are unsealed, and birth families and adoptive families may actually know one another, and in the broader sense of being openly acknowledged — the myth of the "as if" family, "constituted by shared biological heritage, by the 'mystical commonality' of mother and child" (Yngvesson 1997, 71), could no longer be easily sustained.

By the 1990s, these changes in the American social landscape intersected with growing political and economic pressures within China. The one-child policy, the Chinese state's attempt to curtail population growth, called for all couples to limit themselves to a single child. In many areas this became a "one son/two children" policy: parents were allowed to try for a second child, a son, if the firstborn was a daughter. Measures for enforcing the one-child policy included steep fines for "overquota" children, sterilization, and the threat of forced abortion in the event of future pregnancies.

The one-child policy had serious consequences for gender relations. Mothers who gave birth to baby girls might be "subject to verbal and physical assault from unhappy husbands and in-laws," and their little ones suffered, too, "as peasant women discriminated against their baby daughters in order to ensure the birth and survival of a son" (Greenhalgh and Li 1995, 609–10). One form of discrimination was infant abandonment.[7] In the late 1980s, large numbers of healthy abandoned baby girls began to crowd China's state-run orphanages (Johnson 1993, 1996). Kay Johnson, along with Chinese researchers Huang Banghan and Wang Liyao (1998, 467–510), found that in the 1990s most couples expressed the wish to have a daughter and a son but felt under intense pressure if they failed to produce the son. Many couples felt they had "no choice" but to abandon their second or third daughters.[8]

Abandonments, which are illegal, take place in secrecy. The baby is left where parents hope he or she will be found: the steps of a police station or hospital, the side of a well-traveled road, a busy marketplace, a train station, perhaps at the entrance to a house where a family lives who might, especially if they already have one son and no daughter, decide to adopt the child.

Ironically, then, as adoption and the embrace of the birth family in the United States have become increasingly open and encouraged, in China the circumstances of the child's abandonment are profoundly hidden and unknowable. Adoptive parents often express a yearning for connection, a wish for knowledge of a narrative that cannot be complete. Sometimes the painful realities that have created both the possibility and the impossibility of these connections are acknowledged, as longing is laced with a critique of the inequities in the global political economy through which white American parents benefit from the suffering of their Chinese counterparts: "People whose agony over her [the writer's daughter] I cannot begin to comprehend. People whose deep loss produced perhaps my greatest joy," writes Lindsay Davies (2000, 19). "I don't know what to say to a woman whose greatest tragedy is my good fortune," writes Emily Prager (2001, 237) in a similar musing. "That you should have your daughter forced from your arms by a government who I then must pay to envelop her in mine is the stuff of which I have fought against my entire career. That I should end up tacitly supporting this policy is my shame, and yet, my fate. . . . Forgive me, Madam, for my part in ripping off the Women of China and in particular, of course, you."

A More Expansive Sense of Kinship

Two institutions — one real, one virtual — have been critical in shaping and sustaining a sense of kinship and community beyond the family. Families with Children from China (FCC) is a name used by more than one hundred separate organizations that have developed across the United States and Canada since the mid-1990s. Inspired in part by smaller groups founded in the late 1970s by parents of children adopted from Korea, FCC's beginnings can be traced to 1992 when a few of the earliest adoptive parents on the East Coast met in New York's Chinatown to celebrate their new adoptions. Susan Caughman, one of the founders of the organization in New York, described the impulse behind this early FCC: "We felt as if we knew an amazing secret that we had the obligation to tell the world about" (cited in Klatzkin 1999, xiii).

The other powerful force contributing to the shaping of the adoptive Chinese community is the Internet. The Internet and adoption from China began to grow at approximately the same time, and by 2002 the two largest electronic mailing lists for China adoption had a combined membership of over 13,000 subscribers, and more than 350 other lists were devoted to more specialized interests, from *chinaboys* and *China Dads at Home* to born-again Christian lists. There are lists for those whose adoption dossier went to China in a particular month, and well over 100 lists for families with children adopted from the same orphanage or region. Members of orphanage lists may come to think of all children in their child's orphanage as siblings.

The Internet may serve its greatest function outside of cities that already have flourishing FCCs, an array of friendship circles, and countless other forms of face-to-face sociality. But for many, electronic mailing lists provide valuable information, ideas, a space for debate, and a sense of community. Both FCC and the Internet dramatically expand the sense of kinship beyond the domestic sphere: FCC through the many gatherings it sponsors, the Internet by building online relationships that extend throughout the country and internationally as well. In cyberspace, even more than in the face-to-face contact of FCC activities, people may come to feel as though they know each other well — an illusory intimacy, perhaps, but nonetheless a space in which they are comfortable sharing concerns and intimate details about their daily lives, emotions, and their children that they would not easily reveal to ordinary (known) relatives. In response to another list member's announcement that a long-awaited child had been referred, one person wrote "Mazel Tov, Mazel Tov, Mazel Tov! . . . Although we don't know each other I have thought of you and your husband often. I am so happy for you two tonight" (Silverman 2002).

The Question of Culture

The question of culture pervades the discourse of contemporary adoption. Contradictory movements — "erasures of belonging," in Barbara Yngvesson's words, (2000, 177), and its reinscription — permeate and complicate the everyday practices of Chinese and other forms of transnational adoption. Is the child an "open cultural space," or is he or she inextricably "rooted in national soil" (173)?

In an article entitled "Dancing to Her Music," an adoptive mother describes how her daughter, Oona, adopted from China eleven years ago, was provided with opportunities to develop "a deep appreciation of the Chinese art and culture that are part of her native heritage. At home in the San Francisco Bay Area, we wheeled her in the stroller past the exquisite brush paintings and ceramics in San Francisco's Asian Art Museum, stopping afterward for dim sum in Chinatown. We took her to see the Chinese acrobats at the Civic Center and dutifully attended the Chinese New Year Parade (even though she hated it, because of the firecrackers). And when friends began packing their daughters off in frilly tutus and pink slippers for ballet classes after school, we opted for a more international form of movement: gymnastics" (Putnam 2003, 6). In spite of all this, Oona fell passionately in love with, and became extremely good at, Irish dancing.

Like most articles on Chinese adoption, Oona's story was circulated on Internet mailing lists and provoked a range of responses, including some criticisms of Oona's parents. Oona's enthusiasm for Irish dance, one person speculated, was a reaction to the family's overemphasis on China at the expense of a more all-embracing multicultural heritage that would have included her adoptive mother's Irish "culture." To this, Julie Higginbotham (2002) in Chicago asked: "Where do we draw the line between strenuous but appropriate efforts to affirm our status as a minority family, and putting the family into a box where only ethnic activities focused on the child's/children's birth heritage(s) are deemed appropriate? . . . Is the child in the article, so filled with joy at present, being set up for future trauma by spending so much time with ringleted, red-haired, creamy-complexioned sprites, whom of course she can never physically resemble?" A parent whose adopted Indian son was fond of boat racing commented: "Until I read this thread about the little girl loving Irish dancing, I never thought to ask our son, 'Gee, Son, maybe you should only excel at a sport that would somehow reflect your Indian culture.' "

"If constructions of race and culture are contingent processes that are historically open-ended," Ann Anagnost (2000, 391) has written, "we need to consider how current adoption practices do not merely fit into what is historically given, but in themselves produce race" — and, I would add, culture — "in a new form." Anagnost suggests that adoption practices may reproduce the problem of identity and difference anew, "in a domestication of differences emptied of history," or they may be progressive, as "the experience of racism opens the possibility of pushing politics of parenting beyond the family, as the basis of a broader politics of anti-racism." Both trajectories, I argue, are at play.

The challenge to the biologically formed family is particularly clear when adoption crosses racial lines, as it usually does in the case of China.[9] A recurrent theme in the adoption world is how to respond to racist, rude, ridiculous, or simply awkward questions from strangers (or sometimes from friends and relatives). These typically occur in public venues like grocery checkout lines: "Is she yours? Is she real? Is she natural? Where did you get her? How much did she cost? Are they really sisters? In China they don't like girls, do they?" One list member reported a colleague's remark: "What a lovely baby, it's just too bad she's a communist." Responses to such comments range from calm to furious; some parents try to turn these encounters into "teaching moments," others reply with sarcasm. To a common query, "Is her father Chinese?" one mother laughs, "I don't know, I couldn't see his face."

The highly visible, racially marked challenge to the biofamily may contribute to the media's fascination with adoption fron China, accounts of which provide what appears to be a less fraught space in which to deal with race than stories about transracial black-white adoption in the United States.[10] Whereas racial differences were just as striking for earlier generations of Korean adoptees, until recent years the pressure for sameness seems to have suppressed or obscured them. Many adult Korean adoptees recall growing up thinking that they were white like their parents: for example, the "little Scandinavian" invoked by Nathan Adolfson's mother. A survey of adult Korean adoptees reports that as they reached adolescence their ethnic identifications shifted: "Only 28 percent of the respondents considered themselves Korean-American or Korean-European as they were growing up; by contrast, 64 percent of the respondents, as adults, viewed themselves as Korean-American or Korean-European" (Evan B. Donaldson Adoption Institute 1999, 1). In the survey the Koreans described themselves as "Caucasian with a difference," "a white person in an Asian body," and "white middle class, but adopted from Korea"; or as "trying to be white," "not white enough," and "Caucasian, except when looking in the mirror" (18).

It is in part an awareness of the Korean experience that motivates parents of Chinese children to provide something—pride in culture, pride in being Chinese. The sense of responsibility for doing this may begin with social workers who counsel prospective parents about the challenges of forming transracial or transnational families and about the need to acquire "cultural competence" (Vonk 2001, 246). This counseling differs strikingly from the earlier emphasis on matching, assimilation, and denial. It has a counterpart in China: as part of the adoption proceedings, parents must promise the Chinese authorities not only to provide their children with love and care but to impart respect for "Chinese culture." Global discourses reinforce these concerns: the United Nations Convention on the Rights of the Child (1989) and the Hague Convention on Intercountry Adoption (1993) affirm that "due regard shall be paid to the desirability of continuity in a child's upbringing and to the child's ethnic, religious, cultural and linguistic background" (cited in Stephens 1995, 38; see also Cecere 1998).

While there certainly are families who have decided that their children are "just American" or "just New Yorkers," even parents who describe themselves strongly in these terms are aware of FCC and its commitment to culture. Among the most vivid representations of this commitment are "Culture Days." In New York, Culture Day has grown steadily since the mid-1990s, and the event now draws about two thousand people. Performances abound: drum ensembles, shadow plays, bits of Peking opera, and a vast array of dances performed by professionals as well as children. There are crafts and dragon carts and cotton candy, and raffle tickets are sold to benefit Chinese orphanages. In 2002, the Chinese consul general attended and praised the "rich Chinese culture," against a very New York backdrop, as Kay Johnson (personal communication, 2002) noted, of Polish sausages and soft pretzels. Children who arrived early in the day marched under the banner of their home province in China in the "Parade of the Provinces." And throughout the day, on a huge map of China, each child could point to her presumed place of origin and attach a sticker with her name.[11]

The desire for culture is translated into a panoply of cultural productions, representations, and performances. Parents work to connect their children and their families with some relatively accessible form of Chinese culture: dance and dumplings, language lessons, Chinese babysitters and role models. Ann Anagnost (2000, 413) refers to these practices as "culture bites."

Miriam, a New York mother, expressed it this way: "It's all about blending — she's Jewish, she's Chinese, she's American, she's a New Yorker, she's from Kansas." Miriam's daughter studies Hebrew, Chinese, Suzuki violin, and ballet. She attends Passover seders (mostly with other adoptive families and lots of Chinese girls) and Lunar New Year festivals. She has many names: Chinese, Hebrew, and English. Miriam is thinking ahead to her bat mitzvah and wondering whether appropriate Chinese elements could be incorporated. Although the oldest Chinese adoptees are only about ten, ideas are already beginning to circulate. One mother suggested looking at Chinese coming-of-age rituals: "For my daughter's baby naming we hybridized something from a baby boy's thirtieth-day celebration that we saw in a Zhang Yimou movie: Villagers passed the baby through a giant, donut-shaped, decorated steamed bun, so we had a bakery make us a giant donut-shaped challah and passed her through at the end of the naming ceremony to much delight and applause." Chinese friends, she added, "said they'd never heard of the ritual, but were not surprised since China is a large country with lots of regional customs" (Eisenberg 2002).

Culture is seen in part as a way of instilling pride in adopted children, who come to learn impressive things about the glorious civilization of the place of their birth. Art and language and ancient history loom large in the imaginary that is China, and holiday celebrations abound. Far less is mentioned about Chinese politics. This overwhelmingly celebratory view of China and Chinese culture is sometimes questioned, especially by Asian American parents. Some criticize white parents for "exoticizing and mysticizing and obsessing about Chinese culture in China while ignoring the living, breathing Chinese American culture at our doorstep" (Amy Klatzkin, personal communication, 2002). Others contend that providing appealing little packages of culture is in itself a form of racism and "worse than nothing," eliding more painful histories of oppression, colonialism, and Asian American immigration (Kimberly Chang, personal communication, 2001).

In her study of Internet discussions on adoption from China, Anagnost (2000, 391) suggests that "celebratory representations of cultural difference, which are often detached from immigrant histories in the United States," may make it difficult for adopted children to understand their racialization and may even serve to maintain "the separations that constitute racialized boundaries in U.S. society historically." But Anagnost studied discussions on an electronic mailing list that included parents who were waiting or had just received referrals. When babies turn into children, especially school-age children, a very different set of concerns emerges, and both Internet and daily life are filled with talk about race, identity, and adoptive families' ambiguous relationships to other immigrant communities. Conversations about race and racism do not always come easily. When Robin's seven-year-old daughter mentioned to her that a young friend asked if she planned to work in a Chinese restaurant when she grew up, Robin said, "Do you think he asked because that's what I did when I was in college?" Robin's immediate response was to affirm her connection with her daughter; only later did we wonder together whether that might have been a moment to discuss race or stereotypes or immigrant labor. Nurturing "cultural pride" is often seen as the critical ground on which later struggles against racism may be waged. The startling, sometimes shocking, discovery of racism, whether subtle or flagrant, has transformed many parents' consciousness of race in ways they never anticipated. When children are teased for their small noses, flat faces, yellow skin, or short eyelashes, parents wonder if they can truly empathize or help. "What can I say to her?" asked one mother: "I speak with long eyelashes."

The starkness of black and white in racial discourse creates still more uncertainty; many parents simply do not know how to articulate other kinds of difference. What shall I say, a mother asked, when my Chinese daughter tells me she is "white"? An adult Korean adoptee offered this in response: "To tell her that she's not white immediately creates the feeling of difference. To remain silent reinforces a belief that she is, and with that, feelings of entitlement that walk hand in hand, which she does not have. If she is saying she is white because she does not have to move off the proverbial seat (a reference to Rosa Parks), there's a problem because that means she has created racial divisions that are only seen in black/white, and no in-betweens" (Eun Mi 2004).

The question of the relationships of adoptees with Asian America remains unsettled. Some FCC organizations cultivate relationships with Chinese American worlds. In New York's Lunar New Year Parade, an FCC contingent marches with its own banner.[12] While social workers advocate adult role models and "meaningful relationships" in the Asian American community, it is not clear which parts of this "community" would be accessible or receptive. Speakers of Mandarin or Cantonese or Hakka? Students, workers, or second-generation or third-generation professionals — another category of "privileged immigrants" struggling with the nature of their "Chinese American" identity?[13] One white adoptive mother laughed as she described how a highly educated Chinese American friend sought her advice on books about things Chinese for his young children.

Vivia Chen, one of a small number of Chinese American mothers in the New York FCC, recounts a telephone conversation with a white adoptive mother in search of mooncakes, who insisted: " 'You're Chinese, you must have an old family recipe somewhere.' I replied, 'Chinese people don't make their own mooncakes. I mean, who makes their own bagels? It's not done. Just go to Chinatown and buy some.' Silence ensued on the other end of the line. Finally, she spoke: 'Well, I'm sure real Chinese people make their own mooncakes!' " (1999, 17). Chen upset a few of her fellow New Yorkers when she wrote: "I fear that some parents might mistake the colorful trappings of Chinese traditions for the experience of being Chinese-American. . . . I can understand why parents are so intrigued by

FIGURE 1. A girl places herself on the map of China during Culture Day, New Jersey, 2002. (Courtesy Kevin Bubriski)

sword dancing, lantern making, dragon boat racing and mooncake baking. These snippets of Chinese culture are appealing, fun and just more accessible than grappling with the more difficult issue of identity and the race thing." Yet, Chen went on to say, adoptive parents "astound me with how much pride they take in their daughter's birth culture. In fact, they've inspired me to incorporate Chinese art and language into the fabric of my daughter's life" (18).

There is, on the one hand, an inevitably disappointing search for an organic connection with things Chinese or Chinese American and, on the other hand, an unselfconscious pleasure in things imagined to be "Chinese," whether appropriated or invented. The "red thread" for example, has come to represent connections between adoptive parents and their children and among those who share loved ones or children from China. The image, said to be drawn from an old Chinese tale, evokes lovers predestined to meet, connected by an invisible red thread that will never break, or red threads that spring from a newborn's spirit and attach to all people who will be important to the child, shortening as he or she grows and bringing closer those who were meant to be together.

FIGURE 2. Preparing for a dance performance for Culture Day, New Jersey, 2002. (Courtesy Kevin Bubriski)

Ironically, in China the red thread tale appears to have a more limited and not altogether positive resonance. "An invisible red thread attaches you at birth to your future spouse," writes Amy Klatzkin. "With romantic marriage now the norm in China, it has taken on a positive glow, but I think that's recent—and it has nothing to do with adoption. Given that traditional marriages often brought misery and servitude to women, the fate signified by the red thread was not necessarily a happy one." Klatzkin adds: "It astounded me at first to see it morphed into an American feel-good, everything-is-for-the-best ideology of international adoption." In most writing about Chinese adoption, the red thread signifies the destiny that brought parents and children together. Klatzkin questions this as well: "And will our children always feel that they were destined to be with us and only us? Mine certainly doesn't. She delves deeply into the arbitrariness of her fate" (personal communication 2002).

While it is easy to parody the compulsion to consume (to spend lavishly on Asian dolls or to search the Web for panda pajamas) or to scorn the superficiality of a celebratory multiculturalism, many parents strive for some deeper transformation of their own identities and lives. Some parents become local advocates for adoption, revising school curricula, or critiquing media portrayals of adoption. Others work to create a sense of community extending to China, often through efforts to "give back" something, to redress imbalances, as Yngvesson notes, in "a world in which children flow in only one direction" (personal communication 2002). These efforts also represent an activation of ties to China, an affirmation of the child's origins.

Giving back may be a matter of contributing to a growing number of orphanage assistance programs, many of which have been founded by adoptive mothers in the United States who have taken the project of adoption significantly beyond the personal. These individuals often work full-time directing programs that provide foster care for orphanage children or school fees, warm clothing, surgeries, or "hugging grannies," retired women who come to the orphanage to offer stimulation and affection. For other adoptive families, giving back may be as simple as sending photographs, letters, and money to children's orphanages — money that sometimes children themselves have raised by selling lemonade or running campaigns in school. Orphanage directors in China often welcome these connections in emotional terms. In May 2002, the director of one orphanage sent greetings in an e-mail message to "our adopted children and adoptive parents," noting that the orphanage children there would celebrate Children's Day on 1 June and hoping that the adopted children in the United States would "have a good time too." She added: "My staff and I care about all the children that have been adopted. We would like to know how the children are getting along in life. We would like to see your children's pictures. I would like you to tell your children that we still love and miss them."[14]

Longings

Although some parents prefer to adopt in a distant country to avoid the complexities of dealing with birth mothers, especially at the beginning of the process, many adoptive parents come to express deep sadness about their lack of knowledge or possible contact with the birth family. Beyond the efforts to instill a kind of protective cultural pride, it is this sadness and desire, I suggest, that may incite tremendous interest in the child's "culture." In the absence of the mother's body, the longing for origins may be displaced onto the body of the nation and its imagined culture. The genetic lineage of the child is unknown, but the cultural heritage can be studied, celebrated, performed, and embodied. The world of adoption has come up with a term that seems to express this, a paradoxical formulation: *birth culture*.

The shift in domestic adoption, now something to be celebrated rather than shrouded in mystery and silence and to be explored lifelong rather than ignored, has surely helped to create a climate in which it is desirable to search: whether for actual birth families, or for greater knowledge about those families, or at the very least for one's story. This shift has also helped to create a climate in which the adoption of children who look nothing like their parents, as is often the case in transnational adoption, may be accepted and even welcomed and embraced. Yet there is nothing instantaneous or simple about this welcome, and its complexity is compounded by the fact that the child has come from another country, another "culture." Furthermore, the new focus in domestic adoption, to create a narrative of the self that includes genetics and beginnings, does not translate easily to situations when virtually nothing is known of the specific circumstances of a child's abandonment or of her birth parents.

The social pendulum has swung from the virtual denial of adoption and the biological beginnings of the adopted child to an insistent ideology that without an embrace of those beginnings there will forever be a gaping hole, a primal wound, an incomplete self. Betty Jean Lifton (1994, 11), a psychologist and adoptee whose books have been influential in the domestic adoption world since the late 1970s, writes of "the ghosts that haunt the dark crevices of the unconscious and trail each member of the adoptive triangle . . . wherever they go." Lifton has provided the world of adoption with a compelling vision and a language describing "the journey of the adopted self," "the broken narrative," (36) and the "genealogical bewilderment" of the adoptee (68). This vision and this language have helped to make the case for dissolving the secrecy that once surrounded adoption, but they have also helped to create an adoption discourse in which searching to repair the wounded self and broken narrative seems almost compulsory. The activism efforts of adoptees and birth mothers, changes in adoption law in many states, open adoptions of various sorts, the prevalence of searches and reunions and literature describing them, social work discourse, and recent work in genetics all have created a set of new cultural pressures to find the missing genetic link, what Kaja Fink-ler (2001, 235) calls "the kin in the gene."[15] Pressures that originated within domestic adoption now touch the world of transnational adoption as well.

The mysteries that would be part of any adoption are compounded in China by the absence of a narrative and by a political, social, and eco-nomic situation that seems to preclude the possibility of ever learning more. As we have seen, most Chinese adoptions are of a baby who was abandoned at a place where she (sometimes he) would be found and taken to safety — to a Chinese family who might adopt the child or, more proba-bly, to an orphanage. Adoptive parents struggle with contradictions as they seek to imbue a child with a love of China and an understanding of the harsh realities that probably inform her or his personal history. It is not uncommon for adopted children, like eight-year-old Ying Ying Fry, who wrote a book called *Kids Like Me in China* (2001), to have a rather sophisticated understanding of the one-child policy and what Fry calls "the girl thing": the expectation that boys take care of their parents when they are old and pass on the family name. "Sometimes they decide they can't raise another baby girl, no matter how much they love her, because they need to try again for a boy. And then they take that new baby girl someplace safe, where she will be found quickly and taken care of and maybe get a new family — in China or some other country — who can love her and keep her forever. Maybe that's what happened to me," adds Fry. "I don't know for sure" (13–17).[16]

The secrecy that must surround this surrender of the child, and the consequent absence of knowledge of, or possibility of connection with, the birth mother or birth story, may in part impel the proliferation and circulation of parents' personal reflections in the world of Chinese adop-tion. In her essay "Navel Gazing," Lindsay Davies (2000, 18) ponders her daughter's belly button: "Thus for Gemma, a child adopted from China, her navel is the sign on her flesh of her deep loss. It marks an actual physical connection to the woman who gave her life; with the woman whom later, no doubt, she will try to imagine, try to grasp in her mind and heart; for whom she will cry and yet never be able to know. This fleshly knot attaches her to a past she can never access and to people who will remain as elusive as shadows." Davies tries to embrace these shadows and see them as people: "People who contributed the nature part to the nature/

nurture equation of identity. People who are present in her in ways we can never exactly know but which constantly provoke my imagination" (19).

Françoise-Romaine Ouellette and Hélène Belleau (2001, 27) have pointed to the "paradoxical situation that is created for the child who is assigned exclusively adoptive kinship in a society where blood ties are seen as indissoluble bonds of love and solidarity." A strategy for dealing with this paradox, they suggest, is to see biological ties as preceding or external to adoptive ties, "as just one tiny part of the particular history of the child, and not a component of the child's current identity." Although birth ties are "recognized" in documents, photographs, and "souvenirs," Ouellette and Belleau describe these as a "deactivated, objectivized" (27) archive. I contend that, on the contrary, parents seek ways of "activating" the archive and the connection. The quest for a DNA connection with sisters (to which I shall return below) is one example. The return journey is another.

Many parents have undertaken return journeys — sometimes to adopt a younger sibling, sometimes to visit orphanages and foster families, sometimes to give their child an experience of China (and of looking like the majority). As Jane Brown (2002) writes of her six-year-old's trip to China: "We watched as she was enfolded into feeling a sense of belonging and oneness with the kind people she was meeting. Her self esteem grew a foot taller. Her sense of self as a person of Chinese heritage grew a mile. 'I look like everyone else. You two don't!' she would say with an impish grin." Another cheerful version of the journey was developed by Jane Liedtke, an entrepreneurial Beijing-based mother, and involves a traveling "culture camp" in which groups of families visit tourist attractions and child-friendly sites like panda reserves. Such trips create a solidarity among the campers and a sense that China is a real place: huge, complicated, filled with Chinese people. "We specialize in helping your child fall in love with China!" Liedtke's brochure proclaims.[17] Liedtke eventually hopes to convert an abandoned Beijing palace into a "cultural center" for families traveling to adopt or to revisit China, but also as a center for returning adopted teenagers and young adults and even soon-to-be-retired parents who would like to engage in some form of community service in China.

Travel may also take the form of a quest. Even with the knowledge that it is virtually impossible to find birth families in China, the search for something — and the narration of that search — can nonetheless assume nearly mythical proportions. *Wuhu Diary: On Taking My Adopted Daughter*

Back to Her Hometown in China (2001) recounts Emily Prager's journey with her five-year-old daughter, Lulu, back to the town of Wuhu. Hoping to visit Lulu's orphanage and to find some traces, some additional information, to supplement the incomplete narrative of her child's beginnings, Prager writes: "Lulu is now part of our heritages, in the kinship charts. Yet the mysteries of her genetic code . . . are lost to her, probably forever. So anything we can find, any tiny nugget that might lead us back, we will take and store. If paleontologists can build a race from just a jawbone, surely we can glimpse a mother and father from an entire town" (40).

After two months in Wuhu, mother and daughter left China without learning anything more about Lulu's birth parents or her past. Even the orphanage had been torn down and rebuilt, and they were not allowed to visit the new facility. Prager's desire for a connection to the woman who had borne her child is thus displaced onto a town and onto China, the Chinese people, and the history of China. In the preadoption letter that she wrote at the agency's request to her daughter's imagined birth mother, she assures her: "I will also instill in her . . . a love of China, and an identity with the Chinese people. Don't worry. She will know where she comes from, that she was born of a great and ancient tradition. Perhaps some day, she would wish to go back. The history of China is, as you know, wide and long." Prager adds: "As your daughter becomes my daughter, your ancestors become my ancestors, and mine become yours. It is an interesting thing and very modern" (238).

Part of what is "very modern" about Prager's situation is the role of the adoption agency, which asked her to imagine and write a letter to the birth mother of the child she will adopt — even before a child is referred. When a discussion on an electronic mailing list that includes parents of older children turned to the question of grieving and whether grief is overemphasized, a social worker specializing in adoption, Jam Brown (2000), countered that a child adopted as an infant who does not appear to grieve may later learn to grieve for a loss she was too young to experience, understand, or articulate. Although this grief is not "the intense, powerful, time-limited primary grief that someone experiences when someone known and remembered and cherished dies," most adoptees do "grieve the loss of birth parents, connection to ancestry, disconnect from their original culture . . . at the same time that they celebrate and claim the connections that they have to their adoptive parents."

Such emotions are expressed in a cultural and historical field that has changed considerably since the silences of the 1950s, when the possibility of grief on the part of anyone in the adoption triad (child, birth parents, and adoptive parents) or any attention to birth parents was suppressed. The contemporary discourse of American social work and much of the popular literature that has focused on search and reunion frame orphanage travels and the wish to search as a quest for knowledge, as a necessary step in what is constructed as a universal, "natural" process of grieving and healing.

A growing number of adoptive families have returned to China. Some have been allowed to visit the adoptee's orphanage to meet her original caregivers, or to visit a foster mother outside the orphanage. One mother has established a small enterprise that provides photographs of a child's "abandonment site" and other key places in her story. Ironically, thanks to substantial financial support from parents in America, many of the older orphanages have been torn down and rebuilt. Yearning for some tangible connection to their daughters' pasts, two mothers who visited a reconstructed orphanage sought out the original building's site, from which they each managed to retrieve, and carry home to Massachusetts, a single brick. Children, too, may seek something tangible. Jane Brown (2002) wrote that when her daughter, asked by a friend traveling to China what she would like from there, replied, "dirt—I would like some China dirt—so I know it's a really real place." She "treasured that small bag of China dirt," Brown wrote, and when the daughter herself returned to China for the first time at the age of six, she and her family went to the mountainside and "dug up some rich, brown, moist and fragrant earth from Sierra Song E's beloved China."

There is in all of this a sense of multiple, layered longings. In the absence of birth parents (mothers especially), longings may emerge as a quest for place. Parents at Culture Day help their child place her name on the map of China. In China, Prager (2001, 83) tries to reconstruct the scene of her child's abandonment, to render the tale concrete. Staring at the bridge above the canal where she has been told Lulu was found, she muses, "Did people bring her here on a houseboat? Lu, with her love of boats and water? They could have. Did they bring her up out of the houseboat and place her right here?"

In *The Lost Daughters of China*, Karin Evans (2000, 83) also writes of

her longing for fragments of a story about her daughter, Kelly, and wonders about the scene of abandonment and being found. Knowing only that
Kelly was left in a marketplace when she was three months old, Evans
conjures a scene vivid with sensuous detail: "It was mid-winter, a season
of mild weather, I'd been told, but likely to be wet and the market would
have been crawling — filled with buckets of squirming local shrimp, live
frogs in bamboo cages, and tiny shiny eels swimming in tubs. . . . Bok choy
and long beans tied in neat bunches. Piles of oranges. And somewhere in
that large, bustling place, tucked among the produce, maybe, or near the
winter melons, was a baby." She continues to fantasize about the finding
of the child — perhaps by a farmer, reaching for a melon — and then tries to
imagine "all the possible identities for her elusive mother — a farmworker,
a young university girl, a daughter forced to fend for herself when floods
destroyed her family's village, a poor rural woman who came to the city
seeking work and found herself instead with an unexpected child? . . . Was
she sixteen? Or twenty-two? Or forty?" (85). Unable to answer these
questions, Evans turns to something palpable — to geography, to land and
water. She imagines a symmetry between the child's birth mother and
herself: "Just as the rivers in my daughter's homeland defined the physical
landscape . . . there was an invisible human current at work. A rippling
flow of people, poor and prosperous, riding to and from the city on motor-
bikes, bicycles, in trucks and cars. Somewhere back in the Pearl River
Delta, I knew, I had a counterpart" (86).

Belongings

Unlike most previous waves of adoption, adoption from China has further challenged the normative family by creating large numbers of single-
parent families. Adoption from China is not, of course, alone in destabi-
lizing the two-parent biological family model but rather takes its place
among all sorts of contemporary ways of making families and babies:
blended stepfamilies, gay and lesbian parents, parents who conceive with
the help of new reproductive technologies. These new family forms challenge the strength of the symbolic blood tie, that powerful metaphor of
American kinship (Schneider 1968). Is adoption inescapably bound to the
effort to replicate, echo, or mirror the family formed by biological ties? Or
is a more radical transformation possible, as Yngvesson (1997) suggests in

her analysis of open adoption? The practices of contemporary Chinese (and other forms of transnational) adoption reveal both the pull of the genealogical model and the impulse to transcend it and create new forms of kinship beyond blood.

The search for adequate language suggests something of the effort entailed in rewriting kinship. Adoptive parents worry about ways of naming the woman who conceived and gave birth to their children. "Birth mother" is the preferred term of the moment, but discussions about terminology often turn to ways of acknowledging that both adoptive and biological mothers are "real." One electronic mailing list member commented that whatever we call them, it should not be so hard to incorporate the idea of extra mommies: after all, we have grandmothers, godmothers, and stepmothers, and lesbian families already have two mothers. Cynthia Goldberg, the mother of a teenager, expressed her concerns about the singleness of the "one-mom" policy: "I can recall reading, when R was little, about making sure your kid got the 'real mom' right, that the [adoptive] mom was real. But then I figured out that hey, the [birth] mom was very real, too. When we went to Korea when R was 9, we met her foster mom, so R came up with a numbering system. B mom was her first mom, foster mom was second mom, I was third mom. And then she decided that Lynn was fourth mom, and my sister Nancy was fifth mom, and Gail, a close adult friend, was sixth mom. And she was delighted that she has *six* mothers who loved her and cared for her and nurtured her and were the stars in her small constellation. I was a bit worried that I was merely third but after a while I realized that I was quite glad to be counted in the lot of women who have loved her and been loved by her" (Goldberg 2003).

If the birth mother is impossible to find, the longing for genetic connection may be transposed onto a search for sisters. Two families — one in the United States, one in Europe — pursued efforts to determine if their daughters, fifteen months apart in age and adopted from the same orphanage, might be sisters. The girls look so much alike, wrote one mother, "that their photos could easily be mistaken for one another's. It's really astonishing. Even if they aren't siblings . . . it will be very cool to know somebody who looks that much like them." The families met, the girls' DNA was tested, and after six weeks of anxious waiting, the results were inconclusive. Both families were deeply disappointed. Social worker Jane Brown (2000) mused: "In a world where one is genetically all alone, it is a rare thing to have even a chance at making a connection." At the same time, she noted, adoptive families "have to acknowledge that our relationships are not just like those of families who share a genetic history. We can talk openly about how we are the same and how we are different—and that doesn't make our relationships any less authentic and powerful."

If adoptive parents struggle to affirm a kinship that is always in the process of being created, the media is quick to dramatize the romance of genetic kin reunited. The *Seattle Post-Intelligencer* published a story of twins discovered when a couple in Seattle sent a disposable camera to the foster home in China in which their soon-to-be-adopted daughter had spent the first year of her life. On returning home with their child, they developed the film and to their astonishment saw pictures of her with another toddler who appeared to be her identical twin. In this case DNA testing verified the genetic link: "A miracle made possible only by a photograph" (Eggert 2002). Although the second child had already been referred for adoption to another family, the Seattle parents were able to stop those arrangements and adopt the twin as well. The mother said, "I'm very excited, to put it mildly. . . . Twins are supposed to have this bond" (quoted in Eggert 2002).

Oscillations between these discourses—the search for the DNA connections and the bonds that blood relatives are "supposed to have" and the creation of a "different, authentic, and powerful" kinship—appear in other contemporary kinship forms. "Open adoption" may entail knowing about or meeting birth parents, or it may go further and incorporate birth and adoptive families on an ongoing basis (Yngvesson 1997; Pertman 2000). Adoptive parents are on the edge as they struggle to balance assumptions driven by the dominant ideology that everyone has an "innate desire to know about their genetic histories" (Pertman 2000, 11–12) and simultaneously to legitimize the cultural construction of kinship. Kahleah Guibault (2000, 52) who was born in Guatemala and now lives in Quebec, wrote the following passage when she was nine: "There are two ways of building a family, by giving birth to a child, or by adopting a child. Some people do both! . . . Being a member of an adoptive family means having two families. One birth family, and one forever family. Both families are important in different ways. . . . Some people ask me if Mommy and Daddy are my REAL parents and if Tristan is my REAL brother. I answer, "You can't get more REAL than my family!" . . . I wish I could write to my birthmother. If I could, I would tell her: I love her, I am okay, I am happy and loved. I have a family. I hope she is happy and loved . . . I think adoption is a great way to build a family and to make people happy. To me, a family is: people who love each other, take care of each other, help and teach each other, and will always be together."

As I have suggested, there is a movement toward the palpable and the particular among families who have adopted from China. The search for the place of birth and abandonment; the telling of the story of being found; the salvaged orphanage brick that represents an individual's history; the forging of solidarity with others who have been adopted from the same town, or orphanage, or even crib, or at the same moment: all of these substitute for the unattainable "kin in the gene." At the same time, there is a movement that goes beyond the China community to create a broader, more transcendent space. One venue for such efforts is a New York ritual created by adoptive parents' groups, organizations of young adult adoptees, and birth parents. The annual "Spirit of Adoption" ceremony strives to bridge not merely gaps but chasms by representing and celebrating all members of the adoption triad, in both domestic and transnational adoptions. A similar broadening is also evident in New York's Korean adoptee community. The mentorship program created by the largely Korean members of Also Known As (AKA), an organization of adult adoptees, was formed particularly to reach adopted Chinese children. The Culture Day sponsored by AKA was notable for its Korean drummers and dancers who performed along with groups of Vietnamese and Chinese dancers — and even salsa dancers from Colombia — a mix of adopted and hyphenated Americans.

"We're all in the Adoptee Network," concludes each verse in a poem composed by seven-year-old participants in a New York "Playshop" in 2001. As a sort of junior consciousness-raising and empowerment group for adopted children, the Playshop was invented by social worker Jane Brown. The poem's refrain was provided by Brown, but it is an idea that echoes through much of the discourse of contemporary Chinese adoption. "Jane helps our children see that they are part of something big," wrote Amy Klatzkin in describing Playshops, "that they have a role to play in learning what this all means and passing on their knowledge and experience to the children coming after them. She helps them see themselves not as victims of a sad past but owners of brilliant lives whose futures are theirs to create" (Klatzkin 2001). And indeed, as Klatzkin's daughter, Ying Ying Fry (2001, 1), declares in the first paragraph of her book; "There are lots of kids like me who were born in China and adopted by parents from other parts of the world. . . . Wherever we go, we often meet families like ours."

The powerful image of the network, of "kids like me" or "wherever we go . . . families like ours," enacted through the everyday practices of ribbon dance classes or FCC picnics, reflects how significantly the culture of adoption has changed in recent years. Parents of children adopted in earlier decades often note these changes with some awe, wishing that they had had a venue for the complicated discussions of myriad issues that are now the daily staples of adoption talk on the Internet. It is not that the complexities and contradictions of adoption have become any simpler. Performing "Chinese culture" surely does not erase racism; it may reinscribe or reify difference in unintended ways. But many of these complexities and contradictions are now exposed, voiced, and debated, at times to such a degree that some parents wonder if this is not too much: "Are we not scrutinizing every little thing to excess?" one mother wrote.

For many, however, the scrutiny, occurring in the field of a larger collectivity, yields both pain and pleasure. In 2003, I wrote that it is "too soon to know what the growing cohort of adopted Chinese children will eventually have to say about adoption, about birth parents, about culture, race and gender, about China or the world. To date, the voices we have heard are mostly those of parents" (51). As I write today, a year later, venues for children's voices have begun to proliferate. *Narrations*, a "newsletter by and for kids who are touched by adoption," includes stories, poems, and drawings by adopted children from many countries. New York's FCC has launched an annual *Kids Issue* of its newsletter, the first two issues featuring writing and art by more than a hundred children adopted from China.

The narrative impulse in the world of Chinese adoption is being nurtured at an early age, supported by adults with a lot to say, but also by a new and rapidly evolving culture of adoption. That culture includes an array of practices, from play groups and Playshops to the circulation of autoethnographic films and writings by older Korean adoptees. It was *First Person Plural*, the film by Korean adoptee Deann Borshay Liem, that originally inspired eight-year-old Ying Ying Fry to contemplate a film of her own. Fry's mother, a writer, persuaded her that a book would be simpler, and thus the idea for *Kids Like Me in China* was born. In winter 2004, FCC organized a reading of Kay Johnson's book on adoption and abandonment in China, hosted at New York City's elegant National Arts Club. In a separate room, in a "kids-only" session, the children had their own parallel book signing, reading, and discussion. Ying Ying Fry (by that time ten years old) read passages from *Kids Like Me*, while a panel of slightly younger girls, including my daughter, spoke about what it was like to revisit China. That night my daughter felt free to ask new questions about the one-child policy and the fate of children in China's orphanages.

Other children who have begun to write about their lives find an avid readership among their peers and, perhaps especially, adoptive parents. Questions abound in this passage from a poem by ten-year-old Teresa Yun Salvatore (2003, 3) of Brooklyn, written for the FCC *Kids Issue*:

Born in Tianjin, China.
Loved by a mother and father.
Placed in a strange building.
Where do I belong?
Feeling hopeless.
Having bottles, being fed.
By strange people.
I do not know.

Being picked up by a new family.
Being taken care of again.
But by who? Who are these strange people?
Taking care of me?
Who do I belong to?
These people or them?
I need many answers to my many
Questions.
Needing help.

I've found some answers, but not all.
Now some questions I understand.
But some still remain.
I want to know a lot of answers.
But not all are possible.
But I can wait.

Salvatore's "A Poem of My Life" was discovered by the mother of one of the poet's friends, who asked if she might circulate it on an electronic mailing list for adults. The young author readily gave permission. It seems more than likely that Salvatore, and many others in her young cohort of adoptees, will add their voices to future debates about adoption, debates that have already been enriched and complicated as earlier generations have come of age and have begun to define themselves as part of an international community, network, movement, and even "culture." As the mother of an eighteen-year-old Korean adoptee wrote on the Internet, "My daughter says she belongs to four cultures. . . . Korean, American, Jewish and Adoption. It's going to be very interesting to watch how these next few years play out." The interaction between the younger generation of Chinese and other adopted children and their older counterparts from Korea, Vietnam, and elsewhere will no doubt continue to play out in unanticipated ways, reminding us that adoption, like other forms of trans-national kinship, is situated in a moment of increasingly unquiet, criss-crossing migrations.

Notes

I am grateful to Families with Children from China of Greater New York, and especially FCC president David Youtz, for welcoming me simultaneously as eth-nographer and member of the Board. Thanks are due as well to electronic mailing list members, most of whom I have never met, who graciously permitted me to use their words. Many friends and colleagues offered encouragement and helpful feed-back, especially Ann Anagnost, Jane Brown, Sharon Carstens, Lindsay Davies, Faye Ginsburg, Cindi Katz, Laurel Kendall, Eleana Kim, Rayna Rapp, Nancy Smith-Hefner, Margaret Wiener, Barbara Yngvesson, and Charles Zerner. The support of the Ford Foundation is gratefully acknowledged.

1. My field research for this article was primarily carried out in New York City (2001–2002), supplemented by seven years of informal "participant observation" as an adoptive parent in New York and by Internet materials and electronic mail-ing lists that represent a more broadly North American population. Some names have been changed, and identifying information has been omitted for list partici-pants who requested anonymity. This essay does not address differences in com-munities throughout the United States or Canada, nor does it deal with families who have chosen to raise their children as "just American." Nonetheless, member-

ship in FCC as well as Internet participation encompass a very large percentage of adoptive families. Statements in this essay about "most" or "many" adoptive parents or children must be understood in terms of these constraints.

2. For statistics, see http://travel.state.gov/orphan_numbers.html.

3. In the late 1990s, one writer counted more than one thousand articles published in the popular press in a mere two years (Cecere 1998, 82). This interest is paralleled by media coverage of adoption in general. See Hallmark Channel's release in 2002 of the thirteen-hour series *Adoption* (www.hallmarkchannel.com).

4. Whereas adoption from Russia parallels the Chinese case in terms of dates and numbers, issues of race and difference have not emerged with the same salience, nor have the communities that mobilized around Russian adoption become as vocal (Scroggs n.d.). Most adopted Russian and Eastern European children are considered "white" in the United States (although in their birth country they may be stigmatized as Roma) and may to some extent resemble their adoptive parents. Even families with children from Latin America or India, where racial differences are often marked, have not organized as actively and visibly as their China counterparts. In the North American imaginary, China and Chinese "culture" are paradoxically deemed both exotic and accessible.

5. In 1999, the age limit was lowered to thirty years both for foreign adopters and for Chinese parents wishing to adopt in China.

6. Prior to quotas issued in 2001 that limited single-parent applications to 5 percent of each adoption agency's total, such adoptions constituted 25 to 35 percent of the total (Smith and Kelly 2002, 4). An earlier set of regulations prohibited gay and lesbian parents from adopting.

7. Other forms include sex-selective abortion. The growing use of ultrasound scans to determine gender is partly responsible for sex ratios that have become increasingly skewed since 1980. The 2000 census reported a male to female ratio of almost 117 to 100 (Gittings 2001). "The numbers tell a frightening story: little girls are being eliminated from Chinese society . . . on a massive scale" (Greenhalgh and Li 1995, 601).

8. Abandonment has painful consequences for parents, including punishments (fines and sterilization) if they are caught. We know little of the emotional consequences, but Johnson describes one birth mother who "wept silently before we even began to speak; several years after abandoning her second daughter she remained undecided as to whether she would ever proceed with another pregnancy despite the fact that she held a certificate of permission to give birth again and was under great pressure from her husband, and in-laws. She vowed that if she did decide to become pregnant, she would never again abandon one of her babies regardless of the gender" (Johnson, Huang, and Wang, 1998, 480–81).

9. On the West Coast and in Hawaii there are many families with one or more Asian American parent (Wang 1999).

10. Other reasons include the American public's fascination with China — a mix of longings for some mysterious "East" and fear of its contemporary power. Orientalizing and ambivalence take gendered forms with respect to adoption from China. On the one hand, Chinese girls are represented as adorable, even exquisite; on the other, they are viewed as victims of a cruel and oppressive society that devalues women and discards its precious daughters. These representations pose dilemmas for adoptive parents, who see their children as neither "China dolls" nor "abandoned girls."

11. Adoptive parents have no way of knowing their child's birthplace; all they know is where the child was found.

12. In San Francisco, where a third of FCC children have at least one Asian American parent, FCC marches without a banner, merged with the whole parade as members of local schools or Chinese American groups (Klatzkin 2001).

13. At a workshop on transnational adoption at the Spence Chapin Adoption Agency in New York on 6 March 2002, parents responded to social worker Joy Lieberthal's talk about the importance of Asian role models by lamenting the fact that in their virtually all-white communities there were no Asian doctors or teachers; the only Asians worked in restaurants or laundromats. Lieberthal suggested that children should see all sorts of Asians because they, too, will someday be mistaken for the delivery boy (or girl).

14. The influx of resources from abroad to orphanages in China may have unintended, less beneficial consequences, as some officials "have grown accustomed to the benefits of international adoption and seem less than eager to promote the domestic adoption of healthy children" (Johnson 2002).

15. "When you go to the doctor you do not have a medical history and you are not a person," commented an adoptee in Finkler's (2001, 241) study of the medicalization of family and kinship, a sentiment shared by almost every adoptee Finkler met.

16. For girls, the birth policy story offers a partial answer to the question of why their birth parents did not keep them. It is a somewhat comforting possibility that birth parents had no choice but to relinquish their female babies. But for parents of the 5 to 10 percent of adopted Chinese children who are boys, the standard gendered narrative is not helpful. One mother wrote: "I've had parents react to our family as though we didn't 'really' adopt from China because we adopted a boy . . . because we didn't save one of these precious little girls that had been displaced because of the one-child law. I've even had people suggest we should have turned down our referral or perhaps sued our agency for not making us more aware that boys were even a possibility. . . . We were, for the record, one of the many families

each year that writes a gender-neutral application, paints the nursery pink, then gets surprised by the referral of a son. Like most of these families, we got over our shock and went ahead with the adoption and lived happily ever after (except for having to repaint the bedroom)" (Ridenour 2002). This comment raises the question of how inclusive is the adoptive "community" in a world where girls so clearly predominate.

17. The market for such trips is growing rapidly: Liedkte's brochure (2002) offered ten options, including "Yangtze River Camp Cruise" (see your daughter's hometown before it is submerged by the Three Gorges Dam, on a ship outfitted to resemble a splendid palace, offering onboard tai chi, kite flying, and seminars). Other organizations that have for years sponsored Korean and other "heritage" tours have begun to add China to their repertoire.

References

Adolfson, Nathan. 1999. *Passing Through*. San Francisco: NAATA. Video.

Anagnost, Ann. 2000. "Scenes of Misrecognition: Maternal Citizenship in the Age of Transnational Adoption." *positions* 8: 389–421.

Brown, Jane. 2002. International-Adopt-Talk@yahoogroups.com.

Carp, Wayne. 1998. *Family Matters: Secrecy and Disclosure in the History of Adoption*. Cambridge, MA: Harvard University Press.

Cecere, Laura. 1998. *The Children Can't Wait: China's Emerging Model for Intercountry Adoption*. Cambridge, MA: China Seas.

Chen, Vivia. 1999. "No Recipe for Being Chinese-American." *Families with Children from China* 6: 17–18.

Davies, Lindsay. 2000. "Navel Gazing." *Families with Children from China* 7: 18–19.

Eggert, David. 2000. "By Sheer Chance, Chinese Twin Toddlers Are Reunited. *Seattle Post-Intelligencer*, 4 April.

Eisenberg, Freda. 2002. jfwcc@yahoogroups.com.

Evan B. Donaldson Adoption Institute. 1999. *Survey of Adult Korean Adoptees: Report on the Findings*. New York: Evan B. Donaldson Adoption Institute.

Evans, Karin. 2000. *The Lost Daughters of China: Abandoned Girls, Their Journey to America, and the Search for a Missing Past*. New York: Putnam.

Finkler, Kaja. 2001. "The Kin in the Gene: The Medicalization of Family and Kinship in American Society." *Current Anthropology* 42: 235–63.

Fry, Ying Ying, with Amy Klatzkin. 2001. *Kids Like Me in China*. St. Paul, MN: Yeoung and Yeoung.

Gittings, John. 2001. "Lost and Found." *Guardian*, 17 August.

Goldberg, Cynthia. 2002. International-Adopt-Talk@yahoogroups.com.

Greenhalgh, Susan, and Jiali Li. 1995. "Engendering Reproductive Polity and Practice in Peasant China: For a Feminist Demography of Reproduction." *Signs* 20 (spring): 601–41.

Guibault, Kahleah Maria de Lourdes. 2000. "Family and Adoption." *Adoptive Families* (November-December): 52.

Higginbotham, Julie. 2002. International-Adopt-Talk@yahoogroups.com.

Johnson, Kay. 1993. "Chinese Orphanages: Saving China's Abandoned Girls." *Australian Journal of Chinese Affairs*, 30 (July): 61–87.

———. 1996. "The Politics of the Revival of Infant Abandonment in China." *Population and Development Review* 22: 77–98.

———. 2002. "Politics of International and Domestic Adoption in China." *Law and Society Review* 36: (2): 379–96.

Johnson, Kay, with Huang Banghan and Wang Liyao. 1998. "Infant Abandonment and Adoption in China." *Population and Development Review* 24: 469–510.

Klatzkin, Amy, ed. 1999. *A Passage to the Heart: Writings from Families with Children from China.* St. Paul, MN: Yeoung and Yeoung.

———. 2001. greaterNYFCC@aol.com.

Leader, Melinda. 2001. "Citizen Amy: Adopted from China, Five-Year-Old Amy Speth Pledges her Allegiance as a U.S. Citizen. *Ladies' Home Journal*, July, 136.

Lewis, Rose A. 2000. *I Love You Like Crazy Cakes.* New York: Little, Brown.

Liedtke, Jane. 2002. OCDF China tours (brochure). Bloomington, IL: Our Chinese Daughters Foundation.

Liem, Deann Borshay. 2000. *First Person Plural.* San Francisco: NAATA. Video.

Lifton, Betty Jean. 1994. *Journey of the Adopted Self: A Quest for Wholeness.* New York: Basic Books.

Modell, Judith. 1994. *Kinship with Strangers: Adoption and Interpretation of Kinship in American Culture.* Berkeley: University of California Press.

Ouellette, Françoise-Romaine, and Hélène Belleau. 2001. *Family and Social Integration of Children Adopted Internationally: A Review of the Literature.* Montreal: INRS–Univèrsité du Quèbec.

Pertman, Adam. 2000. *Adoption Nation: How the Adoption Revolution is Transforming America.* New York: Basic Books.

Prager, Emily. 2001. *Wuhu Diary: On Taking my Adopted Daughter Back to Her Hometown in China.* New York: Random House.

Putnam, Conan. 2002. "Dancing to Her Music." *China Connection* 9: 6–7.

Rapp, Rayna, and Faye Ginsburg. 2001. Enabling Disability: Rewriting Kinship, Reimagining Citizenship. *Public Culture* 13: 533–56.

Ridenour, Barb. 2002. PostAdoptChina@yahoogroups.com.

Salvatore, Teresa Yun. 2003. "A Poem of My Life," *Families with Children from China Kids' Issue*, 3.

Schneider, David. 1968. *American Kinship: A Cultural Account*. Chicago: University of Chicago Press.

Scroggs, Patricia. n.d. "Building Cultural Bridges for Internationally Adopted Children." Unpublished manuscript.

Shanley, Mary. 2001. *Making Babies, Making Families: What Matters Most in an Age of Reproductive Technologies, Surrogacy, Adoption, and Same-Sex and Unwed Parents*. Boston: Beacon.

Silverman, Lesley. 2002. jfwcc@yahoogroups.com.

Smith, Joann, and Kelly, Joe. 2002. "New Adoption Regulations Set Quotas, Restrict Singles." *Families with Children from China* 9: 4.

Stephens, Sharon, ed. 1995. *Children and the Politics of Culture*. Princeton: Princeton University Press.

Volkman, Toby Alice. 2003. "Embodying Chinese Culture: Transnational Adoption in North America." *Social Text* 74: 29–55.

Vonk, M. Elizabeth. 2001. "Cultural Competence for Transracial Adoptive Parents." *Social Work* 46: 246–55.

Wang, Anne. 1999. "Parenting Identities: America's Adopted 'Chinese' Daughters from China." Master's thesis, University of Hawaii.

Weil, Richard. 1984. "International Adoptions: The Quiet Migration." *International Migration Review* 18: 276–93.

Yngvesson, Barbara. 1997. "Negotiating Motherhood: Identity and Difference in 'Open' Adoptions." *Law and Society Review* 31: 31–80.

——. 2000. "Un Niño de Cualquier Color: Race and Nation in Intercountry Adoption." In *Globalizing Institutions: Case Studies in Regulation and Innovation*, ed. Jane Jenson and Boaventura de Sousa Santos. Aldershot, Eng.: Ashgate.

PART II   **Counterparts**

Chaobao

The Plight of Chinese Adoptive Parents in the Era of the One-Child Policy

KAY JOHNSON

A s a China scholar and the adoptive parent of a Chinese child, I am often asked to give talks to groups of American parents who have adopted children from China. In the course of doing so I have found that above all these parents seek the knowledge that will help them understand their children's birth parents and the circumstances surrounding the abandonment of children in China. Who are the parents of these children, why did they abandon their birth child, how did they feel about it, and what consequences did they suffer?

For the most part the American adoptive parents of Chinese children want to believe the best of their children's birth parents. Most want to put as positive a spin as possible on the story of abandonment. Indeed, many refuse to use the word "abandonment" and are surprised, if not offended, when I do. Many American parents prefer to frame the issues of abandonment as a type of "adoption plan" and speak of their children as "being left somewhere to be found by others." They prefer to see birth parents as "forced" into the act of abandonment, as victims with little or no choice in their actions. Sometimes abandonment is even seen as a "brave act," taken at great risk to the birth parents, to save the child's life from abortion or infanticide or to "give the child a better life." Whether the agent of force is government coercion, the iron grip of culture, poverty, or some combination thereof, seeing birth parents as unwilling victims is a favored way to spin the story of abandonment. What is at stake is how adoptive parents will tell their children the story of how they lost their first families and came into their present families, how they will answer their children's emotionally difficult questions about what happened to them in China. Also at stake is the adoptive parents' need to believe that adopting their child and taking her or him from China was beyond moral question and in the child's best interest, if not necessary for her or his survival.

My own collaborative research (Johnson, Huang, and Wang 1998) gives some support to the positive shaping of the story of abandonment, but it also undercuts it in many ways. Certainly most birth parents who turn to the abandonment of a second or third daughter are under great pressure from coercive government policies and actions. Yet birth parents are not forced in any literal way to abandon a child; indeed it is illegal and a violation of birth-planning policy to abandon any child. Rather it is usually a strongly felt need for a son in the face of severe birth planning pressures that drives parents to abandon a child, a child they would most probably choose to keep, regardless of the penalty, were it a boy. Many other Chinese parents in similar circumstances refuse to take this route out of a difficut situation, despite their desire for a son; to most, abandoning a birth child is unthinkable. Nor is it easy to construe abandonment as a brave act. Abandoning parents are usually not caught by the authorities, and when they are, they are generally subject to the punishment they would suffer for having had the child in the first place — birth planning fines and possible sterilization for an overquota child. In the vast majority of cases, the child is abandoned not to serve the child's interests or needs ("they loved you so much they gave you away so you could have a better life") but to fulfill those of the parents and families who abandon them.

Similarly, the construction of abandonment as a type of "adoption plan" receives only mixed support from our findings. Some birth parents in our research sample of abandoning families did indeed seem to have a well-thought-out "adoption plan" in mind; they carefully determined where they would leave a child in an effort to find her a new adoptive home, sometimes choosing the protected doorway of a childless or daughterless couple, maybe even setting off a firecracker to alert the potential adoptive parents inside that there was something special waiting for them outside. But other birth parents simply left a child on a roadside or under a bridge, hoping for the best yet never knowing if the child found a home or even whether it survived its ordeal. There were even a few who dumped a child recklessly in a garbage heap or hid the child in an empty field, walking away without so much as a glance backward. Those who traveled to a city — the site of abandonment for the majority of children who end up in the large state orphanages that offer international adoption — were par-

ticularly unlikely to know precisely what happened to the child after abandonment. The city was seen not only as a good place for the child to be
found quickly and safely but above all as a place of anonymity, far from the
prying eyes or birth planning concerns of local officials in the birth parents'
hometown.

It is not surprising that American adoptive parents are most interested
in the highly charged issue of their children's birth parents and the act of
abandonment. My initial motivation in doing research on the causes and
patterns of abandonment in China in the 1990s was driven not only by my
desire to understand a social phenomenon that was closely related to my
previous research on Chinese women and rural society, but also by a desire
to learn more about the "story" of my daughter and her cohort. Above all,
I imagined how the information gathered through this research would
allow her to come to terms with her own abandonment and, I hoped, help
her to understand the difficult circumstances that were likely to have
surrounded her birth parents' act so that she could ultimately forgive
them. Understanding, I hoped, would overcome the bitterness and lessen
the sense of loss and rejection that must, at some level, accompany the
knowledge of being abandoned by one's own birth parents.

Discovering Our Counterparts: Chinese Parents Who Adopt Abandoned Children

As my research progressed, the imaginative grip of the birth parents and
their plight gradually gave way in my mind to an increasing appreciation
of and interest in another group: Chinese parents who adopt the children
abandoned by others. Here, as an adoptive mother of a Chinese foundling, I found my Chinese counterparts along with the counterparts of the
American adoptive parents to whom I often speak. I also learned about an
important group of my daughter's cohort who remains in China: the abandoned children adopted by these Chinese parents. I was fascinated with
the Chinese adoptive parents' stories and I often strongly identified with
them. Their motivations to adopt, the joy that they expressed in their
children, and their determination to raise them well all seemed familiar.
Even more, I was in awe of the hardships that many of them endured in
order to adopt and keep their children, hardships that far surpassed anything that I had confronted in adopting my daughter. The stress that U.S.

adoptive parents experience during the bureaucratic "paper chase" of international adoption or the endless wait for INS approval pales in comparison with the political and bureaucratic hurdles some of these Chinese parents face. Similarly the verbal slights that U.S. parents may hear at places like the grocery store, or the other subtle and sometimes not-so-subtle forms of social and cultural discrimination that they and their children experience in school and daily life, seem minor compared with the highly discriminatory legal and political obstacles that confront some Chinese adoptive parents and their children. While international adoption in the United States is considered extraordinarily expensive and thus is open only to solidly middle-class or upper-middle-class people, the expense relative to income is far less than the amount some adoptive Chinese peasants or townspeople of ordinary means must pay in fees and penalties in order to keep their children.

The issue of Chinese adoptive parents is a side of my research that has not gained as much attention from the American adoptive community as have the few insights that I have been able to offer into the motivations of abandoning birth parents and the consequences they suffer. Yet the experience of Chinese adoptive families is part of the larger story of abandonment and of the cohort of abandoned children, of whom only a small percentage are ultimately adopted abroad. Aside from the minority of abandoned children who are in orphanages, little is known of those who remain in China. Indeed, the very existence of a large group of adoptive Chinese parents of abandoned children flies in the face of deep and persistent stereotypes about Chinese attitudes, culture, and customs of adoption. Above all, it undermines the common assumption that it is primarily international adopters who welcome these "unwanted girls," these "lost daughters of China." These stereotypes create an imagined "other" to which American adoptive parents then compare themselves, concluding — inaccurately — that the Chinese are generally unwilling to adopt children to raise "as their own" and certainly far less willing to adopt than Americans and other Westerners. The Chinese are often thought to be especially unwilling to adopt the children of those who are not blood relatives, let alone the children of totally unknown strangers. Afflicted with the strong preference for sons, Chinese parents are presumed to be particularly uninterested in adopting girls, who comprise most of the abandoned children who languish in Chinese orphanages. In contrast,

American adopters are seen (and see themselves) as far more likely to open their hearts to the children of strangers, regardless of gender or race, and to raise these children as if they were birth children. As Ellen Goodman states in an editorial written in 2003, the "beautiful, healthy daughter[s]" adopted from China by Americans have come from "a culture in which [they] faced the options of either an orphanage or America." American adopters, then, can rest assured that these children had no good option except international adoption.

In fact, none of these stereotypes were supported by our research. We found that nearly 60 percent of the roughly eight hundred adoptive families from whom we gathered information between 1995 and 2000 had adopted abandoned children — that is, strangers' children left in public or semipublic places.[1] Only a handful of these eight hundred families had adopted from an orphanage; the majority adopted children before they passed formally into the hands of a government institution. In the 1990s only a few thousand of the estimated hundreds of thousands of domestic Chinese adoptions each year involved orphanages, although the numbers grew at the end of the decade and were greater than the numbers of foreign adoptions.[2] The overwhelming majority of the adopted abandoned children were girls. People who already had sons but no daughters were particularly eager to add a daughter to their family, reflecting a widespread desire among contemporary Chinese to have both a boy and a girl in the family (Greenhalgh and Li 1995; Johnson, Huang, and Wang 1998; Zhang 2001). These adoptions generally were permanent, "strong" adoptions and the children's status in their adoptive families was similar or identical to that of a birth child. Although our fieldwork was primarily based in south-central China, all of these patterns have recently been confirmed by fieldwork conducted by Zhang Weiguo of more than four hundred adoptive families located in various parts of southeastern China, central China, and the north China plain (Zhang 2002).[3]

Even more gripping than the dismantling of false images of domestic adoption were the stories of the adoptive parents of abandoned children who faced huge government penalties and long-term legal discrimination in order to keep and raise their adopted children. Not all adoptive families experienced such problems, and none did from the small number who adopted from state orphanages. But why did a large minority of those who adopted abandoned children outside the orphanages face official and legal obstacles instead of encouragement in adopting homeless children at a time when Chinese orphanages were increasingly overburdened and underfunded? Clearly these parents not only help the children they adopt, sometimes even saving their lives, but also save the government the expense of caring for these children in overcrowded and, in the 1990s, often grossly underequipped facilities (Johnson 1993, 1996). Without the existence of this large group of adoptive families willing to put up with the problems posed by adopting, state orphanages in the 1990s would have been totally overwhelmed with abandoned children. The answers to these questions illuminate another reason, addressed below, why adoptive Chinese parents have received relatively little attention, and why so many of the adoptions we learned about took place outside official channels of adoption and outside the orphanage system, from which all international adoptions take place.

The One-Child Adoption Policy

Current adoption patterns are to a significant extent the product of population control policies pursued by the Chinese government in the last two decades. In the mid-1980s a number of restrictions on adoption began to be enforced by local officials throughout China, backed up by the coercive power of fines and other penalties. These restrictions were a product of the birth planning restrictions that emerged in the early 1980s under the name of the one-child policy. From the outset, the one-child policy was greeted with various efforts to avoid or get around the regulations, especially in the countryside where there was more political, organizational, and physical "space" to do so (Greenhalgh 1994). One of the ways that some peasants got around their birth quota was to adopt out a birth child, usually a daughter, in order to be able to give birth again so as to try for a son. Sometimes these "adoptions" were temporary, intended merely to hide the existence of a child until the desired boy was born. But sometimes these adoptions were real, whereby adoptive parents assumed permanent, full rights and obligations toward the child, and the child assumed the status of a birth child in the adoptive home.

Because of this subversive and at times creative use of "adoption" — sometimes real, sometimes subterfuge — as a means to avoid birth planning restrictions, adoption policy quickly came under the regulatory net of birth planning authorities. To tighten their grip on birth quotas, birth planning authorities not only sought to regulate and punish birth parents who gave away a child in adoption for the purpose of avoiding a fine and/or having another child, but they also sought to restrict the pool of potential adopters by allowing only older, childless, and presumably infertile people to adopt someone else's child. All other adopters were considered in violation of birth planning regulations and subject to penalties and fines. As I will discuss in greater detail below, those who already had birth children and adopted another child were particularly likely to encounter official pressure and penalties. Their adoption was often treated exactly as an overquota birth, or *chaosheng*. Hence this kind of adoption is sometimes referred to as an "overquota adoption" or *chaobao*. Meanwhile, restricting the pool of legally qualified adoptive parents to those who were childless and over a certain age made it less likely that birth parents could find adoptive families or use friends and relatives as a subterfuge for hiding children.

By the late 1980s the interests and needs of population control authorities rather than the welfare of parentless children dictated local adoption regulations. As an unintended consequence, these restrictions led to more outright abandonment and, although such restrictions likely reduced fake "adoptions" and the use of fostering as subterfuge, they also pushed many real adoptions underground or at least away from official channels. Once codified into law, the restrictions also ensured that the numbers of people seeking to adopt from orphanages would remain small or even decline just as orphanages began to bulge with increasing numbers of abandoned children in the early 1990s.

Thus adoption policy in the 1980s evolved to mirror the one-child birth planning policy (Johnson, Huang, and Wang 1998), with negative consequences for abandoned children and for the Chinese parents who sought to give them new homes. Indeed, by the late 1980s adoption policy was even stricter than birth policy. By this time, in most rural areas the so-called one-child policy had become somewhat more lenient. Due to fierce resistance to the one-child policy in the countryside — where, with no social security system, the felt need for a son was particularly strong and the ability to subvert birth planning regulations much greater than in urban areas — most provinces allowed rural couples whose first child was a girl to give birth to a second child after a period of several years (Greenhalgh 1993; White 1991). A few rural areas allowed two children, widely spaced, regardless of the gender of the first child. Yet adoption policy continued to insist that only the childless could adopt, and they could adopt only one child, be it a girl or boy. This restriction applied to rural as well as urban areas. Furthermore, adoptive parents had to meet high age requirements while rural birth parents were usually allowed to have children at a relatively young age as befit the local social norms for childbearing.

In late 1991, in the midst of a massive birth planning crackdown in large parts of the countryside, these adoption regulations were codified in the first national adoption law of the People's Republic of China, which came into effect in April 1992.[4] To international adopters and Western adoption agencies, this law heralded the "opening" of Chinese adoption to the world and hence the liberalization of adoption policy (Cecere 1998), but from the perspective of domestic adoption it represented the final legal codification of severe restrictions and the closing down of spontaneous and customary adoption practices that could have been called on to secure more homes in China for the increasing numbers of abandoned children. Instead of challenging the grip of birth planning policies on adoption policy, and instead of carefully supervising rather than severely limiting domestic adoptions, the government turned to international adopters to help solve the growing problem of child abandonment that rose in the wake of the one-child policy.

The Impact of the One-Child Adoption Policy on Adoptive Families

In the Chinese countryside, practice often diverges from policy, and policy itself is always open to interpretation. Implementation in some areas, at some times, was strict while in other areas it was lax. Moreover, the national adoption law, like the local regulations before it, carefully exempted orphans from the restrictions. True orphans — that is, children whose parents were dead as opposed to children who were abandoned by living parents — could be adopted by relatives, friends, or others regardless of their age or the number of children in the adopting families. The relatively small percentage of families in our sample who adopted orphans (about 10 percent of the whole) encountered no difficulties from officials even if they had birth children or were young. Disabled children were also exempted from the restrictions. We found too few cases in this category to generalize, but the experience of families who adopted disabled children seemed to depend on how serious and irreversible was the disability. In general it seemed that domestic adopters were subject to a much more stringent definition of "disability" than were international adopters.[5] The primary target of the restrictive adoption policy, like the birth planning policy that dictates it, is healthy children whose birth parents choose not to keep them. Slightly less than 90 percent of our sample involved children in this category, whose adoptions theoretically were subject to the legal restrictions of childlessness and the minimum age requirement of thirty-five (which was reduced to thirty in 1999).

In practice we found that underage adoptive parents who were childless were rarely punished for adopting. Often their main difficulty was waiting until they had reached the legal age before they could register the adoption and obtain a household registration (hukou) for the child. In other words, local officials did not seem to take the age requirement too seriously as long as the parents were childless and apparently infertile. Those who encountered the greatest difficulties were parents who already had one or more birth children, a group that comprised about half of our sample of adoptive families. These were the chaobao, or overquota adopters. They were, in effect, regarded by law as if they had had an overquota birth.

Not all overquota adopters in our sample were punished, just as not all birth parents who give birth to overquota children were punished. Many successfully kept their adoptions secret from authorities; others simply lived in areas where the authorities ignored the violation or found it unreasonable to penalize them because it was felt that they had done a "good deed" by providing an abandoned child with a loving, permanent home. But nearly 40 percent of these families were penalized in some way. As the 1990s progressed, it became increasingly difficult for chaobao to escape either detection or penalties, and the percentage subject to penalties increased. In some areas by the late 1990s even underage childless adopters were sometimes fined. Apparently the impending 2000 census led to a tightening of all birth planning restrictions, including adoptions, in many rural areas.[6]

Chaobao adopters faced the full range of penalties suffered by those who gave birth to overquota children, the most common being stiff monetary fines (sometimes equivalent to or greater than a family's yearly income) and, less often, the mandatory sterilization of one of the parents. Wage earners, such as factory workers or state-employed teachers, might be penalized by a reduction in pay or even lose their jobs. In most cases penalties were levied by birth planning authorities rather than by the courts or by the civil affairs office (the bureaucratic arm officially charged with matters such as adoption and child welfare).

Yet chaobao parents also faced a penalty that overquota birth parents never faced: their child might be seized from them and placed in an orphanage or given to another legally qualified family, assuming one could be found. This threat was made even in areas where no orphanage facilities existed or in areas where orphanages were severely underfunded, overcrowded, and virtually unable to handle any more children. Agreeing to fines and/or sterilization usually prevented the seizure of the child, but some adoptive parents simply could not afford the entire fine (which in extreme cases might be double their yearly income or more) and, despite their efforts to keep the child, might have her taken away. On the other hand, some local officials listened to the angry protests of adoptive parents who could not afford the fines but who refused to relinquish the child and let them off with only a token fine or none at all.

Unfortunately, not all officials were so flexible or compassionate, nor could even those so inclined be so in periods when birth planning authorities were breathing down their necks. Some adoptive parents, when faced with the immediate prospect of being caught with an overquota adoption, might themselves feel compelled to abandon their adopted child, thus subjecting the child to a second abandonment. To make matters worse for the child, even passersby who find abandoned children report that if they take a child to the police or to an orphanage, they may be suspected of violating birth planning themselves. To avoid being fined, they might have to prove that the child was not born to them, something that adopters who have avoided official scrutiny for some time cannot always do. Indeed, even if they are not suspected of being the birth parents they may be held accountable for the birth planning fines in any case. As a result, the well-founded fear of punishment encourages some people to leave children by the roadside rather than deliver them safely to authorities. Hence the dynamics of this adoption policy lead to many more "double abandonment" cases than would otherwise be the case, thus subjecting some children to double jeopardy.

A Case of Chaobao

The case of Wang Meiying presents an illustrative, if extreme, case of the experience of a chaobao family in the 1990s. Wang lives in an area of southeastern China where birth planning regulations, including the restrictive clauses of the adoption law, have been harshly implemented. She works in a shoe factory in a suburb of a medium-sized city and her husband works as a laborer outside the area, returning home every few months. Shortly after they were married, both at age twenty-five, in the mid-1980s, Wang gave birth to a son. Like other factory workers in her area, Wang was then required to have an IUD inserted and to sign a certificate pledging not to have another child. She had always wanted a daughter but knew it would be impossible for her to give birth to another child; the penalties for doing so—a ruinously high fine, loss of job, and sterilization—were prohibitive.

Several years later, Wang's mother found an abandoned baby near the steps of a hospital located in her neighborhood. Her mother brought the baby home and took care of her while trying to decide what to do. A neighbor who had only one child, a son, very much wanted to adopt the baby girl and took her immediately to a doctor to see if the child needed treatment. Like most of the adoptive families we met, this woman felt that a child of each gender made a perfect family (Johnson, Huang, and Wang 1998), and she had longed for a daughter after her son was born. Unfortunately the doctor discovered that the infant girl was in extremely poor health and was unlikely to survive regardless of treatment. Reluctantly, the neighbor took the baby back to the hospital and left her on a bench in one of the wards, hoping the doctors would do whatever they could for the child.

When Wang heard about the baby she rushed to the hospital, but the baby had already died. She was heartbroken that they were able to do nothing to save the baby. A few years later another baby girl was abandoned in the same area. No one dared take the child for fear of getting in trouble with the authorities, who were in the midst of a stringent birth control campaign. Although Wang feared legal consequences, she could not bear to leave the child, afraid that it too would die.

Her in-laws were not pleased when Wang brought the baby home, knowing that it was illegal for her and her husband to adopt a second child and that the consequences could be severe. In response, Wang went immediately to the police station and asked permission to keep the girl at least until a childless family could be found. After gathering eye-witness accounts about when and where the baby was found, the police gave permission to register the child in Wang's household, that is, to give her a legal hukou for that area. The police were in fact grateful that the baby was being cared for because it would be difficult and costly for them to provide care. But when Wang took the police report and letter of permission to the local birth planning committee they refused to accept it. They said that she could not register the child because she already had a child; she could, however, volunteer to care for the abandoned girl, at her own expense, while they looked for someone who was childless and over thirty-five to adopt her.

Two weeks later the committee had not found anyone to adopt the child. Yet even after having a meeting to consider allowing Wang to adopt the child, the birth planning committee decided that the child had to be given up to the orphanage immediately. Wang was devastated. She had heard that the orphanage conditions were very bad and she had already fallen in love with the baby. "Every day my love for this child doubled," she said. She could not bear to do as she was told, so she left town with the baby and went to stay with a friend in a distant village. Her friend agreed to keep the child and Wang went back and forth to visit. Gradually, Wang started to bring her adopted daughter home for long visits, telling people that she was caring for her friend's child. Yet during a campaign of renewed enforcement, birth planning officials visited Wang's home and immediately suspected that this child was none other than Wang's adopted daughter. Although Wang insisted that they were wrong, they threatened her with a fine of 20,000 yuan (several times the total of Wang's yearly wages) and mandatory sterilization unless she sent the girl to the orphanage. Defiant, Wang again ran off with the child.

This cat-and-mouse game continued for years, during which Wang's relationship with her husband and in-laws deteriorated. Although her husband also loved the child, he worried about the negative impact of the situation on their older son. He also feared that eventually they would be caught and ruined financially by the fines, and that in the end the child would be seized from them regardless. While birth parents caught hiding an overquota child might be fined, sterilized, and fired from their jobs, in the end the child would still be theirs, even if they could not manage to pay in full. But Wang and her husband, as overquota adopters, did not have this assurance.

Nonetheless, Wang persisted in her determination to keep her daughter, causing great tension in the family. Meanwhile, the daughter, deprived of a proper registration, could not enter school in her parents' area and had to be sent back once again to the village to attend a poor rural primary school that did not require a hukou to enroll. Adding insult to injury, Wang had to pay a tuition fee that was more than double what a legally registered child would pay to attend a far superior school in Wang's urban neighborhood. Wang's daughter also missed several of her inoculations because she lacked a legal identity. Wang was constantly afraid of being discovered with her "black child" and thus she avoided situations where she might be asked to show the child's hukou.

Urban / Rural Differences and the Problem of Hukou

The story of Wang Meiying and her daughter has no particular denouement. As far as I know, they struggled on with this barely tolerable situation hoping for some break that would allow a legal resolution of their status. While theirs is an extreme example, both in the persistence of the adoptive parents and the relentlessness of birth planning authorities to catch and punish them, it reflects a pattern heard again and again from chaobao parents. While adoptive parents feel that they are providing a loving family for a homeless child, saving not only the child but also the government's money, birth planning authorities see these parents as engaging in a practice that threatens their control over the population's reproductive behavior. Neither the policy nor the letter of the law allows room to consider the interests of the children, let alone those of the adoptive parents. Fortunately, in practice, the one-child adoption policy, like other problematic policies, was implemented unevenly by local officials, a pattern that led to lighter penalties or no penalties for adoptive families in some areas, at least in the countryside. Often enforcement of adoption restrictions hinged on whether an active birth planning campaign was being waged in the area. In the late 1990s, as the 2000 census approached,[7] such campaigns intensified in many areas. But in the early and mid-1990s, and wherever birth planning enforcement was somewhat more relaxed, there was greater flexibility in local enforcement.

In the countryside, chaobao families might go undetected or local cadres might look the other way for many years so as to allow a more or less normal life for a family with an overquota adopted child (Zhang 2001). Locally, these parents were perceived as doing a "good deed," not committing a crime. While in the 1990s it became more and more difficult to avoid punishment for a chaobao adoption, the consequences might still be less devastating in rural areas than in urban areas, such as the one where Wang Meiying lived. While birth planning committees in urban areas could offer threats such as job loss, huge fines, and sterilization, most peasants do not have wage-earning jobs to threaten, and fines, while high, were usually pegged to income. But sometimes even in rural cases, birth planning cadres demanded sterilization as the price for keeping an adopted child. We heard of one particularly egregious case in the mid-1990s when an older retired couple found a sick abandoned child, paid for her extensive medical treatment, nursed her back to life, and, unable to find her another family, decided to adopt and raise her rather than deliver her into the hands of government officials who could not provide adequate care. When birth planning officials discovered this they demanded that the nearly sixty-year-old adoptive father be sterilized and the couple pay a 10,000 yuan fine, a huge sum for retired rural school teachers in 1996.

Yet such extreme cases were relatively few in number. More often, when families were caught they were fined and then usually, although not always, allowed to register the child. In one case, a very poor family could not pay the fines, nor were they in the least bit willing to hand over their child of many months, whom they feared might even die in government hands. They stubbornly argued with the officials who came to their home nightly for several days, finally wearing them down. Two years later, they won a hukou for their daughter, and in the end, all agreed that this resolution was the best for everyone. Families with relatively adequate resources might pay their fines, as they would take bitter medicine, and then get on with their lives. One family named their adopted child "Sanqian," meaning "three thousand," the amount of the birth planning fine they had to pay for their overquota adoption. Whatever the fine or the extent of the struggle, we could not help but be impressed with adoptive parents' willingness to endure economic loss and sometimes extreme official harassment in order to honor their commitment to and love for these previously abandoned, mostly female children.

The Problem of Hukou, *Heihaizi*, and the Rights of Citizenship

Despite their dogged determination, many of these families were unable to gain for their child the sin qua non of legal status as a citizen in China — the hukou, or household registration. While most manage over a period of years to buy or otherwise obtain a hukou, some children lack a hukou throughout childhood. Thus many of the adopted children in China fall into the category of "illegal" children known as *heihaizi* (literally, "black children"). The consequences of being without a hukou are not as serious as they once were; a hukou used to be necessary to access many goods and privileges, including grain. Yet the consequences remain significant, the most serious of which involve access to basic childhood immunizations and to schooling, especially beyond the primary level.

In urban areas the lack of a hukou is particularly consequential. A hukou is also much more difficult to obtain in urban areas, where the entitlements of local urban residents are closely guarded against the encroachment of outsiders, especially peasants. In large urban areas even primary school enrollments require hukou, whereas in villages they may not. While some urban primary schools will take a child with a village hukou if the parents pay additional fees, a child with no hukou at all, which is the case for many chaobao children, may simply be unable to attend for any price.

There may also be psychological consequences of living as a heihaizi. Some parents report that their unregistered child senses that she has a lower status than the other children in the family and community, not because she was adopted but because she lacks a legal status in her family and community. Sometimes children are teased by their peers for being heihaizi. When a child also knows that she was abandoned and adopted, the effect on self-esteem of having no hukou or legal status in one's adoptive family must be even greater. By the time a child is of school age the discriminatory status becomes clearer. One precocious girl cried when her kindergarten teacher told her she could not go on to primary school in the city where she lived with her family because she had no hukou; if she was to go to school at all, she had to leave her family to attend a primary school in a distant village. "Why can't I go to school like my friends? Why can't I have a hukou like *gege* (elder brother)?" she cried. The lack of hukou accentuated whatever difference she felt as an adopted child. The parents claimed that being adopted would not in itself be a source of discrimination or distress for this child, but the lack of a legal status for her in the household and community exacerbated her position as an outsider and created a gap between her and other children in the community who were entitled to attend their own school.

While many adoptive families struggle with these problems, finding ways around them through connections, money, or a sympathetic official, the obstacles encountered in trying to raise a heihaizi child, whether in dodging birth planning authorities or in struggling to get one's child an education, can cause some adoptive families to fall apart. I have encountered quite a few cases of "double abandonment" where adoptive parents, after years of raising an abandoned child, ultimately give up the struggle and take the child to an orphanage because they are unable to overcome the problems caused by their child's illegal status. In one instance, the adoptive parents hoped that they could readopt the child after the orphanage gave her a hukou. But the adoptive parents, in lacking any legal claims to the child and by being in violation of birth planning regulations for having adopted her in the first place (they already had a birth son), were not allowed to readopt her. Instead they found out, after the fact, that the orphanage had arranged for their seven-year-old adopted daughter to be adopted by an American family and taken to the United States to live. The American adoptive parents were as shocked to learn the true situation as were their Chinese counterparts. For years, the child and both sets of adoptive parents have struggled with the painful consequences of this situation. Other Chinese adoptive families have also succumbed to pressures and have handed over their children to the authorities who — rather than grant the family a hukou and legal adoptive status for their children — put the children into an orphanage at state expense and at great cost to the children's well-being. Thus the children suffer the loss of a second family due to the political and administrative pressures generated by the state's one-child policy.

The Sunflower Organization

In response to these problems and to a growing sense of injustice, a small group of adoptive parents in Beijing organized an informal group in the mid-1990s to support each other and to pressure the civil affairs office to let them register their children by calling local public attention to their plight. Their organization in some ways recalls the organizations of adoptive families that have sprung up in the United States, such as Families with Children from China (FCC). However the problems the Beijing parents shared as adoptive families were far more immediate and severe than those experienced by their U.S. counterparts. The group, organized by a single mother named Chang Lixin, called itself Sunflower, and its activities were for a brief time reported in local media, including Chinese Central TV.

While traveling in Yunnan province in the early 1990s, Chang Lixin found an abandoned baby. Although she obtained official documents from local police and birth planning authorities testifying to the fact that the child was a foundling and that Chang had permission to take her, the Beijing civil affairs authorities refused to allow her to register the child's adoption and denied the child a Beijing hukou. They said that Chang's single status made it impossible for her to adopt because she could not guarantee that in the future she would not marry and have another child. Even a signed statement to that effect failed to convince them to allow her to adopt her daughter; she was only twenty-five at the time and had many childbearing years in front of her. Although the child had a cleft lip and might have been considered a legitimate "special needs" exemption to the restrictions pertaining to age and childlessness — exemptions that international adopters were often granted under the provisions of the 1992 adoption law — the authorities never considered this option. Because the adoption was illegal, the child was not entitled to a hukou. According to the reasoning of authorities, Chang had brought the child from outside Beijing and thus should return her to the area where she was found.[8]

Several journalists who heard about the case and felt sympathetic to Chang's plight reported her story (although they carefully downplayed certain details that reflected poorly on local authorities and policies). Even Chinese Central TV carried a sympathetic human interest story on how Chang, a single woman, found a frail abandoned infant in a poor minority area of southwestern China and saved her life. Chang was portrayed as a selfless person who had done a "good deed." All on her own, she nursed the child back to health, paid for the repair of the child's cleft lip, and bore the burden of feeding, clothing, and raising the child. In the process she was seen as sacrificing her own future marriage prospects because it was assumed that few men would marry a woman who had already filled her one-child quota with an abandoned girl. And now Chang, like many other adoptive parents, was struggling to gain support and a legal status for her daughter. Her story and the stories of other Beijing adoptive parents, most of them chaobao, were told tearfully.

The near-universal inability of these adoptive parents to obtain hukou made a normal life and education for their children in Beijing extremely difficult. One of the goals of the parents of the Sunflower group was to raise money to start a private school for their children. While some parents, like Chang Lixin, were able to get their children into schools as a result of favors, connections, or sympathy, schooling generally cost families a great deal in extra fees. Further, the position of their children in the Beijing schools was tenuous at best. Some parents complained that their children were frequently teased and made to feel inferior by students and teachers. While Sunflower activists had a lot of energy and some public support in the 1997 to 1998 period, they failed in those years to get permission to register as a legal organization. Chang Lixin herself seemed to weaken and emotionally collapse under the stress of her situation and her inability to attain a legal status for her daughter. In spite of public support for the Sunflower group, the children were often treated as pariahs. To be without a hukou was a status that set one apart, on a lower social level than others. Even at a young age, some children felt this difference. Like other adopted heihaizi that I have learned about, some of these children "looked down on themselves" and sometimes had problems in school and in their neighborhoods. As someone commented about a particularly troubled and troublesome adopted abandoned and unregistered child in Chengdu, "It was wrong that she was born."[9] A young adult woman who had been an overquota heihaizi wrote that she felt her entire childhood that she had to prove she had "a right to exist."

Recent Changes in Adoption Policy and the Limits of Change

In the late 1990s civil affairs authorities and reformers in the government sought to revise the adoption policy to ease some of the restrictions on adoption in an effort to allow more domestic adoptions from overcrowded orphanages. In November 1998, Premier Zhu Rongji presented a revised adoption law to the National People's Congress for approval. The revision proposed to lower the age for adoptive parents to thirty and to strike the childless requirement for those adopting abandoned children. There was considerable debate within the congress about these changes, with the staunch supporters of birth planning concerned that the revisions would weaken population control efforts (Kwan 1998). In the end the revised law was passed, but with stipulations that carefully narrowed the childless exemption to those adopting children "living in state welfare institutions." Moreover, prospective adoptive parents had to gain certification from local birth planning authorities that they had never violated any birth planning regulations. Adoptions that took place outside of state welfare institutions — that is, the vast majority of domestic adoptions in China — were still supposed to be restricted to those who were childless and over thirty.

Nonetheless, some chaobao adoptive parents hoped that the new law would help them legalize the status of their adoptions and obtain hukou for their children. In fact we met several adoptive parents who were able to secure hukou after the revised law came into effect. One such parent was a doctor in a county town in Anhui province who had found a sick abandoned child during the floods of 1992. Because the local government had no one to adopt the child and also had many flood victims to care for, they allowed the doctor to keep the child in his family. Nonetheless, because he and his wife had three older birth children, they were not allowed to legally adopt the girl or obtain a hukou for her. Thus when she turned six years old they found it impossible to send her to school in their town, so they had to send her away to a village school where fees were accepted in lieu of a hukou. The doctor said the girl often cried that year because she did not like being separated from her family and she wanted to attend "the good school" in the town. When the revised adoption law was enacted in 1999 the doctor pursued the matter with county civil affairs authorities who agreed that the new law made it possible for them to legalize the adoption and give their child a hukou.

This case of a successful resolution of a hukou problem through the new adoption law was carried in the local newspaper under the banner "Black Hukou Child Finally Sees the Sunlight" (*New Anhui Evening News* 1999). In that particular county there was a surge of adoption applications after the revised law was announced, as many parents sought to legalize previous adoptions and obtain hukou for their children. In some counties in Anhui and elsewhere the first beneficiaries of the revised law were foster families who had been raising the children with permission from the government, often at the government's behest, but without the ability to adopt because they had birth children. Now many of these families applied to adopt their children, even though this meant in some cases that they lost their subsidies. Thus in the first year after the revised law was passed, legally registered domestic adoptions increased significantly from around 6,000 to 8,000 per year in the mid-1990s to over 56,000 in the year 2000. About 10,700 of those adoptions were domestic adoptions from state orphanages; 37,000 were said to be foundlings adopted directly from society (Gittings 2001; Johnson 2002).

Elsewhere in China, the new law was interpreted differently and previous chaobao adopters were still judged to have illegal adoptions that could not be set right by the new law. In some areas a family who already had children might legally adopt an abandoned child, but only if a strict procedure of reporting and applying to various civil, welfare, and judicial authorities was followed at the time the child was found. Failure to follow the right steps in the right order in a timely manner could jeopardize one's chances. Those seeking to legalize the adoption of an abandoned child after the fact usually found it impossible to do so.[10] As mentioned above, parents who entered their adopted children into orphanages after the passage of the revised law in the hope that they could now legally adopt them as children "living in a government welfare institute" were devastated to learn that they could not qualify to adopt back their own children. In large cities like Beijing, Nanjing, and Shanghai, obtaining legal status and hukou for illegally adopted children remained particularly difficult.

Citizenship, Adoption Policy, and the Rights of Children

When I began this research I was interested in investigating the extent to which social attitudes and cultural values today discriminated against adopted persons and their families, and whether this situation had improved or worsened in recent years. Discriminatory social attitudes certainly continue to exist today. Yet time and again questions about discrimination and other problems led adoptive parents to talk about the far more stark and debilitating political and legal discrimination that they and their children confront. The greatest obstacles that adoptive families face in raising their children are government policies (and the intended and unintended consequences arising therefrom) that conspire to deprive tens of thousands of adopted children of a basic legal status. Access to standard social entitlements such as "compulsory" education and health care, including mandated inoculations, are adversely affected as a result. We have found that many adoptive parents eventually manage to obtain a hukou for their child, but they usually do so only after years have passed and often after expending great effort and money. Rather than being an automatic birth right or entitlement, an official identity as conferred by the hukou and a legally recognized family status has become a right that often must be "earned" or paid for if one is born outside of the planned birth regime of the state.[11] Depriving children of basic rights, even the right to a family, has become a routine way of punishing birth parents and adoptive parents for violating regulations. In effect, these children are deprived of citizenship in their birth country.

Citizenship rights are problematic for many internationally adopted children as well. When children are moved across the borders of nation-states to be adopted into a new family and country, their legal status is often placed in limbo by competing claims and legal regimes. Until recently, children adopted into the United States were not automatically granted U.S. citizenship even after they became legally adopted children of U.S. citizens. Gaining citizenship required a separate, and often time-consuming, bureaucratic process. International adoptees whose parents failed to apply for their citizenship when they were minors entered adulthood with the legal status of resident aliens, deprived of the full protection and legal rights afforded U.S. citizens. They could even be subject to deportation under certain circumstances. Not until February 2001 was this legal inequality remedied, when a new law mandated automatic citizenship to all children adopted by U.S. citizens abroad as soon as they enter the United States. This legal change in U.S. policy was the product of hard lobbying by organized and vocal groups of U.S. families who have adopted internationally.

The Chinese government in its negotiations with other countries has carefully attended to the need to guarantee the rights of Chinese children adopted abroad, including their right to full citizenship in their new adopted country and their right to equal treatment in their adoptive families. However, the same government has done far less to critically address the ways that their own policies inadvertently deprive domestically adopted children of their rights to a full and equal legal status in their country of birth and in their adoptive families. Organizations such as Sunflower have lacked the legal status and clout that U.S. adoptive parents and their organizations have used to demand redress for legal discrimination. We hope that in the future the Chinese government will move more vigorously to eliminate these anomalies inside China, as the authorities become more aware of the serious problems that their own population and adoption policies have created for hundreds of thousands of children, depriving them of rights guaranteed by the Chinese constitution and various other Chinese and international declarations on the rights of the child. Revising these policies with an eye to guaranteeing the rights of abandoned Chinese children to a family and full citizenship would make it possible for more children to secure homes in China rather than doing so abroad.

Notes

1. The first portion of this research was reported and analyzed in Johnson, Huang, and Wang 1998. The patterns found in the 397 adoptive families analyzed in this 1998 essay are similar to those found in the entire sample of 771 adoptive families. Since 2000 I have continued my research on Chinese adoptive families through interviews and other documentary work. The information and stories recounted in this essay come from the large body of personal research that I have done since the early 1990s as well as from the survey data gathered from 1995 to 2000. In some of the individual cases discussed here names and minor details have been changed to protect people's privacy.

2. Relatively few adoptions involved orphanage children partly because of legal restrictions placed on those qualified to adopt through official channels, thus severely limiting the pool of adopters available to orphanages. These legal restrictions are discussed below.

3. This as-yet unpublished manuscript was generously shared with me by the author.

4. The China Center for Adoption Affairs' English translations of the 1991 adoption law (effective April 1992) and the revisions passed in November 1998 (effective April 1999) can be found on the Web site of Families with Children from China, fwcc.org/ccaalaws.htm.

5. A twenty-five-year-old Beijing parent (discussed later in this essay) who adopted an abandoned child with a cleft lip, which she had surgically corrected, was not allowed to legalize the adoption on this basis. Indeed the adoptive mother seemed unaware that a cleft lip and palate might be considered a "disability" because it was a correctable problem. Yet during the same period that this Beijing parent was repeatedly denied registration for her adopted child, many foreign adopters who were underage or who had other children were allowed to adopt orphanage children with cleft lips or palates, or even more minor cosmetic problems, as "special needs" exemptions under the law. Although the same law governed domestic and international adoption, it was implemented far more strictly for domestic adopters because the provisions of the adoption law were aimed above all at population control priorities within China.

6. I would like to thank Tyrene White for pointing out this pattern to me as I tried to understand why birth planning implementation seemed to have become so much tighter in rural Anhui in the latter part of the 1990s, despite signs from Beijing that birth planning was being implemented in a more reasonable, less coercive manner. Professor White said that she had found a similar tightening leading up to the 1990 census as local cadres tried to improve their local record for the census.

7. See note 6 above.

8. This account is pieced together from numerous articles and interviews published in China about Chang Lixin's story and her efforts to organize the Sunflower group. One account appeared in the international edition of *People's Daily* (1997); for an English translation, see He 1999.

9. This comment was made of a twelve-year-old truant heihaizi, who was emotionally buffeted by abandonment, adoption, the death of her adoptive mother, and birth of a brother, all the while lacking a legal status of her own. Her story appeared in the *Los Angeles Times* under the title "Two Families — but No Place to Call Home" (Ni 2000).

10. An example of the problems involved in such an after-the-fact case was covered in a local news story in another Anhui newspaper, *Hefei Evening News* (2000), under the title "The After-Effects Left by an Unclear Certificate."

11. For a general discussion of the category of "unplanned persons," see Greenhalgh (2003).

References

Cecere, Laura. 1998. *The Children Can't Wait: China's Emerging Model for Intercountry Adoption*. Cambridge, MA: China Seas.

Gittings, John. 2001. "Lost and Found." *Guardian*, August 7.

Goodman, Ellen. 2003. "Cloe's First Fourth." *Boston Globe*, July 3, A13.

Greenhalgh, Susan. 1993. "The Peasantization of the One-Child Policy in Shaanxi." In *Chinese Families in the Post-Mao Era*, ed. Deborah Davis and Steven Harrell. Berkeley: University of California Press.

——. 1994. "Controlling Births and Bodies in Village China." *American Ethnologist* 21 (1): 3–30.

——. 2003. "Planned Births, Unplanned Persons: 'Population' in the Making of Chinese Modernity." *American Ethnologist* 30 (2): 1–20.

Greenhalgh, Susan, and Jiali Li. 1995. "Engendering Reproductive Policy and Practice in Peasant China: For a Feminist Demography of Reproduction," *Signs* 20 (3): 601–41.

Hefei Evening News. 2000. "The After-Effects Left by an Unclear Certificate." August 8.

He Ping. 1997. " 'The Sunflower's' Embrace of Love." *People's Daily* (International Edition). January 17.

——. 1999. "China's Sunflower Children: In China, Parents Who Have Adopted Orphans Organize to Give Their Children a Better Life," trans. Shixian Sheng. In *A Passage to the Heart: Writings from Families with Children from China*, ed. Amy Klatzkin (St. Paul, MN: Yeong and Yeong).

Johnson, Kay. 1993. "Chinese Orphanages: Saving China's Abandoned Girls." *Australian Journal of Chinese Affairs* 30 (July): 61–87.

——. 1996. "The Politics of the Revival of Infant Abandonment in China." *Population and Development Review* 22 (1): 77–98.

——. 2002. "Politics of International and Domestic Adoption in China." *Law and Society Review* 36 (2): 379–96.

Johnson, Kay, with Huang Banghan, Wang Liyao. 1998. "Infant Abandonment and Adoption in China." *Population and Development Review* 24 (3): 469–510.

Kwan, Daniel. 1998. "Dispute Flares on Adoption Changes." *South China Morning Post*, October 28.

New Anhui Evening News. 1999. "Black Hukou Child Finally Sees the Sunlight." May 21.

Ni, Ching-ching. 2000. "Two Families but No Place to Call Home." *Los Angeles Times*, 29 March.

White, Tyrene. 1991. "Birth Planning Between Plan and Market: The Impact of Reform on China's One-Child Policy." In *China's Economic Dilemmas in the 1990s: The Problems of Reforms, Modernization, and Interdependence*, vol. 1, U.S. Congress, Joint Economic Committee. Washington D.C.: Government Printing Office.

Zhang Weiguo. 2001. "Institutional Reforms, Population Policy, and Adopting Children: Some Observations in a North China Village." *Journal of Comparative Family Studies* 32 (2): 308–18.

———. 2002. "Child Adoption in Contemporary Rural China." Unpublished manuscript.

Patterns of Shared Parenthood among the Brazilian Poor

CLAUDIA FONSECA

B y the end of the 1980s the increasing presence of foreign adoptive parents led Brazilian policy makers to turn their attention to the plight of the country's children and to refine policies concerning in-country adoption. At the time, Brazil was fourth among the world's largest furnishers of internationally adopted children (behind Korea, India, and Columbia). To the growing consternation of government authorities, by the early 1990s greater numbers of Brazilian children were being legally adopted by people in France, Italy, and, to a lesser extent, the United States (Kane 1993).[1] Rumor had it that even more children were being smuggled illegally over the borders. However, despite lingering tendencies in the poorer and more remote parts of the country, by 1994 the tide of international adoption had turned, reducing the outgoing flow of children to a slow trickle.[2]

This decline of intercountry adoption in Brazil was aided by a series of factors. Influences on the local level included nationalistic zeal against what was seen by many as a predatory threat from abroad, the enforcement of increasingly stringent legislation (including widely publicized jail sentences handed out to public officials involved in irregularities), and the growing popularity of national adoption. Influences on the global level were the international legislation aimed explicitly at curtailing the South-North flow of children,[3] as well as the sudden availability for adoption of an immense number of Chinese and Russian children (see Fonseca 2002a).

Although today Brazil is no longer counted among the world's major furnishers of internationally adopted children, a close look at local child-raising practices and national policies on adoption still raises many issues relevant to the field. For example, fifteen years of intensive intercountry adoptions has left its mark on national legislation. A clause in the country's 1990 Children's Code stating that poverty alone should, under no circumstances, justify the loss of parental authority has been attributed by certain analysts (Abreu 2002) to the reaction against the plundering of Brazilian children by "rich" foreigners.[4] Another even more consequential legacy of Brazil's experience with intercountry adoption concerns the high value placed by contemporary policymakers on in-country adoption and, in particular, plenary adoption, seen by many as the ideal solution for children in dire need.[5] In this sense, it would seem that although the wave of intercountry adoption has receded it has left in its wake, embedded in contemporary legal regulations, certain globalized principles based on the modern nuclear family that may or may not be relevant to many of the country's citizens.

The possible difference explored here between national adoption legislation, in tune with cosmopolitan sensitivities, and local-level practices is highly relevant to general debates in the field of intercountry adoption. In many respects, the ethnographic material presented here portrays a reality similar to that described in other Third World countries that continue to send children abroad.[6] Furthermore, the gap in Brazil between national legislation and local-level sensitivities may be taken as symptomatic of the even wider gap between values embedded in international conventions on intercountry adoption and those of poverty-stricken sending families in Third World countries.

Elsewhere, I have considered in greater detail the attitude of foreign adoptants as well as the evolution of Brazilian adoption laws (Fonseca 2001, 2002a). In this essay, on the basis of my ethnographic fieldwork among the urban poor of Porto Alegre, Brazil, I concentrate on examples that illustrate local child-raising dynamics.[7] In pointing out how extremely poor women resort to a wide range of strategies — from charitable patrons and state-run boarding schools to mutual help networks involving a form of shared parenthood — my purpose here is to contribute to the rethinking of national as well as intercountry adoption from the bottom up.

A Helping Hand

I was drawn to the subject of lower-income families not exactly by design but by force of circumstances. It was in the early 1980s and I had recently settled in Porto Alegre with my ("native") husband and two toddlers. I was home preparing coursework for my first classes of anthropology to be given at the federal university when the doorbell rang. On my front porch I encountered a gaggle of youngsters, ranging in age from four to ten, who appeared to be in a skirmish about who was to hold a slightly dented toy plastic truck. A sprightly preteen, the evident leader of the pack, after attempting to shush her juniors, turned to me in a businesslike fashion: "Good afternoon, neighbor. Could you give us a hand [*dar uma mão*]? Would you have any table scraps, empty bottles, or old newspapers for us to take home?"

This young Afro-Brazilian girl, whom I came to know as Luciana, was my first entrance into the squatter settlement where she lived, about half a mile away. As she and a varying group of youngsters added me to their list of "customers," coming to frequent my house on a near-daily basis, I also moved into their homes. I had not yet acquired the demeanor of the usual upper-class *patrão* (boss), and between my American-style casual dress and halting Portuguese, it seemed that people didn't quite know how to place me. Luciana did her best to teach me how to make black beans more appetizing, and many of her neighbors appeared to take great glee in aping my heavy accent. It took me some time to learn that I had penetrated into what was supposed to be one of the city's poorest and most violent favelas, where most public employees — teachers and health workers — refused to set foot.

Luciana, as it turned out, was a sort of babysitter for her little brothers and occasionally for other children in the neighborhood. To "keep the kids out of mischief [*para não fazer arte*]" she would come home from school, gather them up, and take them on her daily rounds.[8] Everyone, she informed me, pitched in to keep the family going. Her mother often worked as a street sweeper, earning as much as the state-mandated minimum salary (around US $60 per month), although she had stopped for a few months after the birth of her last baby. Her stepfather worked on construction sites, where he was paid on a daily basis and laid off with no pay each time it rained. His highly irregular income would cease with the completion of a building or, simply, when the patrão, temporarily out of funds, would suspend activities. Luciana also had a brother close to her in age who, for half the minimum salary, peddled the town's major daily newspaper. It was, however, Luciana's contribution — of food, clothes, and recyclable junk sold at a nearby depot — that was the mainstay of her family's subsistence.

The "helping hand" that Luciana and her neighbors received from their well-off "clients" who, like myself, lived in middle-cass residential districts close to the squatter settlement, was but one of their extralocal resources. Another important bit of support came from the state in the form of institutional facilities (FEBEM)[9] where children could be left, provided their parents proved sufficient need. I soon discovered that a good number of the squatter settlement residents had "studied" at this "boarding school" (*internato*). Luciana's stepfather, for example, claimed to have learned beekeeping during one of his stints at the orphanage. At the time I met Luciana, one of her older brothers was living at the state orphanage ("Mother says it's the only way to keep him out of mischief") but coming home almost every weekend to visit. Luciana explained that she too had stayed for a while at the orphanage, and she could chime in with personal experience when her neighbors spoke of the place's advantages: regular food (including yogurt — apparently a luxury item), separate beds for each child, and guaranteed schooling.

In fact, Luciana's mother, after separating from her second spouse, had left all four of her children at the institution. Luciana was brought home within a year, however, to help take care of her mother's new baby. Some time later, two of her brothers simply walked off the institution's premises, finding their way back to their mother's house. The younger of the two stayed with his family, but the older brother (who "never got along with our stepdad") opted to return to the orphanage — considered, by this time, a sort of annex to the family abode. The destiny of the fourth "boarded-out" child, however, had not been foreseen by anyone in the family. The youngest — a fairly light-skinned, healthy infant — did not come home. After six months passed with no family visits, he was declared to be "in an irregular situation" and given to an adoptive family. Although neither Luciana nor any of her family had a clue as to the child's whereabouts, they continued to include him in the family count, updating his age and musing about how things would be when (not if) they were once again together.

I was nonplussed by the story of Luciana and her siblings. Although I had long since learned to take with a grain of salt the journalistic hyperbole about Brazil's "thirty million abandoned children,"[10] I found it easier to believe that children living at the state institution, and especially those given in adoption, were genuinely orphaned or abandoned. (Brazil's major childcare institutions are not normally called "orphanages," but the young residents who live there are referred to in public parlance as "abandoned children.") The experience of Luciana's family and others like hers provided me with a different angle on the situation.

Little by little, as I canvassed the next sixty families, or nearly half of those living in the settlement, it became clear that especially among the more poverty-stricken the state orphanage played a prominent role in family organization. Parents — in particular women who had recently separated from their spouses — would thus share child-raising responsibilities with the public services: aiming, in the case of older children, to "give them an education" or "keep them in line," and in the case of younger ones to ensure sheer survival.

Such a use of state facilities is hardly uncommon in the history of poverty-stricken populations. During the nineteenth century, for example, institutional administrators throughout the Western world accused the "undeserving poor" of using the orphanage to shirk their parental duties and, in response, attempted through various measures to narrow the clientele to what they considered their legitimate concern: "genuine" orphans. Nonetheless, the overflow of poverty's victims — those people who normally had little or no access to the minimum of society's benefits (jobs, schools, health care) — continued, until very recent times, to periodically seek relief in these large institutions: orphanages and workhouses (Donzelot 1977; Blum 1998). In other words, state institutions for youngsters have traditionally catered to both the poor and the orphaned. Just how today's concerned observers, from journalists to policymakers, manage to conflate the two categories under the heading of "abandoned" children is more than a question of semantics.

During the 1980s, authorities at the state orphanage, complaining that families used them as a free boarding school, were doing everything possible to discourage this sort of "abuse." In an apparently progressive spirit, the country's 1990 Children's Code (article 101) reinforced this policy, proclaiming that institutionalization was to be seen as a last resort, to be used solely as a provisory and exceptional measure, for children en route to a "substitute" (read "adoptive") family. The state of Rio Grande do Sul was among the first to put the new Children's Code into effect, investing heavily in the reform of the institutional network. The creation of small family-type units now permitted a small number of state wards to enjoy a near-middle-class lifestyle, with comforts ranging from computers to horseback riding. However, as the cost of maintaining a child soared to nearly US $1,000 per month, it became apparent that more than ever the government had an interest in keeping the number of interns to a mini-mum, both by narrowing the definition of those to be admitted and by facilitating the process of those to be discharged. Within this context, adoption — as long as it was by Brazilian nationals — appeared to be a politically correct solution. The sticking point of this policy, however, remains to this day: how to define an "adoptable" child.

Brazil's 1990 Children's Code (article 45) clearly stipulates the need for the parent or guardian's legal consent in order for a child to be adopted. This consent may be waived in the case of parents who are unknown or who have been stripped of their parental authority for having abandoned their child or neglected its basic needs. The question, then, is how to define *abandonment* and *neglect*. Already considered vague in the European context (Manaï 1990), the legal definition of abandonment is even more problematic in poverty-ridden areas of Latin America, where children "abandoned" to state institutional care are not, in general, the out-of-wedlock offspring of adolescent mothers but rather third- or fourth-born children of women who simply cannot afford the extra burden.[11] Poverty today remains widespread, leaving nearly one-third of the Brazilian popu-lation with a per capita income of less than US $2 a day.[12] Although legislation in Brazil expressly states that poverty is not a sufficient motive for stripping parents of their rights,[13] researchers have observed that even when they classify the parents as "caring," social workers may well equate extreme poverty with "abandonment" or "neglect" and recommend a child's removal from his or her home (Cardarello 2000).

A good number of mothers, such as Luciana's, may admit they are at times unable to cope and so would not oppose their child's institutionali-zation. However, whether or not contemporary child welfare policies fur-nish the sort of "helping hand" they have in mind is a question I will consider in a later section. For the moment, however, I will look at infor-mal social networks to investigate other childcare resources to which a woman might have access and the perceptions of family and kinship be-hind them.

Mutiple Mothers

I met Claudiane, a radiant seven-year-old brunette, during fieldwork in 1994 in another working-class neighborhood of Porto Alegre. I had dropped in on Dona Dica, a stately grandmother, to hear more about her thirty-six grandchildren and eighteen great-grandchildren, at least one of which was inevitably there in her company. As she put it, "I've always had grandchildren with me. Sometimes two, sometimes three, sometimes, none at all. They come and go." Imitating the researcher, her present eight-year-old companion, a lad nicknamed Batata (Potato), thrust a micro-phone under his grandmother's chin and demanded, "Tell me about your life." Dica, busy pouring lemonade into narrow plastic cones, scarcely paused before teasing back, "I make popsicles, fight with you (because you're a rascal), sell drinks, and raise chickens and ducks."

By this time, two of Dica's grown daughters had arrived on the scene. Living nearby, they had converged that afternoon at the water faucet in their mother's front yard, where they were dying their hair in new, experimental shades of red. Learning of my interest in child-sharing practices, their reaction was immediate. Calling boisterously to one of the four children playing underfoot, they coaxed her, "Claudiane — come over here and tell this lady . . . How many mothers do you have?" Visibly enchanted at being the center of attention, the little girl bubbled: "Three." And, placing a finger aside her chin to better ponder the question, she added: "The mother who nursed me, the mother who raised me, and the mother who gave birth to me."

Volcira, the older of the two daughters visiting Dica, was quick to fill me in on the details. She hadn't minded helping out when Claudiane's mother, wanting to spend a weekend at the beach, had asked if she could leave her two-week-old daughter for a few days. Volcira, feeling the house a bit empty after the recent departure of her teenage daughter, was married at the time and, what's more, her bus driver husband had a regular income. Having just borne a child of her own, Volcira's younger sister had plenty of milk and so offered to pitch in as wet nurse. Time passed and the little girl just "stayed on": "She's my daughter. She sleeps and eats in my house, and she calls me 'mother.'" Because Claudiane's three mothers were neighbors, a triangular sort of arrangement ensued, which when I met them had been going on for the past seven years.

The point to be gleaned from this ethnographic example is that a mother in difficulty need not necessarily institutionalize her child. Rather, in many cases she can count on a social network in which, between relatives, godparents, employers, and neighbors, she is bound to find an additional mother for her child. Grandmothers are the first to be involved. I have in my notes innumerable stories of young couples who were living with the wife's or husband's parents. In such situations, the grandmother would very likely be the primary caretaker of the couple's first children, and it would not be unusual for a youngster to stay on living with the grandmother even after his or her parents had separated or moved on to an independent abode. One grandmother thus explained the kinship terminology used by her different grandchildren: "I call my oldest grandchild my 'son-grandson' [*filho-neto*] because, after my daughter separated from her husband, I took her kids in to raise. He and his sister call me 'Mother' and refer to my daughter as 'Mother Eloi.' I raised the other grandson since he was born. My daughter, who was living with me, had to work, and I'm the one who took care of him. When she and her husband moved out, he just stayed on. I'm his mother. He calls my daughter [his mother] 'Aunt Elsi.' "

Aside from grandparents, there are always a number of people who may be ready to share child-raising responsibilities. It is no accident that many children are baptized two or even three times. Besides the ceremony in the Catholic church (often put off for years because of expense and bureaucracy), people may baptize their children at home in a domestic ceremony presided over by an experienced friend or relative (Fonseca and Brites 1989) and/or at the Afro-Brazilian cult ceremonies. Each ceremony creates new ties between the child's *compadres* (cofathers) and *comadres* (comothers), thus making official their shared rights and responsibilities in the child's future. Because of the high adult (as well as infant) mortality of previous generations, many people I met had been bereft in early childhood of one or both parents, and so the network of willing tutors had proved to be a lifesaving safety net.

For the outside observer, the nonchalance with which people treat child circulation is striking. I have seen, for example, two young women in the process of getting to know each other complete their list of identifying questions ("On which street do you live?" "Are you not the daughter of so-and-so?" "How many children do you have?") with the final inquiry of

"And are you raising all your children?" A good number of youngsters claim to have decided, they themselves, where they wanted to live. Indeed, it is not unusual to hear even a six- or seven-year-old explaining: "Auntie asked me to visit, I liked it, so I just told my mom I was going to stay on." People will include in their own life histories a list of various households in which they lived as a child — with a predictable variety of commentaries. Some foster parents are remembered as wicked slave drivers and some as fairy godmothers, but most are described in quite matter-of-fact terms. Like Claudiane, many, many people will speak of two, three, and four "mothers" with no particular embarrassment or confusion. Against such a background, one wonders if it makes sense to single out the nuclear family as an analytical isolate.

Just as elsewhere in the Western world (Schneider 1984), biological filiation is considered a fundamental part of individual identity. People have no confusion as to who, among their diverse mothers, is the progenitor. And although, for a variety of reasons, fathers may not be so prominent in a person's biography, one's male genitor still has considerable importance for the definition of personal identity, belonging, and integration into social networks. Nonetheless, the mother-father dyad is not necessarily the fundamental reference in a child's life. On the contrary, household arrangements and the day-to-day decisions involved in raising a child reveal the nuclear family as a fragile unit, frequently overshadowed by the dynamics of the extended kin network, activated for and perpetuated through child circulation.

The historical depth and widespread presence of child circulation in Brazil has been investigated of late by a number of researchers (Fonseca 1993; Meznar 1994; Kuznesof 1998; Goldstein 1998). The discovery, in my own university, of at least half a dozen colleagues raised by "mothers" to whom they had been unofficially confided in infancy convinces me that until a generation or so ago, the practice was by no means confined to Brazil's lower classes.[14] Faced with evidence of a widespread "foster culture," one begins to wonder how legislators managed to draft an adoption bill that is so explicitly oriented by nuclear family values — in the definition of who signs the adoption release (the biological mother and/or father), how many mothers and fathers a child should have (one set), and who is qualified to be adoptive parents (a heterosexual couple or single woman). The following ethnographic example, which takes us back to my first field site, is designed to demonstrate that the very distinction embedded in contemporary law between foster care and adoption is based on a conceptually rigid definition of family that may be difficult for the various relatives of children such as Luciana, Batata, and Claudiane to grasp.

The Negotiation of Terms

Three years had passed since my first contact with Luciana and her family. Having grown to know a good number of people in the neighborhood, I began to appreciate the mutual help networks that crisscrossed the social fabric of the settlement's daily existence. One woman, Nelci, seemed to be an important figure, often mentioned by her neighbors, but I'd had trouble meeting her because in holding down a salaried custodial job as well as cleaning different clients' houses she was rarely at home. That July afternoon, thanks to a World Cup football game, I — as well as many people in the settlement — had a day off from work and so, at last, I found this petite, bespectacled black woman at home.

Nelci's two-room wooden shack, measuring approximately fifteen square yards with a corner kitchen equipped with everything but running water, was indeed one of the nicest in the neighborhood. Nonetheless, in contrast to many of the settlement's other well-off residents — who were preoccupied with marking social boundaries — Nelci, when she was home, kept her door wide open. A neighbor's two teenage boys, evicted from their home by their stepfather, had found a few days' refuge with her. Another neighbor's little sister, ordered to stay home and babysit her three nieces and nephews, had grown frightened by nighttime sounds and fled to Nelci's for help. During the two hours I spent in my hostess's front room, I witnessed a parade of visitors. Aside from two friends in their forties who'd been invited over "for a bit of white wine,"[15] she received a teenage mother who had come to boil water for her newborn child; a scrawny lad (about ten) looking to borrow someone's soccer ball; the local *mãe-de-santo*;[16] and an (unidentified) woman with her two-year-old, both of whom stayed but a moment. Around six, Nelci rose and, responding to the smell of roasted meat that wafted in through the window, yelled to her backdoor neighbor: "Where's dinner? I'm starving!"

My point in giving this description is not only to show how much different households are connected to one another through daily routines but to emphasize the setting in which, just as Marcel Mauss (1950) pointed out, children fit into an exchange system in which all sorts of goods and services circulate. With her narrative energies centered on the long and painful story of how she recently lost a one-month-old child, Nelci herself is fairly succinct on the subject of child circulation. She announces simply that her eldest is being raised by his paternal aunt, the second — who should be home tomorrow for a weekend visit — is "studying" at the orphanage, and her three younger children — a twelve-year-old boy and two daughters (ages seven and nine) — all live with her. Her two guests, however, go into great detail about dealings with the rival moms of their offspring.

The first of the two, Edi — an imposing mulatto woman who flaunts her extra weight with raucous exuberance — abruptly changes her mood to indignation as she recalls the absence of her youngest daughter.

> When I separated from my husband, nine years ago, I was really hard up. I sent one daughter to my mother's, another I placed at the orphanage, and the little one — I left with my comadre. I called that woman "grandmother" and she called me "daughter" because she really loved me. The two boys stayed with me because it's easier to raise them, but you can't have girls running around loose in the settlement. In the beginning, I placed the girls in proper homes because I had to work. But when things got better, I wanted to bring them home. By then, "grandmother" was attached to my little girl and asked to keep her, so we made an agreement, nothing written, but we understood each other. The idea was that my daughter would stay there until grandmother died, and then she'd come back to me. The trouble is that my comadre passed away and I didn't even find out about it. Her daughter didn't notify me because she knew I'd want my little girl back. Now she's gone to the courts, saying the girl is hers!

The second guest, a wan and wiry maiden lady who lives with her married sister, clucks her tongue in sympathy at her friend's plight:

> If I were you, I'd settle things out of court, like I did. Zequinha, you know, is my little boy. I took him in when he was no more than a month old. His mother was only sixteen when he was born, and she had no husband. What else was she going to do? Now she's living over on the next street with her husband and two kids. She's getting along fine these days and I heard rumors she was wanting

Zequinha back, so you know what I did? I hid this big knife in my skirt, and I went over to her house. She was in the front yard and I called her to talk, "Come over here, dearie." When she got close, I grabbed her by the neck, showed her the knife, and said, "What's this story I hear that you're wanting Zequinha back?" And guess what! She said, "Don't be silly. I gave him to you and he's yours, forever."

The two guests and Nelci collapse in laughter. Evidently no one is troubled by the fact that the two friends are pleading their cases from opposite sides of the argument: the first claiming, with everyone's agreement, that *mãe é uma só* (there's but one mother), the second insisting with her audience's equally enthusiastic approval that *mãe é quem criou* (the mother is whomever brings [the child] up). Their lively banter brings out the different principles that must be taken into account in the study of child placements, principles that provide the guidelines for the continual renegotiation of a child's status.

In many cases, child circulation, accompanied by a back-and-forth flow of goods and services, appears to create no undue tensions. A grown son might simply visit his own mother more regularly if she is raising his child, a maiden aunt might feel obliged to help her struggling niece if the latter has made her the gift of a child. Blood ties and generational differences help clarify the terms of the child transfer — establishing a clear hierarchy of a child's different mothers. However, in a context where many adults do not possess a birth certificate or an identity card, and where formal contracts are practically unheard of, the unwritten terms of a particular placement may well give rise to conflicts.

Edi, for example, recognizes that she was in dire need at the time of her daughter's placement. Just as many other mothers refer to such a moment, Edi presents the placement as being to her daughter's advantage. The girl would be safe, go to school, and have regular meals, receiving the minimum benefits that her mother could not, at the time, hope to provide. It was understood that Edi's comadre had taken on the burden of raising the child in order to help. In such situations, however, a change in circumstances may abruptly invert the idea of who is helping whom. Children are, after all, highly cherished for the affection and company they provide. Couples with a fertility problem, young brides who have not yet become pregnant, women who have recently suffered the loss of a child, or grandmothers whose own children have all moved out are all among those who often look for a baby or child to raise "as their own." Thus, a birth mother has every reason to see her child's placement as a "gift," just as much as a burden, in the foster family.

Edi appears to consider that she did her comadre a favor by allowing her daughter to stay on even when there was no longer a pressing need. Just how much contact she then maintained with her daughter is unclear. In other cases I registered, women, having confided their child to what they considered a reliable family, might disappear for a couple of years. If the foster family lived any distance away, the cost of a visit would be considered prohibitive. Also, some women explained their exit from their infant's life by evoking a need to respect the "new" mother's autonomy: "I saw that having two mothers around just wasn't going to work, so I moved out." Edi states repeatedly that she didn't "abandon" her child — that she remained in touch throughout the years — yet one can only wonder why she didn't learn about her comadre's death until some time after it occurred. It is quite possible that, just as I observed in other cases, she did not see physical proximity as a priority issue in the mother-child bond.

The daughter of Edi's comadre did not evidently see things in this light. No doubt, from her point of view, her family had for years treated the child "as their own" and in so doing had collectively acquired parental prerogatives. Moreover, it is quite possible that, having partaken in the child's upbringing, she considered herself a mother to the girl just as much as her own mother had been. Although the placement had started out, by consensus, as temporary, it had in time acquired the aspect of a permanent transfer. Edi, like other birth mothers in this situation, might have marked her presence, even at a distance, by contributing to her child's support. In such cases, it is not so easy for the child's foster family to claim priority rights. However, considering that most mothers have given up their children because of extreme hardship, it is difficult to imagine how they are to assure their child's caretaker regular financial support. Thus, in a process reminiscent of Pacific Island societies (Jeudy-Ballini 1992), as food and shelter build the parent-child bond, the principle *mãe é uma só* may gradually cede to the notion that *mãe é quem criou*.

The fundamental ambiguity can be noted here between the partial and temporary transfer of parental responsibilities involved in foster care and the total and permanent arrangement involved in adoption. The same sort of ambiguity, we might add, fueled Nelci's second guest's worries that Zequinha's mother would want him back. These disputes do not concern a child's geneaological status, which generally goes unquestioned. They are, rather, about parental status. Who shall have the right to custody and, even more, to the child's primary loyalties throughout life? Child circulation produces a sort of double (or multiple) affiliation as the youngster, despite the usual filial affection for his (or her) "real" mother (as the "mother who raised me" is often called), sees himself as authorized at any time to rekindle contacts with his consanguineous relatives. This possibility explains why I would often find adult siblings in the same neighborhood, living side by side, despite the fact that they had been raised in different households.

Local Social Dynamics and Public Policy

The observation of these various disputes, which seem to be an intrinsic part of traditional child circulation, raises key questions for public policy. In the first place, should the government, wishing to mediate childcare practices, concentrate efforts on foster care — apparently quite coherent with local values — rather than adoption? A look at recent policies shows that, on the contrary, legal fostercare has become an increasingly less viable option for poverty-stricken families seeking government aid. In Porto Alegre during the 1980s there existed a variety of child placement programs — some better than others. Besides the large, state-run orphanage, government funds helped to support a series of philanthropic "schools" that boarded young people from economically deprived families. There was also a state-funded program of foster families in which certain women — often those who were already running one of the many informal daycare centers to be found in lower-income districts — received a monthly stipend of half a minimum salary (US $30) per child to look after youngsters whose families were not able to cope with them at that time.

State-coordinated foster care, long considered a poor stepsister to adoption, is today practically nonexistent. A recent study on child placement in the state of Rio Grande do Sul found that in 1994 there were 350 children in institutional care, "awaiting placement in a 'substitute family'" (Cardarello 1996, 89). Just what sort of substitute family authorities had in mind is indicated by a comparison of rates of foster care and adoption. By 1996, three children were being given in adoption for each child placed in state-funded foster care (180 adoptees as opposed to 52 children in foster homes) (Ferreira 2000, 131 and FEBEM 1996, 4). Today, while adoptions remain at some two hundred per year, institutional care is once again on the rise, and foster homes have been all but phased out. Policymakers explain that foster families (generally from the lower-income brackets) are simply not up to present standards. The fact that the one group of substitute mothers created budgetary problems by banding together and demanding minimum workers' benefits no doubt also weighs somehow on the issue. The net result is that policymakers no longer consider foster care an acceptable option for public investments.

It thus would seem that, more and more, poverty-stricken mothers are faced with an either/or situation. Either such a woman keeps her child, hoping for different sorts of "helping hands" to allay the ravages of financial misery, or she gives up her child in legal, plenary adoption, which decrees a total and permanent rupture of ties. The choice is, of course, difficult, but as legislators and social workers point out, mothers do technically consent to these terms. Even when they do not sign the adoption release, they do not generally contest the judicial process that strips them of parental authority. Can this behavior thus be construed as total indifference or even implicit acceptance of the adoption procedure?

My experience leads me to believe that most parents who have been divested of their parental authority do not grasp the finality of this legal measure. The same could be said of the release that a woman signs to allow for her child's adoption. Researchers have demonstrated that even in North America, where the concept of plenary adoption was first generated, birth mothers may complain they did not understand the terms of the adoption process (Modell 1994; Carp 1998). Brazilian mothers — descendants of families in which, since at least the nineteenth century and probably before, child placement has been an integral part of socialization routines — have far more reason to misconstrue the law. In a process completely outside state control, children would be placed by their mother or parents in a substitute household, sometimes for long periods of time.

The substitute parents might try to stipulate restrictive conditions — they might, for example, claim that birth parents should have no further contacts or rights over the relinquished child. But time would usually prove such preventive measures ineffectual, and it was expected (often with reason) that sooner or later the child would renew contact with his or her consanguineous network. How then are such parents to construe the idea of a permanent, irreversible break?

The stories in this essay are not designed to show birth mothers as helpless victims, much less to sanctify the biological tie. There are, no doubt, any number of circumstances that might justify the temporary or even permanent placement of children in a substitute family. Ethnographic studies in Brazil and elsewhere suggest, however, that there are many different ways of administering a child's transferal from one family to another (Yngvesson, 1997). Legal plenary adoption, notwithstanding the widely accepted belief that it "imitates nature," is but one — and, I might add, quite arbitrary — formula.

In this essay, I have implicitly asked if the basic premises of plenary adoption are intelligible to precisely those people who are most concerned: the poverty-stricken families from which adoptable children are drawn. Is it conceivable that a judicial sentence can permanently sever the social ties involved in blood relationships? Or that adoptive parents will substitute entirely for their child's biological parents? For that matter, is the distinction between foster care and adoption — presented as obvious in most legal and many academic debates — so clear to the actors involved?

Legislators and social workers throughout the world have, of late, honed their instruments of perception in order to better separate negligent from "simply" poor parents, and so avoid the abusive use of adoption. Such efforts are certainly laudable. However, I suggest that if this critical reflection is to bear fruit, it must be extended to other tacit assumptions in the field of child welfare, such as the very terms of the adoption contract. By speaking of local-level practices in terms of social dynamics (rather than cultural void), I hope to lend legitimacy to nonhegemonic discourses, to include these "other" voices in contemporary debates, and — consistent with traditional anthropological concerns — to use the confrontation between different worldviews to rethink some of our own rarely challenged truths about family and parenthood in the field of adoption.

Notes

1. According to existing estimates, approximately 7,500 Brazilian children were legally adopted by foreigners in the ten years between 1980 and 1989 (Kane 1993, 330), while in the five-year period between 1990 and 1994, more than 8,000 children left under similar conditions (Fonseca 2002b, 29).

2. In 1990, the Ministry of Justice delivered 2,143 passports to Brazilian children officially adopted by foreign nationals. In 2000, this number had fallen to 463 (Fonseca 2002b, 29).

3. The 1989 United Nations Convention on the Rights of the Child, the 1993 Hague Convention on Protection of Children and Co-operation in Respect of Intercountry Adoption, the 1988 Brazilian Constitution, and Brazil's 1990 Children's Code all contain clauses encouraging policymakers and adoption workers to choose substitute families within the adopted child's original country.

4. One can only wonder, however, what impact this clause has had on actual practice, as researchers point out that to this day many children who are withdrawn from their original families come from homes in which parental neglect is barely distinguishable from the effects of dire poverty (Cardarello 2000; Abreu 2002).

5. Plenary adoption — which decrees total rupture between birth parents and the adoptive family (including the child and its parents) — has been universalized in Brazil through successive legislation. Law number 4.655 of 1965, speaking of "adoptive legitimation," created the possibility of additive filiation. The 1979 Children's Code introduced plenary adoption as one of several forms of adoption, whereas the 1990 Children's Code proclaimed it the country's sole legal form of adoption. For more on this subject, see Fonseca 1993, 2002b.

6. See, for example, the report and conclusions of the Special Commission on the Practical Operation of the 29 May 1993 Hague Convention on Protection of Children and Co-operation in Respect of Intercountry Adoption.

7. Porto Alegre, with a metropolitan population of some three million, is the relatively prosperous capital of Brazil's southernmost state, Rio Grande do Sul. Sporting many social indicators (infant mortality, life expectancy, and so on) with rates well above those of the poorer northeastern parts of the country, the city nonetheless shares in common with other Brazilian capitals an enormous "informal economy" (absorbing nearly 40 percent of the workforce) and a tremendous gulf in living conditions between the rich and poor.

8. Public schools in Brazil never provide more than a half day of schooling. Luciana, at age nine, was still in first grade, attending class ("when it doesn't rain") from 8:30 to 12 noon.

9. FEBEM is Fundação Estadual do Bem-Estar do Menor. Locals normally refer

to the institution by its name. For the sake of clarity, however, I will refer to it as the state orphanage.

10. For a criticism of these numbers, see James and Prout 1990 and Rosemberg 1993.

11. A 1985 survey including over 150,000 Brazilian women who had given up a child before its first birthday found that the great majority had done so because of the sheer misery of their living conditions (Campos 1991).

12. In 1998, approximately 71 million Brazilians were living below the poverty line, with insufficient funds to provide the basic minimum requirements of food, lodging, clothes, and school supplies (Barros, Henriques, and Mendonça 2000).

13. See article 23 of the Children's Code.

14. See Cadoret 1999 for similar episodes among middle-class families in contemporary Spain.

15. Substance abuse, commonly associated with child placement in North America (see Bartholet 1999), is far less relevant in the Brazilian context. There was no evidence of chronic substance abuse among any of the women I describe in this essay.

16. "Mother of saint" refers to the religious leader of one of the many, generally home-based, Afro-Brazilian cults that are a common element of neighborhood life.

References

Abreu, Domingos. 2002. *No bico da cegonha: Histórias de adoção e da adoção internacional no Brasil*. Rio de Janeiro: Relume Dumará.

Barros, Ricardo Paes de, Ricardo Henriques, and Rosane Mendonça. 2000. "Desigualdade e pobreza no Brasil: Retrato de uma estabilidade inaceitável." *Revista Brasileira de ciências sociais* 15: 123–42.

Bartholet, Elizabeth. 1999. *Nobody's Children: Abuse and Neglect, Foster Drift, and the Adoption Alternative*. Boston: Beacon.

Blum, Ann S. 1998. "Public Welfare and Child Circulation, Mexico City, 1877 to 1925." *Journal of Family History* 23: 240–71.

Cadoret, Anne. 1999. "Chronique familiale andalouse et histoires de femmes." *L'homme* 150: 119–37.

Campos, Maria M. M. 1991. "Infância abandonada — O piedoso disfarce do trabalho precoce." In *O massacre dos inocentes: A criança sem infância no Brasil*, ed. J. S. Martins. São Paulo: Hucitec.

Cardarello, Andrea Llamas. 1996. *Implantando o Estatuto: um estudo sobre a criação de um sistema próximo ao familiar para crianças institucionalizadas na*

FEBEM-RS. Department of Anthropology, Porto Alegre: Federal University of Rio Grande do Sul.

Carp, E. Wayne. 1998. *Family Matters: Secrecy and Disclosure in the History of Adoption*. Cambridge, MA: Harvard University Press.

Donzelot, Jacques. 1977. *La police des familles*. Paris: Minuit.

FEBEM (Fundação Estadual do Bem-Estar do Menor). 1996. *Relatório sobre Lares Vicinais*. Porto Alegre, RS.

Ferreira, Katia M. M. 2000. *Estatuto de Criança e do Adolescente na Jusiça de Infância e Juventude de Porto Alegre: análise sociológica dos processos de destituição do pátrio poder*. M.A. thesis, Sociology Department, Federal University of Rio Grande do Sul.

Fonseca, C. 1993. "Parents et enfants dans les couches populaires brésiliennes au début du siècle: Un autre genre d'amour." *Droit et cultures* 25: 41–62.

———. 2001. "La circulation des enfants pauvres au Brésil: Une pratique locale dans un monde globalisé." *Anthropologie et sociétés* 24: 24–43.

———. 2002a. "An Unexpected Reversal: Charting the Course of International Adoption in Brazil." *Adoption and Fostering Journal* 26 (3): 28–39.

———. 2002b. "Inequality Near and Far: Adoption as Seen from the Brazilian Favelas." *Law and Society Review* 36: 236–53.

Fonseca, Claudia, and Jurema Brites. 1989. "Le sacré en famille." *Cahiers du Brésil contemporain* 8: 5–40.

Goldstein, Donna. 1998. "Nothing Bad Intended: Child Discipline, Punishment, and Survival in a Shantytown in Rio de Janeiro, Brazil." In *Small Wars: The Cultural Politics of Childhood*, ed. Nancy Scheper-Hughes and C. Sargent. Berkeley: University of California Press.

Hague Convention on Protection of Children and Co-operation in Respect of Intercountry Adoption, 1993. Adopted by the Seventeenth Session of the Hague Conference on Private International Law (concluded 29 May 1993), I.L.M. 1134, art. 29.

James, Allison, and A. Prout, eds. 1990. *Constructing and Reconstructing Childhood: Contemporary Issues in the Sociological Study of Childhood*. London: Falmer.

Jeudy-Ballini, Monique. 1992. "De la filiation en plus: L'adoption chez les Sulka de Nouvelle-Bretagne." *Droit et culture* 23: 109–35.

Kane, Saralee. 1993. "The Movement of Children for International Adoption: An Epidemiologic Perspective." *Social Science Journal* 30: 323–39.

Kuznesof, Elizabeth Anne. 1998. "The Puzzling Contradictions of Child Labor, Unemployment, and Education in Brazil." *Journal of Family History* 23: 225–39.

Manaï, D. 1990. "La dispense de consentement en matière d'adoption: Autonomie individuelle et contrôle social." *Déviance et société* 14: 275–94.

Mauss, Marcel. 1950. "Essai sur le don." In *Sociologie et anthropologie*, ed. Marcel Mauss. Paris: Presses Universitaires de France.

Meznar, Joan. 1994. "Orphans and the Transition from Slave to Free Labor in Northeast Brazil: The Case of Campina Grande, 1850–1888." *Journal of Social History* 27: 499–516.

Modell, Judith S. 1994. *Kinship with Strangers: Adoption and Interpretations of Kinship in American Culture.* Berkeley: University of California Press.

Rosemberg, Fúlvia. 1993. "O discurso sobre criança de rua na década de 80." *Cadernos de pesquisa* 87: 71–81.

Schneider, David M. 1984. *A Critique of the Study of Kinship.* Ann Arbor: University of Michigan Press.

Yngvesson, Barbara. 1997. "Negotiating Motherhood: Identity and Difference in 'Open' Adoptions." *Law and Society Review* 31 (1): 31–80.

Birth Mothers and Imaginary Lives

LAUREL KENDALL

n the sixth grade my son Henry chose "Korea" as the subject of a school report, for which he wrote this dedication: "To my Korean mother, whom I have never met, and to my American mother, both of whom made me want to learn more about Korea." Henry's American mother is an anthropologist of Korea. His Korean mother is known from a brief description on an adoption case record. This essay is about the anthropologist mother's encounters with women who were the birth mothers of other adopted children and about two children who might have grown up as Korean adoptees in the United States but did not. It is an act of looking back through the mirror to the place and circumstances in which some adoptees from Korea — in particular those now in their twenties and early thirties — were born. These are a few threads in a complex web of experiences and emotions that constitute "Korean adoption" — other roads taken and not taken and people who have lived with the consequences of difficult choices.

Some will undoubtedly see this essay as an act of double exploitation, compounding the privileged position of a white, middle-class, First World anthropologist[1] with the equally uneasy privilege of a white, middle-class, First World adoptive parent of an Asian child (Anagnost 2000). In continuing to work as an anthropologist, I follow Margery Wolf (1992), Lila Abu-Lughod (1991), and Ruth Behar (1996) who, even in their unflinching acknowledgment of the uncomfortable politics of ethnographic writing, affirm that there is value in describing the humanity of otherwise unknown lives and the conditions of class, gender, and global and national politics that inform the living of those lives. But it is from the subject position of an adoptive mother (who happens to be an anthropologist) that I have found myself attempting to make sense of the particular batch of old notes and fragmentary memories that inform this essay. If, as Barbara Yngvesson argues (in this volume), adoption constitutes a "shaking up (and opening up)" of identity's premises (my parents/not my parents, my child/not my child, my country/not my country), and if motherland tours and birth mother reunions do not bring "closure" to these ambiguities so much as a counternarrative to the assumed fixity of family boundaries, then these fragments of the unfinished stories of imagined birth mothers and almost adoptees also belong within the frame of that counternarrative, and "shaking up" is very much a part of the anthropological project in the broadest possible sense.

Shadow Presence

Adoption self-help literature tells us that all adopted children think about their birth parents and some even construct powerful fantasies around them.[2] The adoption guides that were available to me as a prospective parent in the late 1980s encouraged adoptive parents to be accepting of the child's need to know the birth parent, to see a child's curiosity as "normal," and to not be threatened or feel one's own love betrayed when growing children express a need to seek out their birth parents.[3] A decade later these themes were echoed, with even more force, in Joyce Maguire Pavao's *The Family of Adoption* (1998). Reflecting shifting trends in adoption consciousness and practice, Pavao argued emphatically for open adoption records and early reunions with birth parents. The self-help books posit an audience of adoptive parents who are resistant, fearful, or generally squeamish about reunions with birth parents and who need to get over it for the sake of their children.

But many adoptive parents also live with shadow presences. Toby Volkman (in this volume) desecribes a growing number of memoirs by mothers of adopted Chinese children who conjure the birth mother with a mix of guilt, fear, and gratitude. These memoirs are perhaps the full-blown extension of an exercise sometimes requested by adoption caseworkers: "Could you imagine yourself writing a letter to your child's birth mother?" This exercise was presented to us as a form of therapy, a clarification of feelings, and perhaps a reassurance of good intentions toward the counterpart agency in Seoul rather than a literal communication.[4] Korean birth mothers were not commonly in contact with the agency when the adopting family was selected and the child placed, and until the late 1980s, when foreign adoption became a political issue in the Republic of Korea, few birth mothers requested their children's files. Indeed, many did not even know that they had this option or that the agencies would treat them as anything other than shameful women. Even so, and in contrast with the anonymity of most Chinese adoptions in circumstances where the birth mother can almost never be known, for many Korean adoptees and their families, connections are possible, reunions have happened, and some halting and careful relationships have come into being.[5]

In her documentary autobiography, *First Person Plural*, Deann Borshay Liem (2000) brings her two mothers together in one frame with all of the awkward good intentions implicit in such a meeting.[6] Her Korean mother, a worn countrywoman, describes her concern for Liem's early adult unhappiness and her joy when Liem finally got married — how like a Korean mother! Katy Robinson's unmet birth mother haunts her recently published memoir, *A Single Square Picture* (2002) as she tries to unravel the contradictory accounts that her birth father, half-siblings, and maternal aunt provide. Is her birth mother alive or dead? Could she be living in Chicago while Robinson spends a year searching for her in Korea? When Robinson's American mother arrives in Seoul, near the end of Robinson's stay there, her culturally complicated meetings with Robinson's Korean father and brother enable Robinson to highlight the profound differences in Korean and American habitus that she has tried to accommodate in her own being.

Until the Korean adoption agency feels that my son's birth mother is secure in her own adult life, she remains an act of imagination for both Henry and his adoptive parents. Because I have lived in Korea, my imagined portrait of my son's birth mother is an unavoidable composite of other Korean encounters, of schoolgirls her age when he was born who have moved into adulthood as the years have passed. For my husband and myself, our own identity as adoptive parents of a Korean child has thickened many Korean friendships. Our son claims Korean "uncles," "aunts," and "cousins" (addressed with appropriate kinship terminology). Similarly, with Henry's adoption, I became "Namsŏp's Mother," a relief to more than one long-time friend who had considered it awkward in the extreme to continue to call a women past the age of forty by her given name, as if I were still a child. Henry's first-birthday portrait, in Korean dress, hangs with those of other "grandchildren" in the homes of the mother of my village family and of my closest shaman informant. I have never "done fieldwork" on the subject of adoption, but the experience of adopting in Korea is now inextricable from a web of Korean relationships and experiences that thread through my experience as an anthropologist of Korea.

In retrospect, adoption talk was a part of the landscape that I inhabited as a fieldworker in the 1970s and 1980s. By happenstance, I heard the story of a woman who had grown up as an orphan. I met other women who had relinquished children to foreign adoption. Initially, I dutifully recorded such encounters in my notes because they seemed to have something to do with "gender" or "women's status." Adoption was not a personal issue back then. Years later, I took out these bits of memory and poured over them, looking for details, circumstances, the nuances of words, the sentiments behind them. I wanted to see these people clearly, as one tries to reconstruct the face in a faded photograph. I wanted to reassure myself that adoption was "all right," that everyone — including, of course, myself — had acted with the best possible intentions, and that these stories were sad but inevitable. I have learned through my work in Korea that people who do not have many options make hard choices with love and compassion. But there are undeniable elements of cruelty in some of these stories as well.

The history of foreign adoption from Korea has been told in other places. Eleana Kim observes that as Korea has changed profoundly in the half century since the Korean war, typical adoptee profiles have shifted from war orphans in the 1950s and children relinquished by impoverished families, to the children of unmarried factory workers in the 1960s and 1970s, and finally, to the children of young, unmarried students and daughters of the middle class (E. Kim 2000, 44–45, and this volume). In the 1970s I lived among people whose life prospects were very different from the solidly middle-class, university educated, professional Koreans I knew in Seoul or met in the United States. My subjects have been poor farmers, laborers, small-scale proprietors, and low-rung civil servants. For my dissertation fieldwork, I spent more than a year in a rural village on the outskirts of Seoul, a place I have returned to, periodically, over the intervening decades. When I first lived there, village daughters had begun to work in city factories and a few village men were working as contract laborers in the Persian Gulf. Television had just entered the village world. Consumer goods—from appliances to ice cream to cosmetics—were becoming more accessible, seemingly from one month to the next. Older villagers spoke of extreme hardship in the past, including near starvation during the Korean War, and most had not been able to go to school. But their children would be educated, some completing high school, and a very few going on to the university. As the years passed, many of the children of these village families would open small and precarious businesses in town and, most recently, a spate of roadside restaurants in the village itself. My own village family became the proprietors of a short-order Chinese restaurant in a satellite city of Seoul. This village-to-town world became the background for a study of contemporary marriage customs that I began in the 1980s.

It was during this second project, spanning the unseemly long years of my married childlessness, that village friends would suggestively mention a foundling left at the gate of a village household or a foundling left at the mill. "Some maiden got herself pregnant," they would tell me in a stage whisper. The generational shift that had sent village daughters into the factories and to all manner of service employment outside the home also ushered in brave new patterns of courtship outside the gaze of family and village.[7] Seung-Kyong Kim's (1997) ethnography of young women factory workers captures the mix of dreams and pragmatic accommodations with which this cohort began adult life. She and others have observed how the courtships of the working poor were often consummated in consensual unions.[8] Parents, whose own marriages had most likely been negotiated through a matchmaker, responded to their children's arrangements in different ways. Some, relieved to avoid the stress of matchmaking and the elaborate exchanges of ritual goods that such weddings entailed, sponsored modest weddings to give these unions social legitimization.[9] Some received daughters-in-law but were too poor to provide weddings. Others withheld their blessing. In the 1970s, I had already met a village daughter who was paying a terrible price for an early love match.

A Young Woman with a Sad Smile

Early in my first fieldwork, I came into the house of my village family on a cold winter day to find the third daughter, the daughter who worked at home quilting pieces of martial arts costumes, entertaining a friend. I remember the friend as a petite woman with a clear, pale face. I joined them, claiming my corner of the blanket. My village sister introduced her friend and told me, "She's going to *ihon*." My knowledge of the language was still only partial and my hearing imperfect: I confused *ihon*, "divorce," with *yakhon*, "engagement." The friend was young and pretty, so I assumed that she was a prospective bride and offered my congratulations on her *yakhon*. "No, *Ŏnni! 'Ihon'!*" There was embarrassed laughter. I realized my mistake and felt terrible, but my blunder was lost in the rush of indignation my village sister expressed on her friend's behalf. "Her husband is away in the army. Her mother-in-law threw her out and is forcing her to get divorced. Her mother-in-law is sending her baby to a foreign country." I stammered words of sympathy. It was difficult to take this in. "How is it possible?" The young woman cast me a sad, quiet smile, such that Koreans sometimes use to navigate the social awkwardness of grief. This is all I remember of our conversation. Was the child a girl or a boy? A girl, most likely, but I only remember its being referred to as "the baby" (*aegi*). Years later, when I was doing research on matrimony, I would have asked her for particulars, "Was the marriage legally registered? Did you have a wedding?" Most likely she did not. The child belonged to the husband's family; it would have no legal identity apart from the birth father's family register — if the family had agreed to register the birth.

Initially, I remembered this encounter primarily for my embarrassment at being so linguistically inept as to have congratulated the unfortunate young woman on her divorce. In more recent years, she has taken on another identity unknown to me at the time. She is someone's birth mother, someone now in his or her late twenties, a young adult living in Europe or North America, someone who might be trying to locate her. I wish I knew what had happened to the young woman; I wish I knew what her subsequent life was like. Following other women in her circumstance, she might have married an older man, a widower or a divorced man with children in need of a mother. I wish I had thought to ask my village sister about this friend from time to time. I did not realize that her fate would matter so much to me.

The Landlady

In 1989, I was working in Seoul with filmmaker Diana Lee on a project that would become our film *An Initiation Kut for a Korean Shaman*. A young friend of ours, an adoptee who was spending her junior year in Seoul studying Korean, was our "crew." The three of us spent a great deal of time together, with passersby posing their questions in Korean to the two Korean-looking young women who immediately turned to me for translation. We were a walking contradiction. Our adoptee friend was living in a student boardinghouse near her school, but she had just found a more economical perch where she could share a large room with some friendly Korean students, a situation conducive to language learning. When she told the landlady of her boardinghouse that she was moving out, however, the landlady became upset. Counter to my first surmise, her reaction did not seem to be a matter of money. Our friend could not grasp everything that the woman told her, but she did understand something about a daughter who had gone away. Would I please talk to the landlady?

We went en masse to the boardinghouse, which was located on a narrow alleyway in the Sinchon district, down the hill from Yonsei University, a neighborhood where long before I had lived in another student boardinghouse. The landlady, a slim, gray-haired woman, ran an immaculate multistory establishment. I drew a deep breath and began to tell her that our friend had been very happy in her house and had appreciated her kindness, but that she wanted to live with her friends. The woman burst into tears. "When I was young," she said, "I got divorced. It was the marriage before this marriage. I had a daughter. My husband sent her to a foreign country to be adopted. She may have gone to the United States. She may have gone to Germany. I never knew. When I heard about your friend, when they made the arrangement to have her stay here, I felt that it was just like having my own daughter come back to me." I translated her story, feeling myself stretched between the two emotional polarities evoked by this conversation. By now, I was on the verge of becoming a mother by adoption; this "birth mother's" tears were a part of my new universe. My son's foster mother, who had nurtured him through his first three months of life, had already cried at the prospect of giving him over to me in just a few weeks time. At the same time, I was acutely aware of my young friend's discomfort. This was heavy stuff. Only a few days before, she had admitted that she was not yet ready to search for her own birth parents. "Maybe on the next trip, when I can speak Korean better." A surrogate birth mother was not what she wanted or needed on this first trip back to Korea, this first big trip away from home.

In a movie, or in a work of fiction, the young Korean American student and the middle-aged Korean woman would develop a halting understanding of each other that would flower, giving them each a sense of reconciliation with a missing part of their past. If it were a B-grade movie, they would eventually discover, beyond all doubt, that they actually were mother and daughter, but on that September afternoon in the foyer of a student boardinghouse in Sinchon this would not be the scenario. The gray-haired woman was not my friend's birth mother, and my friend was not her daughter. The brief relationship of a landlady and a boarder, the intersecting coincidence of circumstance, did not alter the basic fact of their respective histories, that one had lost her birth parents and the other had lost her daughter. "It would be good if you could visit your former landlady every now and then," I suggested, in the lame hope of realizing the movie or the work of fiction, but knowing better even as I spoke.

I assessed the landlady's age. She must have been in her fifties. The young woman I had met in 1977 would, at most, have been in her mid- to late thirties by 1989. This was not my B-grade movie either, but a more commonplace story of cast-out wives and rejected daughters-in-law. In general, women in such circumstances have little means of tracing their children. The woman who did not know whether her daughter had been sent to Germany or to the United States had been removed from the act of relinquishment; she did not even know the name of the agency that had handled her daughter's case. Like the young woman who was chased out of the house by her mother-in-law, the painful choice was not hers but she lived with its consequences.

Present-day Korean family law is a combination of custom, Japanese colonial law, and postcolonial liberal thinking. As in Japanese family law, a household has a male head; from a woman's perspective a father, a husband, or a son. Every member of the household is registered under his name. The household register is proof of identity and a mark of full citizenship; it is required to enroll children in school, get employment, join the military, get a passport, or satisfy a matrimonial investigation. In 1989, the year of my son's adoption, the Korean Family Code was amended after a long struggle. Since 1991, divorcing women have had the right to a share of the couple's property and to the possibility of obtaining custody over their children (as awarded by the court) (Korean Women and Development Institute 1990, 1; Moon 1998). During the 1988 Olympics, media accounts described adopted babies as Korea's "prime export," which prompted a patriotic furor against international adoption. It is just possible that this controversy tipped the precarious balance of opinion in favor of legal reforms that would make it possible for more women to raise their own children.[10] Even with such options, however, it is doubtful whether the two women described above would have had the material capital and social support to raise their own first-born children.[11]

Anthropologist Chung Cha-whan's (1977, 218) retelling of the picaresque life story of a certain "Ms. Song" conveys the full Catch-22 existence of someone who lacked a legal registration under the old system. In the anthropologist's words, "In all her life of thirty-seven years she has never been registered in the official record as a citizen or even a human being. She does not even have a residential registration number, the equivalent of a social security number in Korea. Orphaned at the age of two, Ms. Song was raised to work as a housemaid, ran away, worked in a wine house, entered a consensual union, ran away again, worked as a prostitute, and eventually found a married male patron who supported her small business enterprises. Realizing that she was barren, she began to think about raising a child to care for her in her old age. On hearing that someone had abandoned a two- or three-day-old baby at a neighbor's gate, she made inquiries and received the baby. Unfortunately, the baby was sickly and died within a month. Because the baby's birth had not been registered, the little corpse could not be taken to a crematorium. Ms. Song and her close friend, Ms. Oh, were forced to take the dead baby and a pick ax, travel by taxi to the outskirts of Seoul, and covertly dig a grave in the frozen hillside, with the loyal friend shielding Ms. Song with her coat while she wielded the pick ax.

Through a doctor, Ms. Song found another baby, a boy, and raised him while operating a tent bar and, later, a small shop. Knowing that her growing child would need to show proof of registration in order to enter school and would encounter many other related difficulties, she begged her patron, a man of fifty-eight, to enter the child on his own registry. By Korean law, this required his legal wife's consent. When the patron was reluctant to face his family, the plucky Ms. Song went to the wife herself. The wife agreed to register the baby out of gratitude to Ms. Song for tending her errant spouse. Her good intentions were thwarted, however, when it was obvious to the staff at the ward office that the sixty-one-year-old legal wife was too old to bear a baby. A second attempt to register the child as the son of the patron's first son was more successful. In Chung's summation: "As a result, a baby of unknown parents, raised by an orphan girl who had never been officially married, was registered as the son of the son of the illegal husband of his adoptive mother" (217).

An Orphan Bride

Against the imagined identity of a birth mother is the imagined story of an orphan child growing up in Korea. My assistant and I photographed Mrs. So's wedding in the agricultural cooperative on a weekday morning in 1985. The attendance was spare, less than twenty, but it was, after all, the middle of the week. The bride was slim and looked so glamorous in her bride's makeup and upswept hair that my assistant and I began to refer to her as the "*miin sinbu*," the "beautiful bride." Armed with a small stack of photographs and an address that someone in the wedding party had hastily scribbled for us, we attempted to find her house.[12] Unable to do so, when we asked in the neighborhood for "the new bride, the beautiful bride," the neighbors were unresponsive. When we showed them the wedding photographs, we still drew no response. By chance, we posed our query to the groom's sister who led us to Mrs. So.

When she came out to greet us, we could barely recognize her, so great had been the transformation worked by the wedding hall's illusions of costume and makeup. The face that had been radiant with cosmetics was now pale and worn, but not otherwise unpleasant. The slim figure that had been elegant in white lace was now a bony frame for baggy work clothes. Weary though she seemed, she was pleased to see us and beckoned us into a small dark apartment, under lines of laundry, to sit beside two small children sleeping soundly on the floor.

Our questions brought forth her story, told while she choked back tears.

She was an orphan raised in an orphanage. She never knew her parents and has only vague memories of an old man who delivered her to the orphanage on a rainy day. After completing middle school, she went to work in a factory, and when she was twenty-five years old she met her husband. They began to live together and the bride put her small savings toward the key money on their rented room. At first, she was ashamed to admit she was an orphan; she thought that her lover would abandon her once he knew the truth. Eventually she told him, "This is the sort of person I am. If you want to live with me, stay, and if you don't, leave me." He stayed. The groom's father sought them out where they were selling produce beside the road and invited the couple into the family home. Her mother-in-law was critical at first, but once the bride became pregnant the mother-in-law treated her with kindness.

The groom's parents emigrated to the United States, and for five years the younger couple tried their luck at various jobs, none of them particularly successful. The parents' venture flourished, however, and they were now able to invite their son and his wife to join them. It was the mother-in-law who decided that there would be a wedding; she wanted her eldest son to "put up his hair," to become an adult. To arrange the wedding she returned to Korea and took care of everything: the wedding hall, watches and rings for the couple, a suit for the groom, and a Korean dress for the bride. The bride was overwhelmed with gratitude. She summed up her life with tears in her eyes.

> I'm really no better than chaff (because I have no family). There isn't anyone who would want a woman like me for a daughter-in-law, but my mother-in-law provided everything. There isn't anyone like my mother-in-law. She's helped us out, both with money and affection. As long as she lives, I intend to serve her to the best of my ability.
>
> I used to bear a grudge against my own parents (for abandoning me) but now that my life has changed, I feel that it was fated and I don't bear a grudge against anyone. It was my good fate that I met such a fine husband and mother-in-law. I don't envy people with parents of their own anymore.[13]

I conjure Mrs. So against my unease when adult Korean adoptees describe profound feelings of alienation and loss.[14] It is all too easy to compare the lives young adult Korean adoptees in middle-class American homes with imagined antiautobiographies, particularly when they are cast in an older, poorer Korea. I recall a couple of young women enrolled in a college summer session I was teaching in Korea who spent a long weekend in the "ville," the commercial strip on the periphery of an American military base, observing the club scene. They told me that it was important for them to see this life firsthand because had they remained in Korea they might have ended up as prostitutes. But this wasn't necessarily so. There are other possible stories, other might-have-beens. Mrs. So's story had a happy ending. To find another one, I need look no further than the Korean family I have been encouraged to think of as my own.

Ŏmŏni and Minja

On lunar New Year's Eve, in February 1977, I became the classificatory daughter of a village household—my Korean "family" ever since. The village elders had made this arrangement for me. I suppose that they had chosen this particular household for two reasons: "Ŏmŏni," "Mother," as I called her from the first, was known for her even disposition, tidy housekeeping, and excellent cuisine; and besides, this family needed the rent money. There were five daughters. The oldest was long married and had children older than her youngest sister, Minja, who was not yet in school. Kkachi, the oldest unmarried daughter, had gone to work in a factory but had stopped working when she became pregnant. Ŏmŏni wanted her daughter to have a proper wedding in the spring, before the child was born, and that would take cash resources. The family paid out school fees for Sukja, the next-to-youngest daughter, and would be paying them, soon enough, for Minja, the youngest.

This spread of five daughters over a period of more than twenty years was easily read. The baby, Minja, would have been the product of a last unsuccessful effort to produce a son. On my very first day in her home, by way of introducing herself, Ŏmŏni told me that her sons had died in childhood, and that she had cried and cried until she had no more tears. One had died from a birth defect, something that would be correctable in the next generation, and one, old enough to go to school, had died of a sudden fever, possibly meningitis. In all the years that I have now known her, Ŏmŏni defines herself as a woman without sons. It was for this that her husband cursed her as he drunkenly anticipated a favorite daughter's wedding. Sonlessness was the condition that she would brood on in her widowhood when, after Minja's marriage in 1999, she lived alone rather than served by a daughter-in-law in a son's growing family. Sonlessness is the salient fact by which her friends and neighbors describe her. It is the central tragedy of her life.

On this first evening I sat with the family, stuffing circles of dough to make dumplings, scores and scores of dumplings, for the *ddŏk mandu kuk* that we would all eat on New Year's Day. We sat on thin cushions, covered up to our knees with a common blanket to hold in the heat that radiated up from under the heated floor. Tiny Minja pointed to the blanket and told me, "I came back home in a *tamyo*." I looked confused: "*Tamyo?*" I did not know the word. She pointed to the blanket for emphasis, squawking with childish impatience, "*Tamyo! tamyo!*" *Tamyo* must mean blanket. I understood. But what did she mean by, "I came back home in a blanket"? Ŏmŏni told me the story: "When she was born, we were so poor. There was an American GI with a Korean wife, and we gave her away to them. She would have a good life. They came out to the house. They brought nice things to dress her in and a blanket, everything just so. I cried and cried, and they took her away. We heard the taxi drive away, and a little while later we heard the taxi come back. The GI and the woman had quarreled. He said that no one would believe this was his child, not with her tiny little black eyes. He wasn't going to go through with it. So they brought her back to us. They said that we could keep all of the clothing, even the blanket."

Minja grew up pert and pretty, the indulged and amusing youngest child. She graduated from high school and became a postal clerk. In 1998 she had become a glamorous twenty-something with fashionable rhinestone clips sparkling in carefully curled hair and a lilt to her voice. In 2002, she is married with a pretty daughter of her own, continues to work in the post office, and has learned to drive the family car. She seems radiantly happy. Would her life have been better had that taxi not turned around? By what measure? Was Minja damaged by the knowledge that she had been (at least temporarily) given away? I doubt it. The story was told in an atmosphere of love and familial warmth. Did it matter that her prospective father had rejected her on the basis of her Asian features? I doubt this as well. Within the family, Minja was always known as the prettiest daughter. She was not a rejected child. It had hurt to give her up. She could easily have vanished, but when she came back she stayed.

Ŏmŏni said that she kept the blanket folded away in a cabinet for Minja to take with her when she married, a part of Minja's own history. I think of this sometimes when I find in the drawer the little set of Korean baby clothes that Henry Sheldon Namsŏp Williams (aka Kim Namsŏp) was wearing when he came to us, a part of his own history.

But for the taxi turning around, Minja's story would have been of a piece with the adoptee stories now portrayed in autoethnographic documentaries (Kim 2000) and memoirs (Cox 1999; Bishoff and Rankin 1997; Robinson 2002; Trenka 2003). Families in difficult circumstances gave children up for adoption, sometimes for the sake of their other children, always in the belief that the child would have a better life in the United States, a place much mythologized in South Korea starting from the end of the Korean War through the 1970s. Among the very poor, there had been pragmatic adoptionlike arrangements in the past. One poor family might sell a daughter between the ages of six and nine to another family who would raise her not as a daughter but as a prospective daughter-in-law, and thus one poor family was spared the burden of raising a daughter who would one day marry out. Another poor family was spared the cost of a wedding and had the added labor of a daughter who would not need a dowry. The logic sounds cold and pragmatic, but as a lived experience, it could mean many different things. Some families sadistically abused these little girls; others loved them as true daughters.[15] Happenstance had a hand here, as much as it did in the taxi turning around and bringing Minja home.

Final Reflections: Imagining Minja's Other Life

Each of the stories told above has a mirror image in possible might-have-beens: mothers-in-law who might have been more tolerant, relationships that might have worked, or taxis that might not have turned around. What if the taxi bearing Minja, wrapped in the new blanket, had continued its course as the first leg on a very long journey? Would Minja have tried, in her adult life, to find Ŏmŏni again? And if she had found her family, would she have felt as did Deann Borshay Liem (1997, 120) "that during the past thirty years they have had a very full, productive life. This is a disturbing and sad realization because I was not and am not a part of that life." Ŏmŏni, I can be almost certain, would have grieved for Minja as she did for her dead children, and if Minja had come back to find her, Ŏmŏni would have folded her quickly into the full embrace of her mothering. I know this because she was able to make a "daughter" of even more exotic material, me. In the village where I did fieldwork, I am still known as Ŏmŏni's *suyang* daughter, a metaphorical approximation of the affection, loyalty, and reciprocity between a fictive mother and daughter that we have maintained for a quarter century. When Henry was adopted, Ŏmŏni went to the market to buy baby clothes. The shopkeeper asked her, "Aren't your grandchildren too big for these?" She answered, "My daughter in America has had a baby." I had "given birth" to my adopted child whose fictive Korean "grandmother" was buying him baby clothes.

In the end, it is impossible for me to extricate my identity as an adoptive mother from that of a writer of ethnographic encounters with birth mothers, the constructed kinship of adoptive parenting from the ambiguity of life in and out of Ŏmŏni's family. It is as the mother of an adopted child that I recall the Korean women I met who lost or nearly lost their children and the woman who grew up in Korea without parents. But I could only have met these women through my experiences as an anthropologist, a resident in a Korean village, a "daughter" of a village family. If, following Yngvesson (this volume), adoptees and their families live "in the eye of the storm" wrecking havoc on the received certainties of identity, anthropologists have also inhabited this space, albeit less consistently, and the shattering of commonsense perceptions has been our work for a very long time.

As adult adoptees make kinship among themselves, seizing the power of the idiom even while rejecting a prefabricated affinity of nation (Kim, this volume), they might find one possible vision that rattles the certainty of idiomatic or plural kinship among anthropologists and their fictive families. I would not elide the critical distinction between anthropologists, who enter these relationships as consenting (if sometimes naive) adults, and adoptees whose multiple identity claims were not a circumstance of their own choosing. The anthropologist's fictive kinship — whatever the local idiom — is wholly volitional for all parties, does not usually impinge on their relationships with their families of origin, and, for many, is a limited commitment that vanishes once the fieldwork is done. For some, however, even these minor tremors to the structure of common sense are not without emotional significance. Such relationships carry a sense of paths and possibilities. In anticipating the future of families like my own, I consider both the plasticity and potency of idiomatic kinship a hopeful sign.

Notes

Mrs. So's story appears in my *Getting Married in Korea: Of Gender, Morality, and Modernity* (1996), and is reprinted here with the permission of the University of California Press. This essay began as a lecture to the 2000 meeting of the Korean American Adoptee Network (KAAN); I am grateful to Lindy Gelber for issuing the invitation to me and Sarah Brezavar for encouraging me to write in this direction. Toby Alice Volkman gave me a helpful early reading of this essay. I alone am responsible for the shortcomings of this work.

1. For insightful and much-cited discussions about the ethics and power implications of a female ethnographer working among far less privileged women, see Abu-Lughod 1990; Behar 1993, 1996; Ong 1995; Stacey 1988; Visweswaran 1994; and Wolf 1992.

2. See for example Melina 1982, 161; and Plumez 1982, 126. Jill Krementz (1982, x) prefaces her anthology of adoptee interviews, *How It Feels to Be Adopted*, with the statement that while the children and young adolescents she interviewed express a range of feelings, the majority "regardless of whether or not they wanted to meet their birth parents, certainly had given the question careful thought." Several of her young subjects express sensitivity to the hurt that their curiosity about their birth parents might cause their adoptive parents.

3. For example, Melina 1982, 153, 155, 161; and Plumez 1982, chapter 12.

4. See Enrico's (1999) letter to her child's Korean birth mother. The author is herself an adoptee. Some agencies in Korea and elsewhere do keep letters and photographs on file in anticipation of birth mothers seeking more information about their children. In one instance known to me, adoptive parents' contributions to the agency that placed their child can be earmarked for the maintenance of these files.

5. For adult Korean adoptees' personal descriptions of reunions with their birth parents, see Liem 1997; Hall 1999; Chappell 1997; and Robinson 2002. There have also been encounters initiated by adoptive parents on behalf of younger children. To my knowledge, memoirs of these Korean encounters are not yet represented in adoption literature (except reports in agency newsletters), but see Yngvesson (this volume) for family reunions of adoptees from Chile, their birth mothers, and their Swedish adoptive parents.

6. Family reunions are also a significant subject in Nathan Adolfson's documentary, *Passing Through* (1999) and Tammy Tolle's *Searching for Go-hyang* (1998).

Eleana Kim (2000) describes these and other films made by Korean adoptees as a burgeoning genre of "Korean adoptee autoethnography" that weds individual autobiography to circumstances that have global dimensions.

7. It is generally acknowledged that without a pool of cheap, educated, and initially docile female labor, the Korean "economic miracle" would not have taken place (Amsden 1989; Cho 1987; Koo 1987). Spencer 1988 and especially S. K. Kim 1998 describe the new lives of young women workers in the 1970s and 1980s. Kim provides a particularly detailed account of changing notions of femininity, sexuality, courtship, and marital aspirations.

8. See also accounts of working-class courtship and marriage in Kendall 1996, 122–27; E.-S. Kim 1993, 205, 23; Pak 1991; and Yoon 1991.

9. The legal registry of a marriage is distinct from a socially recognized wedding that confers full adult status. Many legally registered couples do not consider themselves fully "married" in the eyes of kin and community until they have a wedding, while in other instances registration may follow a wedding by weeks or even months.

10. An article by Susan Chira (1988) appearing as a human-interest piece in the *New York Times* under the title, "Babies for Export: And Now the Painful Questions," described local concerns both that babies were being callously "sold" for profit to foreign parents (the article contained counterevidence) and the abiding Korean concern that adoptees are severed from their cultural and linguistic roots. While the article reflected the growing Korean critiques of foreign adoption, such high-profile foreign press coverage while Korea geared up to present a burnished new image at the 1988 Seoul Olympics precipitated an explosion of concern in Korean media and tagged foreign adoption as a matter of national shame. E. Kim (2000, 63n. 7) cites similar fallout from a 1988 report by Bryant Gumbel on NBC's *Today Show*.

11. Relinquishment after divorce is a part of the personal histories retrieved and recounted by two adult adoptees in Keith 1999; Nelson-Wang and Han 1999.

12. Korean houses are numbered by the sequence of their construction rather than by their spatial relationship to other houses on the street. Needless to say, finding an address can be challenging.

13. Originally published in Kendall 1996, 127–28.

14. This is a dominant theme in the filmed "autoethnographies" analyzed by E. Kim (2000), in the *Voices from Another Place* anthology of adoptee writing edited by Cox (1999), and most painfully in the *Seeds from a Silent Tree* anthology edited by Bishoff and Rankin (1997). Robinson 2002 describes an eventual reconciliation with both her Korean and her American pasts.

15. An analysis of this practice and several firsthand accounts by women who were themselves adopted-in daughters-in-law can be found in Harvey 1983.

References

Abu-Lughod, Lila. 1990. "Can There Be a Feminist Ethnography?" *Women and Performance: A Journal of Feminist Theory* 5: 25.

———. 1991. "Writing against Culture." In *Recapturing Anthropology: Working in the Present*, ed. Richard G. Fox. Santa Fe: School of American Research.

Adolfson, Nathan. 1999. *Passing Through*. San Francisco: NAATA. Video.

Amsden, Alice H. 1989. *Asia's Next Giant: South Korea and Late Industrialization*. New York: Oxford University Press.

Anagnost, Ann. 2000. "Scenes of Misrecognition: Maternal Kinship in the Age of Transnational Adoption." *positions* 8: 241–389.

Behar, Ruth. 1993. *Translated Woman: Crossing the Border with Esperanza's Story*. Boston: Beacon Press.

———. 1996. *The Vulnerable Observer: Anthropology That Breaks Your Heart*. Boston: Beacon Press.

Bishoff, Tonya, and Jo Rankin. 1997. *Seeds from a Silent Tree: An Anthology by Korean Adoptees*. Glendale, CA: Pandal Press.

Chappell, Crystal Lee Hyun Joo. 1997. "Now I'm Found." In *Seeds from a Silent Tree: An Anthology by Korean Adoptees*, ed. Tonya Bishoff and Jo Rankin. Glendale, CA: Pandal Press.

Chira, Susan. 1988. "Babies for Export: And Now the Painful Questions." *New York Times*, 21 April.

Cho, Hyoung. 1987. "The Position of Women in the Korean Work Force." In *Korean Women in Transition: At Home and Abroad*, ed. E. Y. Yu and E. H. Phillips. Los Angeles: Center for Korean-American and Korean Studies, California State University.

Chung, Cha-whan. 1977. "Change and Continuity in an Urbanizing Society: Family and Kinship in Urban Korea." Ph.D. diss., University of Hawaii.

Cox, Susan Soon-Keum, ed. 1999. *Voices from Another Place: A Collection of Works from a Generation Born in Korea and Adopted to Other Countries*. St. Paul, MN: Yeong and Yeong.

Enrico, Dottie. 1999. "To My Daughter's Birth Parents: A Korean Adoptee Writes to the Birth Parents of Her Adopted Korean Daughter." In *Voices from Another Place: A Collection of Works from a Generation Born in Korea and Adopted to Other Countries*, ed. Susan Soon-Keum Cox. St. Paul, MN: Yeong and Yeong.

Hall, Sung Jin. 1997. "And Now and Then a White Elephant: Thoughts on the Evening of August 16, 1997." In *Voices from Another Place: A Collection of Works from a Generation Born in Korea and Adopted to Other Countries*, ed. Susan Soon-Keum Cox. St. Paul, MN: Yeong and Yeong.

Harvey, Youngsook Kim. 1983. "*Minmyŏnuri*: The Daughter-in-Law Who Comes of Age in Her Mother-in-Law's Household." In *Korean Women: A View from the Inner Room*, ed. Laurel Kendall and Mark Peterson. New Haven, CT: East Rock Press.

Keith, Tonya. 1999. "A Journey Back." In *Voices from Another Place: A Collection of Works from a Generation Born in Korea and Adopted to Other Countries*, ed. Susan Soon-Keum Cox. St. Paul, MN: Yeong and Yeong.

Kendall, Laurel. 1996. *Getting Married in Korea: Of Gender, Morality, and Modernity*. Berkeley: University of California Press.

Kim, Eleana. 2000. "Korean Adoptee Auto-Ethnography: Refashioning Self, Family, and Finding Community." *Visual Anthropology Review* 16 (1) (spring/ summer): 43–70.

Kim, Eun-Shil. 1993. "The Making of the Modern Female Gender: The Politics of Gender in Reproductive Practices in Korea." Ph.D. diss., University of California, San Francisco and Berkeley.

Kim, Seung Kyung. 1997. *Class Struggle or Family Struggle; The Lives of Women Factory Workers in South Korea*. Cambridge: Cambridge University Press.

Koo, Hagen. 1987. "Dependency Issues, Class Inequality, and Social Conflict in Korean Development." In *Dependency Issues in Korean Development: Comparative Perspectives*, ed. K. Kim. Seoul: Seoul National University Press.

Korean Women and Development Institute (KWDI). n.d. "Sex-Discriminatory Family Law is Finally Revised." *KWDI* Newsletter—Korean Women Today 26: 1.

Krementz, Jill. 1988. *How It Feels to Be Adopted*. New York: Knopf.

Liem, Deann Borshay. 1997. "Remembering the Way Home: A Documentary Video Proposal." In *Seeds from a Silent Tree: An Anthology by Korean Adoptees*, ed. Tonya Bishoff and Jo Rankin. Glendale, CA: Pandal Press.

Liem, Deann Borshay. 2000. *First Person Plural*. San Francisco: NAATA. Video.

Melina, Lois Ruskai. 1982. *Raising Adopted Children: A Manual for Adoptive Parents*. New York: Harper and Row.

Moon, Seungsook. 1998. "Begetting the Nation: The Androcentric Discourse of National History and Tradition in South Korea." In *Dangerous Women: Gender and Korean Nationalism*, ed. Elaine H. Kim and Chungmoo Choi. New York: Routledge University Press.

Nelson-Wang, Mea Han. 1999. "Purpose." In *Voices from Another Place: A Collection of Works from a Generation Born in Korea and Adopted to Other Countries*, ed. Susan Soon-Keum Cox. St. Paul, MN: Yeong and Yeong.

Ong, Aihwa. 1995. "Women Out of China: Traveling Tales and Traveling Theories in Postcolonial Feminism." In *Women Writing Culture*, ed. Ruth Behar and Deborah A. Gordon. Berkeley: University of California Press.

Pak, Sukcha. 1991. "Tosi chŏsutŭkch'ungŭi honinyangt'ae" (The marriage mode of the urban poor). In *Chabonjuŭi sijanggyongjewa honin* (The capitalist market economy and marriage), ed. Hyojae Yi et al. Seoul: Tosŏch'ulp'an, Tto hanaŭi munhwa.

Pavao, Joyce Maguire. 1998. *The Family of Adoption*. Boston: Beacon Press.

Plumez, Jacqueline Hornor. 1982. *Successful Adoption*. New York: Harmony Books.

Robinson, Katy. 2002. *A Single Square Picture: A Korean Adoptee's Search for her Roots*. New York: Berkley Books.

Spencer, Robert F. 1988. *Yŏgong: Factory Girl*. Seoul: Royal Asiatic Society, Korea Branch.

Stacey, Judith. 1988. "Can There Be a Feminist Ethnography?" *Women's Studies International Forum* 11 (1): 21–27.

Tolle, Tammy. 1998. *Searching for Go-hyang*. Film. New York: Women Make Movies.

Trenka, Jane Jeong. 2003. *The Language of Blood*. Saint Paul: Minnesota Historical Society Press.

Visweswaran, Kamala. 1994. *Fictions of Feminist Ethnography*. Minneapolis: University of Minnesota Press.

Wolf, Margery. 1992. *A Thrice Told Tale: Feminism, Postmodernism, and Ethnographic Responsibility*. Stanford: Stanford University Press.

Yoon, Hyŏngsuk. 1991. "Sŏulgŭn'gyongnongch'on ŭi kyŏngjewa kyŏrhon" (The economics and matrimony of a village on the periphery of Seoul). In *Chabonjuŭi sijanggyongjewa honin* (The capitalist market economy and marriage), ed. Hyojae Yi et al. Seoul: Tosŏ ch'ulp'an, Tto hanaŭi munhwa.

PART III   **Representations**

Images of "Waiting Children"

Spectatorship and Pity in the Representation of the Global Social Orphan in the 1990s

LISA CARTWRIGHT

n the mid-1990s, Frances Cairncross (1997, 4) wrote, "The communications revolution is profoundly democratic and liberating, leveling the imbalance between large and small, rich and poor. The death of distance, overall, should be welcomed and enjoyed." These thoughts were inspired by a climate of international trade liberalization and a burgeoning global information economy that justified conservative jubilance about the expansion of markets in a world newly imagined to be borderless. Cairncross's words can be aptly applied to describe changes in the representation and economy of orphan welfare and exchange during the 1990s. With the expansion of the global economy, transnational adoption became a burgeoning market in which all parties, viewed in Cairncross's logic, stood to gain. Waiting parents got children, orphans got families and homes, and struggling orphanages and local government ministries got subsidies in the form of adoptions fees euphemistically termed "charitable donations." The transnational management of the Romanian orphanage crisis in the early 1990s is a case in point. With the execution of Nicolae and Elena Ceausescu in 1989, Romania became open not only for economic reform but also for foreign patronage, media scrutiny, and the "enjoyment" of the goods and opportunities available in this newly opened market. Among the goods were children, and among the opportunities were foreign humanitarian investments in the national health and social service sectors. Looming among the crises exposed by the press in North America and in Western Europe was the issue of the large number of Romanian children abandoned to the state and languishing in poorly supported orphanages. Although many in the orphanages were children without living parents, there also were large numbers of "social orphans,"[1] children whose parents were alive but unable to support them. An estimated 753 out of every 100,000 of Romania's children aged three years or younger resided in orphanages in 1989, suggesting that the state had become the default custodian of a startlingly large number of the children produced under the Ceausescu state's reproductive mandate.[2]

Romania was not the only country targeted in Western media reports about human rights violations in state orphanages, nor was it the only industrialized country experiencing a crisis in child welfare (Cornia and Danziger 1997). Human Rights Watch, citing Chinese government statistics of 1989 showing that the majority of abandoned children admitted to the country's sixty-seven state-run orphanages were dying in institutional care, published detailed evidence of starvation, neglect, and abuse of Chinese orphans. Collected in a thick monograph, their documentation generated a wave of media attention focused on China's orphanage policies and practices (Human Rights Watch 1996). Supporting media included *The Dying Rooms* (1995) and *Return to the Dying Room* (1996), the British Channel 4 television news magazine stories by Kate Blewett and Brian Woods that were aired internationally. To produce the first of these reports, Blewett used a false identity to visit a Chinese orphanage and, carrying a hidden camera, visually documented the condition of children, including detailed visual evidence of the emaciated body of a child called Mei Ming ("No name") who, the filmmakers alleged, was placed in a "dying room" ten days before the footage was shot. In an effort to counter the documentary's allegations, the Chinese government issued a response film, *The Dying Rooms: A Patchwork of Lies*, and a letter from Harvard literature professor Alice Jardine was quoted in the *New York Times* stating that the Chinese government was "working as hard as is humanly possible in a third world situation" to care for its institutionalized social orphans (*New York Times* 1996).

Similar documentation and debate during this period about the circumstances of social orphans in Russia and other countries in economic transition that, like Romania, had become open to foreign investment and trade, suggest that moral investments, taking the form of foreign humanitarian witnessing, evidence gathering, and intervention, constituted a transnational phenomenon. Techniques of visual mediation, facilitated by advances in global news media, computer and digital imaging, and image reproduction technologies, played a major role in the emergence of a global social movement dedicated to the care of the social orphan as a transnational entity of riveting concern in the 1990s. *Dying Room* producer Brian Woods has remarked that he and Blewett knew that their idea was important but also knew that the public would believe their story "only if we could get the evidence of [the abuses] on film" (*New York Times* 1996). The use by Blewett of a hidden camera to provide visual evidence of the physical conditions suggesting neglect and abuse of Chinese orphans, and the reproduction of Woods and Blewett's documentation internationally through television news magazine shows and (later) Web sites, suggest the extent to which changes in technologies of mediation facilitated a new sort of visibility and circulation of the social orphan, constituting this subject as a global object of Western concern.

In this essay I consider the role of visual documentation, specifically the television news magazine show, as it emerged as a means of narrativizing and of marketing visions of social crises in the 1980s.[3] My specific concern here is the proliferation of a transnational response network that addressed the social orphan crisis as it was unveiled by the media in multiple national sites that were newly opening their borders to global trade in the 1990s (e.g., Romania, the former Soviet republics, and China). The economic and communication "borderlessness" of the sort imagined by Cairncross in that decade allowed for the exposure of internal conditions to an international media audience and to an international network of humanitarian advocacy groups situated across Western national contexts (e.g., the United States, Israel, England, and France). In 1961 in *On Revolution* Hannah Arendt (1990 [1961], 73) wrote that "to avert one's eyes from the misery and unhappiness of the mass of mankind" was no more possible in the industrial cities of the eighteenth and nineteenth centuries than it was in the present day in "some European, Latin American, and nearly all Asian and African countries." With this long history of a Western gaze riveted on distant human suffering in mind, I consider the visual classification and management of the global social orphan in terms of a transnational politics of pity at the end of the twentieth century.

In his monograph on morality, media, and politics, pragmatics sociologist Luc Boltanski (1999, 3) describes Arendt's politics of pity as distinct from a politics of justice. Pity politics, he explains, is based first on a distinction between those who suffer and those who do not. Second, it entails a focus on "what is seen and looking" on the spectacle of suffering. My aim here is to interpret the spectacles of social orphan suffering in news media of the 1990s as a moment in the formation of a mediated transnational politics of pity articulated through humanitarian aid efforts to rescue social orphans. Scholarship on news media and on documentary tends not to regard news images as classificatory in nature. News stories provide evidence of events and circumstances or give profiles of individual or group life. Typically, representations of people in the news do not fall into the same genre of typology as, for example, photographic identification, fingerprinting, or the classification of persons for purposes of individual identification or, at the other end of the spectrum, population management (e.g., national refugee registers, census reports). This essay follows a discussion of photographic classification (see Cartwright 2003) and is intended to suggest that news media images work in tandem with technologies of social classification to create ways of organizing and managing children in states of crisis. My purpose in bringing together these different forms of documentation is to suggest that they are interconstitutive in the production of the global social orphan and, within that global category, of particular subject positions — identity subsets complexly grouped according to unstable signifiers of race or ethnicity, nationality, ability, and health.[4]

The discourse constituting the social orphan can be characterized in two words: compassion and pity. Boltanski (1999, 6) reminds his readers of Arendt's reading of the two terms in *On Revolution*. Compassion, a response triggered by a spectacle of suffering, entails a local response to individualized suffering and is mute in its enactment. Whereas a response of pity, Boltanski explains, "generalizes and integrates the dimension of distance" through discourse and geography, compassion is heavy in its articulation of proximal emotion and feeling. Citing Max Shleler's (1967, 23) writing on forms of sympathy, Boltanski notes that we do not say that a father and mother who weep over the body of their child experience pity, because they themselves also suffer. Pity takes the practical, transformative form of, for example, charitable action at a distance — responses that do not entail the proximity of shared, intersubjective suffering. In light of this, my concern throughout this essay is the role of the spectator in response to the televised global social orphan. This spectator is an actor who engages variously in relationships of proximal compassion that intersect with mediated, distanced pity in response to, and in the reconfiguration of, the social orphan as global type, and social orphans as subjects requiring differentiation or classification to emerge as objects of Western care. How to "read" and classify a child subject placed outside its original family structure, and by what criteria to identify and emotionally bond with that child in a distant state undergoing major political, economic, and cultural transitions are questions that throughout the 1990s were addressed by Western audiences as well as by prospective adoptive parents and the agencies that served their interests (Cartwright 2003). These questions were addressed in part through the systems of social organization made possible with advances in digital and computer technologies, a system whose users were the "waiting parents" engaged in the spectatorship of social orphans from afar. The play of distance in responses of compassion and pity, referenced in the quote from Cairncross above and in Boltanski's theorization of a politics of pity evoked by media spectacles of distant suffering, is a major concern throughout this essay, particularly with reference to distance's "death" and what that implies for the construction of a global social orphan through action elicited by news media reports. If in a politics of pity distance is traversed by words and money, what happens when that distance collapses and the exchange is no longer mediated by distance? What is the means and rate of exchange not only for the "gifts" of words and money that are traded "in person" across differences of language and currency but also for the objects and services uniquely proffered in adoption — namely, love, a new familial bond, and a new national and cultural identity?

"The Shame of a Nation": Transnational Child Mediation in a Borderless Romania

The Romanian social orphan problem was one outcome of a 1984 decree of the Ceausescu regime making abortion punishable by incarceration or death for the woman and for her doctor, and mandating that each Romanian family should produce five children or suffer penalties including taxation of up to 30 percent of their income. Ceausescu's plan was designed to increase, within a decade, the number of "pure-blooded" Romanians available to serve the party from the 1984 estimate of 10 million to 40 million. In the months immediately after the "revolution," in 1990 and early 1991, Romania lacked the infrastructure to manage the social or-phan crisis generated by this mandate. Ceausescu's population policies had been paralleled by his regime's dissolution of the very social service agencies that might in a bankrupt economy have helped to sustain familial support for children as well as support for institutionalized children (Klig-man, 1995; Groza, Ileana, and Irwin 1999). Privatization of the economy eliminated state subsidies of food, utilities, and housing in a market that saw inflation rates of over 300 percent each year, resulting in conditions that made almost inevitable the continuation of the practice of child aban-donment to the state even after the dissolution of the mandate to re-produce (Groza, Ileana, and Irwin 1999, 52).

Romania's infrastructural instability made it an easy target for for-eign intervention in child welfare. Foreign adoptions had occurred under Ceausescu through a system requiring presidential authorization, and pri-vate baby selling was rumored to have occurred under his regime as well (Groza, Ileana, and Irwin 1999, 53). Months after the death of the Ceau-sescus, the presidential approval policy was eliminated and a state com-mittee was established to oversee adoptions. Effective adoption policies were drafted in late 1991, laws regarding child abandonment and adop-tion were passed in 1993, and an organized domestic adoption program was instituted in 1997. A series of moratoriums on adoption were in-stituted throughout the 1990s, concluding in a 2001 partial moratorium established to comply with the then fifteen-country European Union's demand that Romania cease its participation in a system that had posi-tioned that country as a world marketplace for children, a demand that the United States, France, and Israel opposed.[5] The 2001 moratorium culminated in 2004 in the passage of a law making the ban on interna-tional adoption permanent in all cases except those involving the adoption of children by their biological grandparents living in another country. This compliance with the EU demand suggested that the transition of Romania from communist to EU bloc was all but complete.[6] This compliance is not surprising, given that in the immediate aftermath of the "revolution" in 1989, the newly "borderless" Romania was temporarily without ade-quate infrastructure to manage the social orphan crisis internally, much less to stave off ad hoc foreign criticism and intervention.

The social orphan situation in Romania existed but was virtually invis-ible outside Romania until early 1990, when the media began to investigate the issue on the heels of health and human rights workers who had entered the country shortly after the death of the Ceausescus. Stories about Romanian social orphans began to appear as early as a month after the Ceausescus were shot (Groza, Ileana, and Irwin 1999, 51). The relationship of publication origin to national context reflects the uniquely transnational nature of the situation. For example, the *Chicago Tribune* (1990) reported on Australians seeking Romanian orphans; the *Independent* in London reported on South African couples on an "orphan spree" in Romania (Carlin 1990); the *Los Angeles Times* (1990) reported on Romanian children adopted out to France; and the *Times* in London reported on Romanian adoptions in Britain (Hodges 1990).

In the midst of these reports, ABC brought the crew of its news show *20/20* to Romania for the first of five trips made over a three-year period for the purpose of collecting documentary evidence of orphanage circumstances.[7] Initially, the network's aim was to investigate rumors of child selling and to expose the previously hidden living conditions of the tens of thousands of children warehoused, starving, and neglected in orphanages throughout Romania. The footage shot by the ABC crews resulted in a three-part series titled *Orphans of Romania*. This series, and especially its now-classic first episode "Shame of a Nation," which aired on 5 October 1990, exposed the dire and previously obscure conditions of orphanage life in Romania. The detailed visual documentation was a major source of fodder for the seemingly crystal-clear public vision on the spectacle of child suffering. "Shame of a Nation" would nourish the emergent politics of pity among aid workers and a lay media public whose previous exposure had been largely through short, static news photographs. The video images of "Shame of a Nation" revealed the malnourished and physically impaired bodies of children, dirty and despondent and with listless gazes. They also revealed physical circumstances that in terms of esthetics could be described as a kind of visual obliteration. Romanian adoption researchers Victor Groza, Daniela Ileana, and Ivor Irwin (1999, 33–34) recall that "the orphanages were colorless, shockingly quiet and devoid of any of the usual visual or auditory stimulation that children usually receive from bright colors, pictures and displays. Walls were painted in dark browns, to hide the dirt. The paint absorbed any light." Groza, Ileana, and Irwin were not alone in suggesting that the "colorless" darkness and the lack of visual stimuli in the state homes added up to an environment that could "suck the souls out of children" already malnourished and weak, dying at rates of up to 40 percent in the cold winter months (34). Media exposure escalated a transnational campaign to rescue children from this plight, a response already in progress at the time of the ABC crew's arrival. The spontaneous rescue mission to Romania was composed primarily of nonprofit nongovernmental humanitarian aid groups along with volunteer groups and individuals. The mission included close to four hundred nongovernmental organizations providing humanitarian assistance to Romania between 1990 and 1992. By the end of 1992, most of the remaining groups had made connections with foreign government aid organizations to sustain their work. Adoption agencies also became involved in this milieu, constituting a quasi-commercial sector with close links to nonprofit humanitarian aid organizations.[8] Many of the aid groups working in Romania failed to register with the government, which amounted to a situation that was chaotic, unregulated, and, in the words of Groza, Ileana, and Irwin, "reactive and emotionally driven" (51).

The reactive and emotionally driven quality of the Western response to the Romanian social orphan crisis was amplified by the 20/20 "Shame of a Nation" visual exposé. The documentary had some of the impact of both reality television and "snuff film," genres that play on the visual shock value of extreme behaviors and circumstances performed before the observational camera. These genres evoke both horror and fascination on the part of the audience, with graphic representations of real moral infractions, subjective suffering or demise, and an absence of measures of intervention, discipline, and justice.[9] The term graphic is an interesting one in this context: it can refer to pictorial or written representations alike, with the common factor of vividness or clarity. The term is widely used to describe pictorial extremes, obviousness to the degree of the obscene, as in graphic violence or graphic sex. In response to graphic violence we turn away in consternation or repulsion, or we stare in fascinated horror. Covert pleasure is one response to graphic violence or sex, moral consternation is another. I want to suggest here that "Shame of a Nation" and subsequent broadcasts invoked responses to its graphicness in all of these senses, eliciting from its viewers extreme and complex emotional reactions, notably a sort of compassion borne of horror. The images invoked horror and consternation in viewers, but they also invoked concern and even obsessional love. Revulsion toward the inhumane circumstances and suffering depicted in the program provoked a rescue response driven by the desire to save the social orphan; the children imaged in the broadcast became the object of an obsessional fantasy. In the sexual fantasies invoked by pornography the live object of obsessional looking is usually not available to the viewer, and in snuff films evidence suggests the object is obliterated or rendered unattainable (as was also the case for the child Mei Ming in *The Dying Room*). What was unique about "Shame of a Nation" is that the parental fantasies of saving the child who was imaged *could* be realized, if only for a few parents who sought and found the child they spied on the television screen.

Before considering the scenario of saving the specific child, it is necessary to consider the functions of compassion and pity more closely. The *Orphans of Romania* series provoked a response of compassion that was precisely reactive and emotional, insofar as some viewers were compelled by it to act with immediacy. After each of the three *Orphans of Romania* episodes aired, adult viewers reported reacting to the broadcasts with overwhelming emotion, some of them experiencing the images of the children they saw as a personal call to action and an invocation of their potential identities as parents who might step in directly to help the children. Some of these viewers bought airline tickets to Hungary and drove across the recently opened border to Romania, thus collapsing the distance between spectators and faraway on-screen subjects. In some cases, these moral witnesses returned home with a child adopted from an orphanage or obtained by direct or indirect transaction from a destitute family, although in the great majority of cases the child was not among those viewed on television. The televised child images served in most cases as fantasy substitutes, motivating the search for a child "like" those witnessed on screen.

In this sense, "Shame of a Nation" served as advertisement of a surplus of available children. In the "borderless" economic politics of the early 1990s, this amounted to the kind of "win-win" opportunity heralded by Cairncross, where everybody gains: in an opened international adoption market, "waiting children" are matched with "waiting parents." Groza, Ileana, and Irwin note that the earliest news stories about the orphan crisis emphasized not only the circumstances of the children and the inability of the state to address their needs, but also the relative bureaucratic ease and low cost with which foreign adoptions could occur in Romania (59).

Adoption statistics suggest that the surge of news stories and broadcasts paralleled, if not amplified, a surge in actual adoptions out of Romania. In 1990, 121 immigrant visas were issued to orphaned children entering the United States from Romania. In 1991, after the first 20/20 broadcast of *Orphans of Romania*, the number of visas shot up to 2,594, making Romania the country from which in that year the largest number of documented immigrant orphans entered the United States. Indeed, the figure for 1991 almost equaled the total number of adoptions from Romania to the United States for the remainder of the decade, reflecting Romania's subsequent efforts to regulate this market. Overall, however, the number of transnational adoptions into the United States rose steadily and dramatically throughout the 1990s, suggesting a correlation between media exposés and actual adoptions in that decade.[10]

Boltanski (1999, 18), in describing a moral politics of pity in the spectatorship of distant suffering, observes that viewers do not literally rush to the sides of sufferers they perceive at a distance on media reports. Speech or money, he suggests, are the more obvious venues for moral intervention in response to the type of televised suffering that is witnessed from afar. Boltanski's account emphasizes the status of the sufferer represented in the media as a stranger at a distance, and the response of the spectator as one that maintains physical and personal distance. The spectator's efforts, taking the form of a charitable donation or a written or spoken intervention, would not aid the individual sufferer depicted, but might indirectly help a host of others "like" her or him down the line. The sufferer is symbolic of a distant collective on whose behalf an act of charity can be undertaken. For Boltanski, moral action performed on the basis of media witnessing maintains a distance between sufferer and spectator that is both geographic and conceptual. This is distinguished, in Arendt's terms, from the response of compassion that, Arendt explains, "consists in gestures and expressions of countenance and not in words" (cited in Boltanski 1999, 6).

Spectator reactions to "Shame of a Nation" in late 1990, however, suggest a different sort of response to media spectacles of suffering than the indirect action at a distance that is described by Boltanski. Muteness, gesture, and expression were precisely the communicative forms taken, keeping in mind the impact of the episode's many shots of suffering children apart from the voiceover and expert witness speech on the soundtrack. Viewers, some of whom before the show aired had not been con-templating children, were hailed by the child images in the broadcast and responded to the emaciated bodies and vacant stares of the social orphans portrayed — the "mute" gestures — as waiting parents who might step in to help. They traveled to Romania, thereby playing out the collective fantasy of direct transnational crisis intervention and becoming parents as an act of humanitarian aid. In a few cases, individual children spied by viewers on television became the target of a rescue campaign that resulted in a direct impact on these children's lives. The viewers who acted in this manner of immediate and direct action were not vast in number but they did provide for the spectators who stayed at home the symbolic image of the sort of collapse of distance made possible and the kind of immediate, hands-on, gestural and expressive intervention available to them in a context where language and cultural differences limited speech interactions. In the case of the Romanian social orphan rescue campaign, the distance that collapsed between spectator and sufferer was not only physical but also cultural and personal. News and its compelling visual evidence had become vehicles for intimate encounters and for private, even familial, transformations involv-ing bodies and intimacy not unlike the kinds promised by personals adver-tisements, Internet relationships, and dating shows. However, unlike these other forms, the interventions made by spectators who felt compelled to act on behalf of the suffering they witnessed had transnational political implications. In the Romanian social orphan rescue mission compassion was enacted with immediate implications for transnational politics.

The story of filmmaker John Upton's role in the 20/20 broadcasts illus-trates the direct intervention by spectators made possible through visual mediations of the social orphan. Upton was among the small number of television viewers hailed as waiting parents by "Shame of a Nation" who sought and found the one child who had captured their heart on the broadcast. The Emmy-award-winning filmmaker would play a starring role as symbolic father and hero in later episodes of the series as he sought out the child who had become, for him, an obsession. Reporter Tom Jarriel, in his narration for the final episode of the *Orphans of Romania* series (aired in 1993), explains Upton's progression from private and local father to public and global father: "Upton is an unlikely candidate as a champion for Romania's unwanted children. At 36, the EMMY Award winning filmmaker was living the American dream in San Diego with his wife Suzanne and their *three healthy children*. His world revolved around luxury cars, the country club, and a home in an affluent neighborhood." The Web transcription of the episode highlights *three healthy children*, linking that phrase to images confirming Upton's American dream life: three smiling, blond children in their Sunday best pose before a winter-blooming hibiscus under the San Diego sun. Continuing on the thread of the Upton family story, Jarriel relates that "The television screen intruded into Upton's comfortable life in October 1990, as he watched 20/20's report, 'Shame of a Nation' on the so-called *unsalvageable* children of Romania. As image after image flashed by Upton spotted the face of one youngster who seemed to personify everything that was wrong: 12-year-old *Elena Rostas*, with one leg grotesquely twisted over her head." The images of Romanian orphans shown in the broadcast and linked to the word *unsalvageable* on the series' Web transcript page contrast dramatically with the photograph of the smiling, healthy Upton kids dressed in their Sunday best. Clicking *unsalvageable* brings up a photograph of an emaciated child with twisted legs. The name *Elena Rostas* links to another image, a girl lying on her back, her distended belly protruding. Her leg doubles back, pressing against her torso.

Upton's voice breaks in to describe the first moment he spied this image on the "Shame of a Nation" broadcast: "I saw Elena [in the broadcast] and I saw the way that she scooted around on her bottom, and I just had an overwhelming feeling to try to do something to help her, to get her out. I started pacing the floor and my wife said to me, 'You're going over there, aren't you?' and I said, 'I have to.'" Seeing Elena's body on the screen was a powerful prompt. Upton's "overwhelming feeling" motivated him to spend two years, and two trips to Romania, struggling to find and rescue this one girl he'd spied on screen. Subsequent episodes carried the story line of Upton's quest for the one child as a strong narrative motivation for the series. In the series his reaction of compassion is transformed before viewers' eyes into a more organized politics of pity in which his obsessive search for Elena generates the energy to save others along the way. In the final episode of the series, Upton is featured holding Elena in his arms as he whisks her, along with eight other children, out of the orphanage. He leaves against the protests of the nurse in charge. A Romanian boy left behind is captured on film, raising his eyes imploringly to the filmmaker: "Johnny, I go to America?" Upton turns to the Romanian translator and asks, "How do you say, 'I'll try'?" For Upton, and for the many spectators who followed and identified with his mission, compassion was transformed into sustained collective humanitarian action with a mission and a plan. Collective in this case refers not only to the number of child sufferers but also to the number of waiting parents unified in their goal of completing the narrative chain begun in Upton's story. Spectators at a distance are there with Upton, ready to step in and continue the narrative; ready to "try" for that one boy left behind or for another one "like" him.

Even as Upton wonders if the shock of a new life might not be worse for the severely disabled Elena who has spent her life inside the walls of an orphanage, he explains to viewers that it is "because of Elena" that he has made this mission. In rescuing her, he helps to bring to America scores of other children "like" her, a group for whom he believes he is doing "the right thing." The question of which children became social orphans, which children "like" Elena this mission was organized to save, is an important one. I propose that disablement was a striking if unstated characteristic of the global social orphan represented in the media (a claim on which I elaborate in the conclusion of this essay). In contexts like post-Ceausescu Romania where state support did not exist for the care of children with disabilities within families, such children often were the ones abandoned to the state for care over those who could grow to help the family in their efforts to survive. Thus children with disabilities were overrepresented in the social orphan population. So too were other marginal subject positions: for example, the Roma and the other ethnic minorities who were undervalued in the mentality of the Ceausescu regime. Inadequate nutrition and physical care and deficits of contact and emotional caregiving in orphanages played a major role in the development of the sensory, physical, emotional, and cognitive impairment in children who entered these institutions without disabilities. Thus, in Romania and other similar contexts, physical disability was one discernible if unstated characteristic of the social orphan represented in the Western media. As I explain below, one of the tasks of the transnational movement organized to save social orphans was medically to classify and treat the multiple physical and psychological conditions that became apparent in this class of child on its arrival "home" in the West.

In the first half of the 1990s, special children "like" Elena and Mei Ming—neglected and, significantly, disabled and near death—were captured on Western film in countries including Romania, China, and Russia and broadcast in the West. Human-interest stories of these distant sufferers were brought home to television and news media audiences by identificatory parental figures like Upton and Blewett. These children were the late-century emblems of the political mission to recognize the figure of the child as being in need of international protection beyond what its home state could provide.[11] Along with this construction of the distant child in need emerged a protective body of public parents, moral spectators whose concepts of justice and rights responded to the death of distance heralded by Cairncross as an unprecedented opportunity for investment, a category in which I include the emotional investment of humanitarian action. The death of distance made possible a kind of media witnessing and intervention that would finally go beyond the action at a distance captured in Boltanski's description of distant spectatorship, a model that was outdated even as his monograph on distant suffering was published. What made the transnational adoption scene of the 1990s different from that of previous decades was precisely the immediacy of death — not the death of children per se, but the death of distance between viewers and child subjects made possible through communication innovations of the late twentieth century. In the 1990s, "waiting parents" increasingly used technologies of mediation to close the gap, to touch and even to take as their own the disabled child they witnessed on television screens in the first half of the decade and, increasingly after mid-decade, on computer screens.

The Late 1990s: Rescue Gone Awry

Physical disability was readily visible in the images shown in series like 20/20's *Orphans of Romania*. Less apparent to spectators and to prospective parents traveling to foreign countries to adopt was the presence of cognitive, developmental, and psychosocial impairments in the children encountered in orphanages and adopted out. Physician Barbara Bascom and journalist Carole McKelvey, professional participants in the first wave of humanitarian aid missions to Romanian orphanages, included in their 1997 guide to international adoption an extensive account of the developmental and psychosocial problems encountered in some of the children adopted out of Romania in the early 1990s. Romania, they explain, is "used as a model" (94) throughout their guide, and the Romanian social orphan is used as a "paradigm" of "neglected child populations throughout the eastern bloc" (115). Bascom, interviewed on the "Shame of a Nation" broadcast in 1990, had spent seven years in Romania by the time of the guide's publication. The authors' findings, based largely on their own work in Romanian orphanages and with adoptive children in the United States, were supported by decades of postwar research in psychiatry and social work on orphans in a range of populations by professionals including Rene Spitz (1945), John Bowlby (1940, 1951, 1953), and more recently Ronald Federici (1998) (see also Cartwright 2004 and forthcoming).

Professional and participant discourses intersected in the 1990s with the emergence of advocacy groups dedicated to archiving, disseminating, and promoting research on the postinstitutionalized child. An example is the response of Thais Tepper and Lois Hannon, mothers of children adopted out of Romania in 1991. Tepper and Hannon formed an organization, the Parent Network for the Post-Institutionalized Child (PN-PIC), in 1993 to facilitate the exchange of information among parents and medical professionals devoted to managing the psychological problems emerging among some of the Romanian and Russian adopted children. The PN-PIC organization is typical of the consumer health networks that rose up in the 1990s, which were facilitated by the rise of the Internet and the restructuring of medical care into networks of managed care. The acronym PIC (post-institutionalized child) emerged with this dialogue between parents and professionals — psychiatrists, medical doctors, and social workers — devoted to the care of adopted children. The literature devoted to the PIC includes a newsletter (Hannon 1995–2001), a book (Hannon, Tepper, and Sandstrom 1999), and a Web site (www.pnpic.org) with links to the growing literature addressing the PIC's medical and psychosocial problems and the responsibility of adoption agencies in disclosing and screening for such problems (see for example Jenista 2001). With the PIC acronym as an entity gaining informal medical usage in the 1990s the psychiatric category of Reactive Attachment Disorder (RAD) also emerged, a classification that earned its own treatment centers and professional training institutes, including in the 1990s the pioneering Colorado-based Evergreen Psychotherapy Center and Attachment Treatment and Training Institute (Levy and Orlans 1998). In tandem with the emergence of these semipublic resources was the publication of a series of press accounts starting in 1993 that narrated for lay audiences outside the adoption context the unfolding circumstances of Romanian and Russian children rescued from orphanages in the early 1990s. Media stories of the mid-to-late 1990s told about children whose medical, developmental, or psychosocial impairment or "damage" was revealed to parents days, months, and even years after adoption, thereby countering medical record claims of good health and leading parents to cry out against the adoption agencies they believed to have deceived them regarding the mental health status of the child (Brink 1996).

"The Perfect Child," a sequence within the magazine news story *The Darker Side of Adoption*, was one example of this display of public consternation about unclassified damage.[12] Airing in February 2000, this episode of the CBS magazine news series *48 Hours* features Crystal and Jesse, an upper-middle-class suburban couple who had traveled to Russia in 1997 to adopt a toddler boy and a nine-year-old girl (for whom CBS used the pseudonym Samantha "to protect her identity"). The story revolves around Samantha, a girl whose photograph the couple first spied on the Internet in a listing of available orphans. The girl's identity required protection in the view of the network because she had become the center of a legal suit brought by Jesse and Crystal against their adoption agency, an affiliate of the Frank Foundation, a nonprofit charitable organization with strong ties to adoption networks in Russia and the former Soviet republics. The couple alleged that the agency failed to disclose information about Samantha's psychological state.

In "The Perfect Child" series narrator Troy Roberts explains that Samantha turned out to have "deep emotional problems" that were not reflected in her medical documentation. Jesse and Crystal, seated on the couch in the family room of their large home — their adopted son playing nearby — relate the story of the girl's transition to the United States. Family photos and home video punctuate the tale. Samantha, blonde and pretty in her photograph, was incorporated into the family as her parents' "little princess." We see idealized flashback footage of Samantha and Crystal performing in mother-daughter roles. However, the couple relates, within a few months of her arrival home, Samantha became angry and withdrawn. Crystal alleges that Samantha behaved destructively, and that she began to steal items such as jewelry. Samantha told her mother that she heard voices and, according to Crystal, threatened to injure or kill family members. Crystal then relates the climactic story of witnessing Samantha dangling her toddler brother over the rail of a deck thirty feet above the ground, threatening to drop him. Diagnosed as a homicide risk, Samantha was hospitalized for four months. On her return home, the family installed surveillance cameras to track the girl's movements throughout the house as a means of protecting themselves from assault. An attempt to strangle the family dog was among the actions that provoked Crystal and Jesse to begin proceedings against the adoption agency and ultimately to return Samantha back to her orphanage in Boravici, where they left her without explaining that they would not be back to retrieve her.[13] "We've been here every day." explained Crystal in retrospect, "loving her, nurturing her, helping her. And we couldn't save her." Crystal, when asked about Samantha's reaction to being abandoned for a second time, provides an explanation that is startling in its apparent lack of remorse, its cold disaffection: "I believe she might be waiting for us, but she's not waiting for us as parents. She doesn't love us. She doesn't know what love is."

The 1990s began with transnational news stories and a transnational humanitarian movement dedicated to saving the global social orphan, the child at risk in states incapable of providing adequate care and protection. Images of children with physical disabilities in environments that visually and materially "sucked the souls" and lives from children inspired compassionate acts of rescue that in some cases transformed into the performance of a collective politics of pity, a transformative movement of action at a distance. But the decade ended with the rescue fantasy gone awry. Samantha's photograph and the *48 Hours* news magazine story about her are emblematic of the invisible dangers posed by the social orphan image as seductive lure. Children brought home with the fanfare of transnational rescue were revealed to be at risk of developing unforeseen medical, cognitive, developmental, or psychosocial problems, the management of which parents were entirely unprepared (Jenista 2001; Bascom and McKelvey 1997). Adoption disruption, so dramatically narrated in "The Perfect Child," was hardly a new phenomenon (Barth and Berry 1988). But with the dramatic rise of transnational adoption in the 1990s, and the distance and difference that factored into those circumstances, the potential for invisible problems became more pronounced. The damage so blatantly showcased in televised images of children "like" Elena, children whose physical disabilities were featured on-screen as the emblem of need and the call to action, by the end of the 1990s symbolized the threatening potential for hidden impairments in a generation of children adopted out of transitional states in crisis. It was this sort of hidden problem—the specter of the pretty, physically "normal," and apparently healthy child like Samantha who could not be saved by compassionate action—that motivated the response of spectator disaffection in the late 1990s, a condition dramatized in the extreme by Crystal and Jesse.

Samantha's case was far from the norm in transnational adoption. Jesse and Crystal's response was newsworthy not because it represented actions taken by significant numbers of adoptive parents, but because it symbolized public anger and dismay about the representation of children and need in news stories earlier in the decade. This consternation was articulated in the euphemistic terms of medical disclosure. By bringing legal action against their agency for not giving available information about Samantha, Crystal and Jesse place their right to be informed over the humanist perception of Samantha's right to a better life. The story, though not representative of a wide state of affairs, brought into the open an undercurrent of fear and anger, and acted out for viewers the fantasy of rejecting the rescue response. This antihumanist response would have been unthinkable, unrepresentable a few years earlier.

How does compassion devolve into steely disaffection? Crystal and Jesse initially react to Samantha's image with compassion. Drawn in by the photograph of a smiling, lovely girl with long blonde hair, they close the distance and make Samantha their own in an act of palliative aid for which the childless couple is rewarded with children. Throughout their narration Jesse and Crystal affirm their interest in participating in a broader politics of pity. They want to help not just Samantha but children like her. Samantha's suffering, however, could not be contained. As is the case for the parents invoked by Max Schleler (1967), who witness their child's suffering and in so doing experience suffering with her, Jesse and Crystal suffer along with Samantha. Or, we might say with Jesse and Crystal, Samantha inflicts suffering on her family. Because Samantha "doesn't know what love is," the child cannot be integrated into the relationship of proximity required of compassion. Samantha violates the unspoken contract of compassion by maintaining a psychic breach even when physical distance is overcome at great cost. Moreover, she threatens direct violence against her family. Jesse and Crystal thus disavow their legal and emotional connections to the girl in reaction to this breach of an unwritten, perceived emotional contract between waiting parents and social orphans: that the spectator's gift of proximal love will be appreciated and returned; that certainly the gift will not be met with aggression or contempt.

At the end of the episode's sequence on their saga to Boravici and back, Jesse and Crystal explicitly turn their backs not only on the individual child but also on both the sentiment of compassion and the politics of pity that Samantha's picture had evoked in them. The humanist impulse behind the politics of pity in which they tried to engage broke down with the distant sufferer's refusal to accept the gift of the spectator, the gift of proximal care. This gift was conveyed not just in money and words but also through the obsessional love for which the money and words were substitutes. The footage of Jesse and Crystal's home and family life with Samantha makes explicit the report's unstated point that, for Jesse and Crystal, material goods and physical admiration were the primary signifiers of a love they were dying to bestow on Samantha. This message is underscored by the episode's subsequent interview with an older pair of siblings with disabilities whose initial adoption was disrupted. They were subsequently placed in a loving home devoid of the consumerism and idealistic expectations so prominent in the portrayal of the lives of Jesse and Crystal.

This second vignette of *The Darker Side of Adoption* fails to address a crucial difference from the first vignette: the girls who are readopted into a reciprocally loving home have disabilities that are physical, not emotional or mental. Their disabilities are evident on screen, and they were apparent to their parents before their adoption. There is no evidence that they lack the ability to return love. The show's representations of the adoptive parents' home exhibits no signs of the displaced signifiers of love in the form of material goods, and we hear nothing indicative of idealized expectations on the part of the parents. These girls were not expected to be the "princesses" of a fairy-tale home life. All of these messages embedded in the juxtaposition of sequences that comprises *The Darker Side of Adoption* obscure the fact that it is Samantha's hidden disability, her mental illness that presumably results from pathological parenting and institutional care, that makes her seemingly incapable of loving attachment.

For viewers ten years out from *Shame of a Nation*, Samantha embodies the threat of the truly "unsalvageable" child, the child who cannot return the gift of love bestowed on her because she has not developed the ego required to see herself as worthy of life much less of love. Ironically, Jesse and Crystal respond not only by withdrawing their gift, but also by leading an unsuspecting Samantha through a punishing ritual of abandonment that repeats the girl's earlier experience of parental neglect and abandonment to the state. Samantha's sense of worthlessness is articulated in her psychotic state, a condition of death-in-life that, the episode leads viewers to believe, was an outcome of neglect and abuse suffered at the hands of both the state institution and of her mentally unstable alcoholic birth mother who was tracked down and interviewed by the news crew.[14] The tragedy of Samantha, we are led to see, is that she had never been given the opportunity to emerge as a psychical subject capable of selfhood. Samantha died long before Jesse and Crystal came along to save her.[15] In rejecting their children, what the Crystals and Jesses of the 1990s reject is the promise of Cairncross: that the death of distance delivers the goods and that the goods can be freely enjoyed. Responsibility and the proximity and guilt that such an event entails were not part of the promise.

"Special" Children and the Politics of Pity

What I have suggested here is that distance, the mode of media spectatorship described by Boltanski in 1999 as a component of a politics of pity, collapsed with the borderlessness that made possible a compassionate rush to the side of Romanian orphans in the early years of the 1990s. A politics of pity emerged out of a response of compassion in this mediated construction of the global social orphan as an object of transnational concern. Action at a distance precludes risk insofar as money and words in response to suffering come with some assurances against the sort of infection of the family by a "damaged" child, as related in "The Perfect Child." But the death of distance made charitable action risky. By the mid-1990s, news stories were explicit in their warning of the medical risks of transnational adoption. By 1996 the press was reporting on the chance of acquiring a child, for example, with undiagnosed or unrecorded HIV or HCV infection from social orphan populations where vaccination needles had been shared (Brink 1996). Waiting parents were alerted to proceed with caution, to seek out as much medical information as they could, and still to prepare for the possibility of a child with unforeseen conditions. More difficult to manage, however, was the prospect of adopting a child who might develop psychosocial problems as a result of years of institutional deprivation. This is the specter that gave rise to the term "unsalvageable" used in the 20/20 series to describe the children of Romanian orphanages, the child symbolized in terms of physical disability. Upton symbolized the obsession to do the impossible, to salvage the "unsalvageable" child. But his saga fails to tell us what *48 Hours* describes as "the darker side of adoption," the lack of preparation among adoptive parents for addressing the psychical sequelae of institutional life in conditions of economic collapse.

Conclusion: A Politics of Consternation

With the rise of PIC discourse, well documented in the literature of the Parent Network for the Post-Institutionalized Child, we see the emergence of a politics of consternation among some of those parents who most strongly identified with the compassion reaction and the politics of pity during the early 1990s. One of the achievements of the humanitarian movement dedicated to saving the global social orphan was to create a class of parents and advocates professionally trained to address the unique psychical problems of these adopted children. In the late 1990s, under pressure from these parents, some agencies and social work organizations instituted their own parent training sessions to informally certify parents for the task of raising the PIC. A transnational public culture was forged across parent networks, agencies, and medical practices devoted to the post-institutionalized child around the figure of the social orphan in its subsequent identity as post-institutionalized child. One of this PIC network's achievements has been to temper the compassion reaction among "waiting parents" with information aimed to foster apprehension and caution in response to the promise of borderlessness and an open market in children, and to foster critical reserve in response to the compelling images of suffering proffered by the media.

The postwar literature on attachment disorders launched by British psychiatrist John Bowlby (1940, 1951, 1953) and carried forward by Michael Rutter (1972) was revitalized with force in the mid-1990s (Federici 1998; Levy and Orlans 1998). It might be said that the function of the new focus on attachment disorder (or RAD) in the PIC is precisely to counter the unreflective humanism elicited by the media coverage of social orphans in the early 1990s, to create highly regimented protocols for the therapeutic parenting of children unable to properly adapt to the requirements of social proximity, to familial love (Federici 1998). The images of the 1990s, however, were complicit in fostering another sort of attachment disorder: a disorder in which spectators of child suffering were compelled to live out an obsessional relationship with the child image, only to be taken by surprise by the reality of the child's life. What made the social orphan rescue mission of the 1990s different from other charity responses to crises of that decade was the degree to which "death of distance" became literal in its drawing together of spectators and objects of the gaze.

Waiting parents, initially the connoisseurs of suffering, became seasoned actors in a global politics of pity that extended beyond the climax of adoption into the politicized space of the private adoptive home. The proximity of attachment, of love, that characterizes this relationship makes representation a more slippery prospect. Many participants in the politics of pity in the early 1990s became actors in a politics of consternation, reacting against the use of the image as lure, and against the rhetoric of borderlessness charity that had compelled them to draw the sufferer into their hearts. For those who, unlike Jesse and Crystal, held fast to their "disordered" children, the home of the post-institutionalized child became the training ground for the attachment-disordered parent, curing the parent of a romantic attachment to the rescue fantasy.

Botlanski (1999, 192) proposes that the humanitarian movement stay close to compassion, the immediacy of the present that drives this response, even as the framework of a politics of pity remains unsurpassed. He concludes that the present has the unique privilege of "being real" and deserves its own "politics of presence." Throughout his monograph, speech is privileged as an intervening form of action. I would caution that, in the case of the humanitarian movement devoted to the management of the social orphan crisis, the response of presentist compassion facilitated by images fostering a mediated death of distance is deeply troubling. Until we can address the nature of the real in all of its mediated forms including the visual, and with all of the troubling immediacy of impact that the visual brings, we cannot specify a right means of political action relative to that riveting object, the social orphan. Some lessons about the visual are offered to us in the politics of consternation enacted in the network of parents engaged in the care of the post-institutionalized child. One of the shames of "Shame of a Nation" is our failure in the United States to see the problems inherent in action at a distance in an era of virtual immediacy.

Notes

1. I use the term "orphans" as given in the 1998 Human Rights Watch report (Hunt and Whitman 1998), which states that orphans are "children who are abandoned to the state, including the vast majority of 'social orphans' whose parents are living. It is used interchangeably with the term 'abandoned children.'" The report also notes that "children with severe disabilities . . . often become abandoned children and thus enter the population of 'orphans.'"

2. The number dropped to 582.7 in 1990, 595.4 in 1991, and then began to rise throughout the first half of the 1990s, reaching above 1,000 in 1994 and 1995 (see UNICEF 1997).

3. On the emergence of the television news magazine show in the 1980s as a financially lucrative format for television news media, see Hallin 2000; Campbell 1991; and Benthall 1993, chapter 5.

4. Bowker and Star 1999 contains an excellent account of the social impact of classification by medical organizations and by government agencies.

5. See Kirka 2002; Knox 2004; and the Web site of the Romanian National Authority for Child Protection (http://www.copii.roleindex.htm) and of Prochild, a federation of U.S. and Romanian nonprofit groups working to support transnational adoptions out of that country (http://www.prochild.ro).

6. See "Law on the Legal Status of Adoptions," 2004, Parliament of Romania, posted at http://www.copii.roleindex.htm.

7. All quotes from *Orphans of Romania* were taken from the transcript by Janis Tomlinson, ABC News, 19 March 1993, http://www.johnupton.net/2020transcript.htmabc.

8. The relationship among nongovernmental organizations, government aid organizations, and the media is addressed in detail in Benthall 1993.

9. Snuff is defined on the *American Heritage Dictionary* Web site as a movie genre of explicit pornography culminating in the supposed actual violent death of a participant in a sex act (http://dictionary.reference.com/search?q=snuff+film). Controversy exists over whether the deaths are actual or simulated, and the films

themselves trade on the claim of realism. Here I mean to suggest that the social orphan subgenre of documentary capitalizes on audience fascination with subjugation and death on film and violates the extreme taboo of documenting children in the process of dying, even for the purpose of preventing such suffering and death. My aim is not to fault the series for a moral transgression but to analyze these desires.

10. The total number of immigrant visas granted to Romanian orphans in the period 1992–1999 was 3,169, with year-to-year fluctuations (low of 97, high of 895) relative to policy changes and moratoria ("Immigrant Visa Issues to Orphans Coming to the U.S.," 2004, posted at http://www.copii.roleindex.htm).

11. Elsewhere I address the history of international policy and law relating to the emergence and management of the social orphan, and the question of visual classification: see Cartwright 2003, 2004, and forthcoming.

12. All quotes from "The Perfect Child," *48 Hours*, were taken from the transcript from CBS News, 2000, http://www.theadoptionguide.com/48hours/theper fectchild.html.

13. Groza and Rosenthal (1998) note that less than .1 percent of adoptions are contested each year, and more than 98 percent are not terminated after legalization. The percentage of adoption disruptions overall is estimated to fall between 3 to 53 percent (Barth 1988), with figures varying according to the category of adoption being studied. Rates of disruption are higher among older child adoption. Groze (1986) places special needs adoption disruptions at 14.3 percent.[12]

14. This interview introduces to viewers the potential to read Samantha's psychosis in terms of genetic inheritance.

15. On ego emergence and the formation of psychopathology in children reared from infancy and early childhood in institutions or by primary caregivers exhibiting pathological techniques of care, see Spitz 1945, 1946; Bowlby 1940, 1951, 1953; Rutter 1972; Winnicott 1974; and Cartwright 2004 and forthcoming, chapter 1.

References

Arendt, Hannah. 1990 [1961]. *On Revolution*. Harmondsworth, Eng.: Penguin.

Barth, Richard P., and Marianne Berry. 1988. *Adoption Disruption: Rates, Risks and Responses*. New York: Aldine de Gruyter.

Bascom, Barbara B., and Carole A. McKelvey. 1997. *The Complete Guide to Foreign Adoption: What to Expect and How to Prepare for Your New Child*. New York: Pocket Books.

Benthall, Jonathan. 1993. *Disasters, Relief, and the Media*. London: I. B. Taurus.

Berebitsky, Julie. 2000. *Like Our Very Own: Adoption and the Changing Culture of Motherhood, 1851–1950*. Lawrence: University of Kansas Press.

Blair, D. Marianne. 1993. "Liability of adoption agencies and attorneys for misconduct in the disclosure of health-related information." In Joan Hollinger, ed. *Adoption Law and Practice*, 1–150. New York: Matthew Bender.

———. 1992. "Lifting the Genealogical Veil: A Blueprint for Legislative Reform of the Disclosure of Health-Related Information in Adoption." *North Carolina Law Review* 70, 681–779.

Boltanski, Luc. 1999. *Distant Suffering: Morality, Media, and Politics*, trans. Graham D. Burchell. Cambridge: Cambridge University Press.

Bowker, Geoffrey C., and Susan Leigh Star. 1999. *Sorting Things Out: Classification and Its Consequences*. Cambridge, MA: MIT Press.

Bowlby, John. 1940. "The Influence of Early Environment in the Development of Neurosis and Neurotic Character." *International Journal of Psychoanalysis* 21: 1–25.

———. 1951. *Maternal Care and Mental Health*. Geneva: World Health Organization; London: Her Majesty's Stationery Office; New York: Columbia University Press. Abridged version; *Child Care and the Growth of Love* (2nd ed. 1965). Harmondsworth, Eng.: Penguin.

———. 1953. "Some Pathological Processes Set in Train by Early Mother-Child Separation." *Journal of Mental Science* 99: 265–72.

Brink, Susan. 1996. "Too Sick to be Adopted?" *US News and World Report*, 2 May 1996, 66–69.

Cairncross, Frances. 1997. *The Death of Distance: How the Communication Revolution Will Change Our Lives*. Boston, MA: Harvard Business School Press.

Campbell, Richard. 1991. *"60 Minutes" and the News: A Mythology for Middle America*. Champaign-Urbana: University of Illinois Press.

Carlin, John. 1990. "South African Couples on Orphan Spree." *Independent* (London). January 18.

Cartwright, Lisa. 2003. "Photographs of 'Waiting Children': The Transnational Adoption Market." *Social Text* 73: 83–109.

———. 2004. "'Emergencies of Survival': Moral Spectatorship and the 'New Vision of the Child' in Postwar Child Psychoanalysis." *Journal of Visual Culture* 3 (1): 35–49.

———. Forthcoming. *Moral Spectatorship*. Durham: Duke University Press.

Chicago Tribune. 1990. "Australia Seeks Romanian Orphans." 5 January.

Cornia, Giovanni Andrea, and Sheldon Danziger, eds. 1997. *Child Poverty and Deprivation in the Industrialized Countries, 1945–1995*. Oxford: Clarendon Press.

Federici, Ronald S. 1998. *Help for the Hopeless Child: A Guide for Families.* Alexandria, VA: Dr. Ronald S. Federici and Associates.

Freundlich, Madelyn, and Lisa Peterson. 1998. *Wrongful Adoption: Law, Policy, and Practice.* Washington, D.C.: CWLA Press.

Groza, Victor, Daniela Ileana, and Ivor Irwin. 1999. *A Peacock or a Crow: Stories, Interviews, and Commentaries on Romanian Adoption.* Euclid, OH: Lakeshore Communications.

Groza, Victor, and Karen F. Rosenberg. 1998. *Clinical and Practice Issues in Adoption: Bridging the Gap between Adoptees as Infants and as Older Children.* Westport, CT: Praeger.

Groze, Victor. 1996. *Successful Adoptive Families: A Longitudinal Study of Special Needs Adoption.* New York: Praeger.

———. 1986. Special Needs Adoption. *Child and Youth Services Review*, 8, no. 4, 363–373.

Hague Convention on Protection of Children and Co-Operation in Respect of Intercountry Adoption. 1993. Adopted by the Seventeenth Session of the Hague Conference on Private International Law (concluded 29 May 1993). I.L.M. 1134, art. 29.

Hallin, Daniel. 2000. "Commercialization and Professionalization in the American News Media." In *Mass Media and Society*, 3rd ed., ed. James Curran and Michael Gurevitch. London: Arnold Publishers.

Hannon, Lois, ed. 1995–2001. "The Post: The Newsletter of the Parent Network for the Post-Institutionalized Child." Meadowlands, PA: PN-PIC.

Hannon, Lois, Thais Tepper, and Dorothy Sandstrom, eds. 1999. *International Adoption: Challenges and Opportunities.* Meadowlands, PA: PN-PIC.

Hodges, Anthony. 1990. "Orphans May Come to Britain." *London Times.* 5 January 1990.

Horn, David G. 1994. *Social Bodies: Science, Reproduction, and Italian Modernity.* Princeton: Princeton University Press.

Human Rights Watch. 1996. *Death by Default: A Policy of Fatal Neglect in China's State Orphanages.* New York: Human Rights Watch/Asia.

Hunt, Kathleen and Lois Whitman. 1998. "Abandoned to the State: Cruelty and Neglect in Russian Orphanages." New York, London, Brussels, Washington, D.C.: Human Rights Watch.

Jenista, Jeri Ann. 2001. "Commentary." *Newsletter of the Joint Council for International Children Service.* Reprinted at http://www.pnpic.org/jcics.htm.

Kirka, Danica. 2002. "Abandoned Baby Typifies Romania's Adoption Ban." *Napa Valley Register*, 28 June, posted at http://www.napanews.com/templates/ index.cfm?template=story_full&id=6B121A14-CCA7-4EAB-9ED7-65D4 E11249DC.

Kligman, Gail. 1995. "Abortion in Ceausescu's Romania." In *Conceiving the New World Order*, ed. Faye Ginsburg and Rayna Rapp. Berkeley: University of California Press.

Knox, Noelle. 2004. "Romania to Ban International Adoptions Permanently." *USA Today*, posted 6/15/2004 http://www.usatoday.com/news/world/2004-06-15-romania-adoptions_x.htm.

Lalvani, Suren. 1996. *Photography, Vision, and the Production of Modern Bodies*. Albany: State University of New York Press.

LeMay, Susan Kempf. 1998. "The Emergence of Wrongful Adoption as a Cause of Action." *Journal of Family Law* 27 (2): 475–88.

Levy, Terry M., and Michael Orlans. 1998. *Attachment, Trauma and Healing*. Washington, D.C.: Child Welfare League of America Press.

Los Angeles Times. 1990. "Adopted Romanian Children Met by New Families in France." 7 January.

New York Times. 1996. "China's Orphanages: A War of Perception." 21 January.

Ressler, Everett M., Neil Boothby, and Daniel J. Steinbock. 1988. *Unaccompanied Children: Care and Protection in Wars, Natural Disasters, and Refugee Movements*. New York: Oxford University Press.

Rutter, Michael. 1972. *Maternal Deprivation Reassessed*. Harmondsworth, Eng.: Penguin.

Schleler, Max. 1967. *Nature et formes de la sympathie: Contribution á l'etude des lois de la vie affective*. Paris: Payot.

Sekula, Alan. 1986. "The Body and the Archive." *October* 39: 3–64.

Tagg, John. 1988. *Burdens of Representation: Essays on Photography and Histories*. Minneapolis: University of Minnesota Press.

Spitz, Rene A. 1945. "Hospitalism: An Inquiry into the Genesis of Psychiatric Conditions in Early Childhood." *Psychoanalytic Study of the Child* 1: 53–74.

Spitz, Rene A., and Katherine Wolf. 1946. "Anaclitic Depression: An Inquiry into the Genesis of Psychiatric Conditions in Early Childhood." *Psychoanalytic Study of the Child* 2: 313–42.

UNICEF. 1997. *Children at Risk in Central and Eastern Europe: Perils and Promises*. Florence, Italy: United Nations Children's Fund, International Child Development Centre.

United Nations General Assembly. 1948. "Universal Declaration of Human Rights," G.A. res. 217A (III), U.N. Doc A/810 at 71 (1948), article 25, provision 2. Reprinted at University of Minnesota Human Rights Library, http://www1.umn.edu/humanrts/instree/b1udhr.htm.

———. 1989. "Convention on the Rights of the Child," G.A. res. 44/25, annex, 44 U.N. GAOR Supp. (No. 49) at 167, U.N. Doc. A/44/49 (1989). Reprinted at

University of Minnesota Human Rights Library, http://www1.umn.edu/human rts/instree/k2crc.htm.

———. 1992. "Plight of Street Children." G.A. res. 47/126, 47 U.N. GAOR Supp. (No. 49) at 200, U.N. Doc. A/47/49 (1992).

Winnicott, Donald W. 1974. "Fear of Breakdown." *International Revue of Psychoanalysis* 1:103–7.

Phantom Lives, Narratives of Possibility

ELIZABETH ALICE HONIG

> At first Matthew suggested getting a "Home" boy. But I said "no" flat to that.
> "They may be all right — I'm not saying they're not — but no London street
> Arabs for me," I said. "Give me a native-born at least. There'll be a risk, no
> matter who we get. But I'll feel easier in my mind and sleep sounder at nights
> if we get a born Canadian."
> — L.M. MONTGOMERY, *Anne of Green Gables*, 1908

Anne of Green Gables is still, after nearly a century, the English-speaking world's favorite orphan story. It is the tale of an ingenious, imaginative redhead who longs for a family and whose bright and loving spirit converts an isolated, somewhat curmudgeonly couple into warm, adoring parents. Such tales of transformation are staples of orphan fiction: Mary's arrival from India in *The Secret Garden* (Burnett 1962 [1911]) opens every twisted, hardened heart at Misselthwaite Manor, just as abused Will's fostering in *Goodnight Mr. Tom* (Magorian 1981) turns sour old Tom into a doting dad, and Will himself into a confident young artist. Children today are still brought up on these tales of emotional fulfillment through adoption, stories in which delightful children blossom in the care of wise, sensitive adoptive parents who are sometimes explicitly portrayed as "better" for the children than their birth families would have been (Johnston 1994). Very rarely is an adoption portrayed as problematic (Neufeld 2002); almost always, love conquers even the saddest and most troubled minds. No wonder, then, that the readers of these books grow up to become the prospective parents whose applications flow into American adoption agencies.

The world of fiction has not, however, caught up with reality on one score: neither transnational nor transracial adoptions have become a common subject for young adult novels, despite their ever-increasing and very visible occurrence.[1] Only in books for younger children do we read about situations like a little Chinese girl who is unhappy because she doesn't look like her Caucasian adoptive parents (Say 1997). Such books are explicitly written as identity models for young adoptees, unlike earlier orphan novels. But when those adoptees reach adolescence or adulthood, what sorts of fictions will they be reading? And, more important, what fictions will they be inventing for themselves?

Transnational adoption has been on the margins of cultural consciousness for many generations. Readers today of *Anne of Green Gables* must pick up only rarely on Marilla's comment when she mentions Matthew's interest in getting a "Home Boy" that she is talking about a precursor of transnational adoption. For centuries, England sent its "surplus" children to colonies overseas in order to provide the cheap labor that was hard to come by in rural communities. Had Marilla and Matthew taken one of those children instead of the perky Anne, they would have been one of the one hundred thousand families that did so between 1869 and 1939 in Canada alone.[2] Isolated, traumatized, often abused (in an estimated two-thirds of all cases), and enduring lifetimes of discrimination, the "Home Children" long remained voiceless, and their stories are rarely absorbed into the history of transnational adoption. And yet their struggles for identity, for acceptance, and above all for access to their own true histories—the personal records that had been falsified and kept from them—resonate with the struggles of more recent groups of transnational adoptees.

A different early story of transnational adoption (transracial as well, in the terms of its times) is that of the Kindertransport. Starting in 1938 Jewish children, ranging in age from infancy to early teens, were brought from Germany to England to save them from Nazi persecution. In less than a year, from Kristallnacht in November 1938 until the outbreak of war in September 1939, nearly ten thousand children came to Britain, speaking no English and leaving behind parents whom most would never see again. In their new "homeland" they were sent to foster homes or orphanages. Most found comfort, sympathy, even love, but others were ignored and abused. Some would spend the rest of their lives in England; others moved on to America, Canada, or Israel. Their tale is better known than that of the Home Children, and is seen perhaps as an uplifting epi-sode within the broader Holocaust story, and yet it too is not widely mentioned in histories of international adoption. It is true that neither of these episodes provides the equivalent of the post–Korean War model — the childless couple yearning for an infant to love and treasure as its own, often turning to a foreign country because (unlike Marilla) they feel safer with an Asian or Russian baby than an American one — but I would argue that despite the different structures of these child migrations, there is a similarity of effect in their results. The words of an adult Kindertransport child would strike a chord with later generations of transnational adop-tees: "I am conscious of my origins; I am not a genuine Englishman — but I am also not German any more. I do not feel homesick. It is a yearning for something that no longer exists, something like a pain in a leg after it has been amputated."[3]

Many transnational adoptees live with phantom lives, lives defined as possible but unlived. Those adopted at older ages, like most Kinder-transport or Home Children, may carry a memory on whose fading image that phantom life is constructed in fantasy, while those adopted in infancy must weave their possible lives out of individual threads gathered from many sources: travel books, photographs of the adoption journey, culture camps, the face in the mirror. From these scraps, a story is invented, one that begins "what if. . . . " "What if my birth mother had been able to keep me? What if I had stayed in Vietnam and had not been brought to this place where I am so different? What if I were growing up in China right now? What if a family in India had been able to adopt me? What if my grandmother hadn't died, if my uncle hadn't taken me to the orphanage, if my adoptive parents hadn't seen my face on the photolisting?" The possi-bilities are endless. Such narratives of possibility are familiar to anyone who has experienced a tremendous trauma, particularly one in which they were in fact powerless: "What if I had stayed home that evening, I could have saved my sister from the fire." But the narratives seem most powerful in adoption and especially in transnational adoption, because the stakes are so high, the differences between lived experience and another possible life so extreme, and the possibility perceived, at least, as so genuine.

While the recognition that their lives could have been different is com-mon to many transnational adoptees, the story each tells himself or herself about what that difference would have meant is intensely personal. The narratives are often fiercely owned and held to: an individual dispossessed of his or her past can at least have control over a narrative of possibility. Such narratives are by definition amorphous, infinitely changeable, and always shifting to absorb new facts or to be inserted into new situations, new levels of self-awareness. The story that works for the adolescent ("my birth mother would have loved me better") may no longer work for the young adult constructing an identity ("I would have been happier in a Korean orphanage because everybody would have been like me") and this again may change when that adoptee becomes the parent of biological or adopted children. Each stage of life generates new narratives that are always only fictions. But they are strong fictions, fictions through which identity is tested, adjusted, and redefined.

Return journeys to the adoptee's country of origin are so important and yet so difficult because they are moments when a somewhat settled narrative of possibility is strikingly tested against a great deal of new information, and almost certainly has to be revised. That revision cannot, however, be confused with resolution. No matter what new information is gathered in the homeland, even through a reunion with the birth family, the course of history has not been changed and the alternative past remains always only a fiction. In this volume, Eleana Kim and Barbara Yngvesson describe the narrative disruptions of return journeys, the presentation of official counternarratives of possibility in the face of which the individual must struggle to retain his or her personal story. The Korean adoptees whose journeys Kim describes are confronted with a political master-narrative of national maternity that attempts to supplant their own understandings of loss, separation, and what Kim terms "disidentification." Similarly, Yngvesson's returning Swedish Chileans experience the "simultaneous fascination and terror evoked by what might have been," asking themselves "what would have become of me had I remained there?"

Most members of the group of returning adoptees with whom Yngvesson traveled are accompanied by their adoptive parents, parents who did not originally make the journey to adopt their children because of diplomatic issues between sending and receiving nations. To these parents, as Yngvesson remarks, the trip seems to serve almost as momentous a function as it does for their children. Lacking an early experience of contact with the country of origin, they have never been able to serve as mediators of that origin for their children, a role that Toby Volkman's and Kay

Johnson's essays show most adoptive parents now assuming. Yet, as these authors also recognize, the role of mediator of birth culture is a paradoxical one for an adoptive parent. The parents may, as Yngvesson says, have "become a bridge between there and here," but in what sense does that give them access to their child's culture, and what exactly are they supposed to transmit to their children? The Hague convention speaks, with amazing optimism, of continuing a child's ethnic, religious, cultural, and linguistic background. The assumption seems to be that culture is homogenous, belonging equally and unproblematically to all citizens of a nation, and that adoptive families can somehow provide a "true" sense of that culture. This is one of the official fictions of transnational adoption.

Adoptive parents, now encouraged to preserve a heritage they have witnessed but in which they have no social investment or position, develop their own fictions of possibility around the lives of their adopted children. These acts of narration begin, as Lisa Cartwright points out in her essay, with attempts to read a whole life and a whole past from a single photograph, glimpsed on a Web site or accompanying a referral. They continue with stories about the child's birth mother, comforting tales in which that shadowy figure's life story may be made parallel to the adoptive mother's (Volkman, citing Evans). At the very least, writes Johnson, the stories tend to involve a loving birth family acting in the child's best interests by abandoning it in such a way that it will be adopted — preferably by a family from the West. This is balanced by a counternarrative of impossibility: that there were no good options for the child apart from being adopted out of country, a tightly held fantasy that Johnson's and Laurel Kendall's essays go some way toward refuting. Within this tale, explanatory elements labeled as historical or "cultural" tend to take precedence over those seen as political, and it is the cultural — pretty, colorful, distant, lacking any taint of immediate responsibility — that marks the stories that parents, as mediators, tell their adopted children.

The "what if's" that adoptive parents themselves entertain are carefully delimited to justify their participation in transnational adoption. One could imagine a whole series of possible narratives: "What if my child had stayed with his birth family? What if she had been adopted by a family in her original country? What if another Western family had adopted her? What if he had remained in the orphanage?" While the first narrative must at some point have been a real possibility (although in the typical story, abandonment is presented as somehow inevitable), and while the second is the little-known possibility that Johnson and Kendall reveal to us, and while the third is quite plausible, most adoptive parents focus on the last possibility — life in the orphanage — because it is the one most easy to imagine as the negative counterpoint of the life they have provided for their child. In many sending countries, prospective adoptive parents spend considerable time visiting the orphanage, and it becomes what they witnessed of their child's previous life: it is, in fact, their version of his or her culture. These parents may hold a picture in their minds of some degree of abuse, neglect, or deprivation, qualities sometimes falsely measured against Western standards of material abundance and childcare but sometimes also quite accurately assessed by adults well versed in comparative cultures. "*That* was the life my child would have lead, had I not brought her to America where she is loved and nourished and educated." A possibility.

Narratives that adoptive parents tell about their children may not coincide at all with those the children tell about themselves. While a parent may see a child's phantom life as located in a grim and soulless orphanage and followed by a life of street crime, the child's phantom life may take place within the bosom of a poor yet loving family. Parents who indulge in tales of tragic averted possibilities can be confused when confronted with the child's more idealistic imagined autobiography, to use Kendall's term. And adoptees whose phantom lives are negative, like Kendall's Korean American college students who imagine their alternative lives as being prostitutes, assume a burden of gratitude that is, in fact, based on a fiction.

While the fictions (and the realities) of birth mothers are less well known than those of adoptive parents and adoptees, Kendall gives us some insight into their tales of possibility. She shows us birth mothers in Korea who are nearly as powerless as the children they bear and lose, and whose imaginings may include that same impossible resolution for which some adoptees hope when they search for their birth family. The disconnect between these fantasies, the different gaps they attempt to fill, can lead to complete breakdowns in reality. In the film *Daughter from Danang* (Dolgin and Franco 2002), a young woman adopted from Vietnam to the United States returns to her birthplace expecting to regain her stolen childhood, while her biological family expects the responsible behavior of a long-lost adult family member.

Heidi Bub, the central figure in *Daughter from Danang*, was brought to America at age seven. This is an age of full consciousness, and most children who have a significant life experience at that age will retain memories of it. Yet Heidi's assimilation is total. She is so "101 percent American" that she has passed as white for most of her life. When she begins to construct a sense of her other, lost, possible life, it is created seemingly out of nothing, written on a blank slate. In another work, Jane Jeong Trenka (2003), who struggled to establish a true and continuing narrative linking her two lives, meditates on how such erasure could have happened in her book *The Language of Blood*. While Trenka was adopted as an infant, her sister was four and a half when they came to America. Trenka imagines a film of the mind of her sister Carol being "cleansed" of all memories of Korea as they ride in the car to their new home: "Each scene in Korean language plays for fewer than five seconds before it is faded into black and the next scene plays. Scenes are various memories, showing an account of her young life so far. They include playing with her sisters and friends; eating with her family; sleeping next to her mother. . . . At the end of the movie sequence, the Korean memories are completely erased, and the reel-to-reel projector shows blank frames and white noise . . . CAROL has willed herself to become a girl with no history and is now ready to start her new life" (17).

Heidi Bub and Carol represent an earlier generation of transnational adoptees. Like Deann Borshay Liem, whose film *First Person Plural* presents a similar erasure of memory and history, they were pressed into what Yngvesson calls the "clean break" model of adoption, which emphasized complete assimilation to the adoptive culture. Today, older adoptees are stimulated to retain, rather than to discard, their memories. While all the models of "imagined autobiography" represented in this volume assume the fictionality of phantom lives, some of the adopted adults of tomorrow will have a kind of continuity of life narrative, along with a consciousness of the moment it was diverted, that will inevitably alter the stories they tell themselves. Here, the stories of Home Children and Kindertransport children with which I began this essay will be particularly relevant, for most of them were of an age to be conscious of their situations and were not encouraged to reject memories of their past.

As adoptive parents accept the persistence of memory, as they encourage the duality of identity and the exploration of birth culture, they discover the inadequacy of their own narratives of their child's alternative life. Perhaps no reflective parent can avoid creating phantom lives for their adoptive child, but they can also be aware of both the plurality and the fictionality of those stories and can accept that their child will invent entirely different and utterly personal fictions of their own, fictions essential to identity. Parents, in drawing on what are assumed to be "deep cultural" or "ancient historical" aspects of their child's birth culture — the Red Thread tale, for example, in Chinese adoption — have sometimes used such tropes to overwrite more flexible narratives. While claiming to validate the adoptee's birth culture, such stories ignore both political reality and personal possibility; but as adoptees mature, it may be the political reality that they want to reconcile with individual imaginings. As Kim concludes in her essay, it will be the collective countermemories that are mobilized when adoptees find a political voice.

My own two daughters, adopted from Kazakhstan at ages five and six, have wept when the cruel foster parents called Anne of Green Gables "trash." They have sung along with Shirley Temple in her orphanage; they have beamed with relief when Rumer Godden's Holly and Ivy found one another and a home; they have listened in agonized silence to the young narrator's hopeless search for the mother who abandoned her in Eve Bunting's *Train to Somewhere* (1996). Anglo-American culture holds up to their experiences a peculiarly relentless mirror. They have the ability to assess these outside fictions against reality because they have memories, vivid ones, of life in an orphanage. Fierce in their concern for ill-treated orphans, anxious that a resolution involve the unification with friends or families, they also have always shown a need to narrate, to explore possibility, and to reconcile their stories with political rather than "cultural" realities. My older daughter has pointed out to me, calmly and without accusation, that had I not adopted her somebody else would have. That possibility is one I seldom entertain, yet it is one of her own phantom lives.

A few months after we arrived home from Kazakhstan, my younger daughter, Alice, came upon me reading the *Economist* at the breakfast table. "I'm reading an article about Kazakhstan," I told her, "and it says that Nazarbayev [the country's long-term president] is bad." "No mama, no!" she exclaimed, passionately, "Nazarbayev is *good*!" Clearly this was what she had been taught at the orphanage. But later that day she suddenly interrupted a swimming lesson and, standing in the shallow lake water, asked me, "Mama, why paper say Nazarbayev bad?" Then and there, we had a quick discussion of freedom of the press ("presidents need to listen to other people's good ideas") and inequitable distribution of wealth in developing nations. Soon after, Alice's life narrative had incorporated this episode: "My birth mother couldn't keep me because Nazarbayev was bad, he stole poor people's money, so mamas can't buy food for their babies." Some day she may be telling herself narratives of what might have happened in a different world, a world of social justice, a world in which her birth mother had enough money to feed a baby. That fiction, and those of her compatriots, will have formidable political power.

Notes

1. One exception is John Neufeld's disturbing book from the 1960s, *Edgar Allan*, about a white family who attempt the (domestic) adoption of a black child. The only young adult novel I know of about a Korean orphan — Linda Sue Park's *A Single Shard* (2001) — concerns a child in medieval Korea. Within the large body of children's literature on the Holocaust there are some books about Kindertransport children, such as those by Irene Watts.

2. On the "Home Children" see Kenneth Bagnell, *The Little Immigrants* (2001 [1980]). The exportation of children from England to Australia and South Africa continued after World War II as well. Only in the late 1990s did the Labour government announce an investigation into Britain's involvement in postwar child migration.

3. Paul M. Cohn, interview from 1980, published at http://www.rrz.uni-hamburg.de/rz3a035/kindertransport.html. Many Kindertransport children have been interviewed as part of more general holocaust survivor research, but there is a considerable literature specifically on the Kindertransports as well (see Harris and Oppenheimer 2001).

References

Bagnell, Kenneth. 2001 (1980). *The Little Immigrants*. Toronto: Dundurn Press.

Bunting, Eve. 1996. *Train to Somewhere*. New York: Houghton Mifflin.

Burnett, Frances Hodgson. 1962 (1911). *The Secret Garden*. Philadelphia: Lippincott.

Cartwright, Lisa. 2003. "Photographs of 'Waiting Children': The Transnational Adoption Market." *Social Text* 74: 83–109.

Dolgin, Gail, and Vicente Franco, 2002. *Daughter from Danang*. Berkeley: American Experience and ITVS (Video).

Godden, Rumer. 1987 (1957). *The Story of Holly and Ivy*. New York: Penguin.

Harris M. J., and D. Oppenheimer, eds. 2000. *Into the Arms of Strangers: Stories of the Kindertransport*. London: Bloomsbury.

Johnston, Julie. 1994. *Adam and Eve and Pinch-Me*. New York: Penguin.

Liem, Deann Borshay. 2000. *First Person Plural*. San Francisco: NAATA (Video).

Magorian, Michelle. 1981. *Goodnight Mr. Tom*. London: Kestrel Books.

Montgomery, L. M. 1995 (1908). *Anne of Green Gables*. London: Everyman's Library.

Neufeld, John. 1969. *Edgar Allan*. New York: Signet Books.

———. 2003. *The Handle and the Key*. New York: Phyllis Fogelman Books.

Park, Linda Sue. 2001. *A Single Shard*. New York: Dell Yearling.

Robertson, Struan. 2000. "A History of the Jews in Hamburg: Kindertransport." Regionales Rechenzentrum, Universiteit Hamburg http://www.rrz.uni-hamburg.de/rz3a035/kindertransport.html.

Say, Alan. 1997. *Allison*. New York: Houghton Mifflin.

Trenka, Jane Jeong. 2003. *The Language of Blood: A Memoir*. St. Paul, MN: Borealis Books.

Contributors

Lisa Cartwright is an associate professor of communications and science studies at the University of California, San Diego. She is the author of *Screening the Body: Tracing Medicine's Visual Culture*, coauthor of *Practices of Looking: An Introduction to Visual Culture*, and coeditor of *The Visible Woman: Imaging Technologies, Gender, and Science*.

Claudia Fonseca is a professor of anthropology at the Federal University of Rio Grande do Sul, and author of *Caminhos da Adoção* and *Família, Fofoca e Honra*. Her current research focuses on law, kinship, and working-class culture in Brazil.

Elizabeth Alice Honig is an associate professor of the history of art at the University of California, Berkeley. She is the author of *Painting and the Market* as well as many articles on images and gender, society, and economic thought in early modern Europe.

Kay Johnson is a professor of Asian studies and politics at Hampshire College. A China scholar, her current research is on the impact of population policy on women and children. She is the author of *Wanting a Daughter, Needing a Son: Abandonment, Adoption, and Orphanage Care in China* and *Women, the Family, and Peasant Revolution in China*.

Laurel Kendall is an anthropologist and the curator of the Asian ethnographic collections at the American Museum of Natural History. She has written several books on Korea, including *Shamans, Housewives, and other Restless Spirits: Women in Korean Ritual Life* and *Getting Married in Korea: Of Gender, Morality, and Modernity*.

Eleana Kim is a Ph.D. candidate in the department of anthropology at New York University. She is writing her dissertation on Korean adoption and the adult adopted Korean network. Fieldwork conducted in the United States and in South Korea informs her examination of the social and cultural production of an emergent Korean adoptee identity formation. Her research has been supported with grants from the James West Memorial Fund, the Social Science Research Council, and the Fulbright Commission.

Toby Alice Volkman is the deputy provost of New School University. An anthropologist, she is the author of *Feasts of Honor: Ritual and Change in the Toraja Highlands* and other publications on Indonesia, area studies, and ethnographic film. She coedited the special issue of *Social Text* on which this volume is based.

Barbara Yngvesson is a professor of anthropology at Hampshire College. She is the author of *Virtuous Citizens, Disruptive Subjects: Order and Complaint in a New England Court* and coauthor of *Law and Community in Three American Towns*. Her current research focuses on movements of children between families and nations in adoption, the power of law in constituting these movements, and the hierarchies of belonging and exclusion (racial, familial, national) that they produce.

Index

Library of Congress Cataloging-in-Publication Data

Cultures of transnational adoption / Toby Alice Volkman,
editor.
p. cm.
Includes bibliographical references and index.
ISBN 0-8223-3576-X (cloth : alk. paper)
ISBN 0-8223-3589-1 (pbk. : alk. paper)
1. Intercountry adoption. 2. Cognition and culture. 3. Kinship.
4. Transnationalism. I. Volkman, Toby Alice.
HV875.5.C86 2005
362.734—dc22   2004026187